MEMORY, IMAGINATION, JUSTICE

Through the creative use of literary analysis, *Memory, Imagination, Justice* provides a critical and highly original discussion of contemporary topics in criminal law and also in bioethics. Author David Gurnham uses popular and classical texts, by authors including Shakespeare, Dickens, Euripides, Kafka, the Brothers Grimm, Huxley and Margaret Atwood to shed fresh light on such controversial legal and ethical issues as passionate homicide, life sentences, child pornography and genetic enhancement. Gurnham's overarching theme is the role of memory and imagination in shaping legal and ethical attitudes. Along this line, the book examines the ways in which past wrongs are 'remembered' and may be forcefully responded to, both by the criminal justice system itself and also by individuals responding to what they regard as gross insults, threats or personal violations. The volume further discusses the role of imagination as a creative force behind legal reform, in terms of the definition of criminal behaviour and the possible future development of the law. These ideas provide a useful and highly original perspective on contemporary issues of crime and society as they resonate both in legal and literary discussion.

For my parents, Richard and Harjinder

Memory, Imagination, Justice
Intersections of Law and Literature

DAVID GURNHAM
Manchester University, UK

ASHGATE

Published by
Ashgate Publishing Limited
Wey Court East
Union Road
Farnham
Surrey, GU9 7PT
England

Ashgate Publishing Company
Suite 420
101 Cherry Street
Burlington
VT 05401-4405
USA

www.ashgate.com

British Library Cataloguing in Publication Data
Gurnham, David.
 Memory, imagination, justice : intersections of law and
 literature. -- (Law, justice and power series)
 1. Law and literature. 2. Criminal law--Interpretation and
 construction. 3. Justification (Ethics). 4. Justification
 (Law).
 I. Title II. Series
 340.1'1-dc22

Library of Congress Cataloging-in-Publication Data
Gurnham, David.
 Memory, imagination, justice : intersections of law and literature / by David Gurnham.
  p. cm. -- (Law, justice and power)
 Includes index.
 ISBN 978-0-7546-7103-9 -- ISBN 978-0-7546-9107-5 (ebook) 1. Law and literature.
2. Law in literature. I. Title.

PN56.L33G87 2009
809'.933554--dc22

2009004330

ISBN 978-0-7546-7103-9
e-ISBN 978-0-7546-9107-5
Reprinted 2010

Mixed Sources
Product group from well-managed forests and other controlled sources
www.fsc.org Cert no. SA-COC-1565
© 1996 Forest Stewardship Council
FSC

Printed and bound in Great Britain by
MPG Books Ltd, Bodmin, Cornwall.

Contents

Table of Cases

Table of Statutes

Introduction[1]

1. Memory and Imagination in Legal and Moral Critique

There can be little doubt that both memory and imagination are important faculties for reflecting on the moral and legal questions of our time. When in Dickens' *A Christmas Carol* Jacob Marley and the Christmas ghosts return from the grave to save the pathologically selfish Ebenezer Scrooge from eternal damnation, they do so by forcing the old man to remember his past, to look at his present and to imagine his future. Somewhere in the combination of these three revelations that collectively horrify him, Scrooge finds the motivation to change his outlook and to mend his ways. It is a heart-warming story about the redemptive power of memory and imagination, but how could such a turnaround be possible? Despite having lived a life utterly devoid of the positive human qualities of generosity, kindness and care, Dickens wants us to believe that Scrooge is nevertheless equipped to interpret the scenes shown to him by the ghosts in the required way, and therefore to understand what is lacking in his character and in his life. Was Scrooge in fact a good man all along, who just needed a nudge in the right direction to realize it? Set against the background of Victorian London, Scrooge's interpretive task might be assumed to be made a little easier by the relative obscurity of respectable alternatives to Christian moral frameworks. However, in the context of contemporary critical scholarship, this evokes something highly problematic in trying to engage with legal or moral issues through literature. Although important, the faculties of imagination and memory are by no means sufficient for critique: if the literary imagination is to tell us anything very interesting about law or morality, then it needs a good deal of interpretive labour. A discussion of the moral content of law in a world in which religious and other metaphysical certainties are no longer so self-evidently persuasive is therefore left with an uphill struggle. We are unlikely to glean the kind of revelatory truths experienced by Scrooge unless we are prepared to believe that the visions of the literary imagination can be clearly understood in the context of a modern society that admits many different kinds of ethical imperatives. It would be naive to suppose that an engagement between law and literature could be without bias, but if there is any commonality between the many and various scholarly accounts of what has become known as 'law and literature', it might be the modesty of its promise. With this in mind, the method

---

1   Many thanks to Paul Raffield, John Harrington, Ummni Khan, Melanie Williams and John Coggon for their helpful comments and advice on early drafts.

employed by Marley's ghost may yet be helpful for a critical engagement with legal and moral issues through literature, though without its redemptive purpose.

This anxiety about the difficulty of interpreting the visions of the literary imagination may be a symptom peculiar to 'law and literature' as a discipline that sits awkwardly alongside literary and legal scholarship. Within the more traditional discipline of 'serious' jurisprudence, theories of justice tend obliquely to confirm the significance of memory and imagination, whether through the imaginative ways in which they construct theoretical approaches to law and morality, or by the assumption that the imagined actors of their theorizations are themselves imaginative beings. Dworkin (1977) possibly gave us the most vivid example of such a move in Hercules, his heroic ideal judge standing aloof on Mount Olympus ready to make sense of the entire vast vista of legal authority. In his idealization of what a judge ought to aspire to, Dworkin is appealing to his readers' powers of imagination. There are many other examples. In his discourse theory of law and morality, Habermas (1997) insists that the key to realizing the liberal democratic promise of a universal legal and moral framework lies in human beings' capacity to engage in an unfettered discursive process for the testing and affirming of ideas and propositions. We are invited to look at the world, as Habermas presumably does, as a vast public forum in which every person will somehow find the voice to have their say in the universal discussion. Furthermore, such a theory demands that the people involved are capable of sometimes great feats of imagination which might move them to care sufficiently about participatory liberal democracy: they must be able to form an idea as to what an *ideal* speech situation might be like, and must further imagine themselves as potential constitutive elements of it. Likewise consider Rawls' *Theory of Justice* (1999), which envisions a mythical 'original position' wherein strange disembodied creatures equipped only with abstract reasoning powers are asked to select the most rational and reasonable first principles of justice from behind a 'veil of ignorance'. Such a myth of liberal democracy demands no less of both those creatures and the readers. Such jurisprudential approaches to the problem of justice give a specific role to the imagination inasmuch as the abstractions presented must appeal to some sense of what an ideal system might look like. Habermas and Rawls may disagree on many things, but they both share with *A Christmas Carol* an ending which, if not exactly inevitable, certainly leads the reader towards a destination that, once the premises are accepted, ought to seem natural and self-evident. Rawls' original position is designed in such a way that, were *we* to somehow find ourselves separated from the world by a 'veil of ignorance', then we too would find Rawls's first principles of justice irresistible. Similarly, Habermas' ideal speech situation is essentially a set of conditions that we could not fail to choose if we wanted to conceive of a situation in which discourse might be fully free, fully representative and fully democratic. To choose otherwise would imply a failure of our own ambition as much as a failure of Habermas' powers of persuasion. Dworkin's discussion of Hercules too is full of imperatives – Hercules *must* consider this, he *must* consider that, or he would not adequately grasp the full range of legal sources and would thus not be Hercules the superhuman judge. These deployments are designed to teach the reader that, deep down, they already know the truth about the preconditions for justice and just need to be nudged in the right direction to be fully convinced. Of course, to judge these patriarchs of liberal legal thought as either right in all their claims or else wholly wrong would be to ask too much of them for critical engagement. But for those commentators, imagination is a tool for constructing theory of justice. In this book, by contrast, imagination plays a slightly different role, inasmuch as the idea is not to construct a theory as much as to reflect and interpret its effect on ideas of justice. As a book falling broadly within the field of law and literature, imagination must naturally take a central billing at least in the form of the writing, since the book as a whole goes about the business of legal and moral critique through a discussion of various works of western literature. But imagination also plays a more *substantive* role in the last third of the book. Part 3 (Imagination, or Ghosts of Violence Yet to Come) examines the role of the imagination in creating moral anxieties and grounding a perception that legal prohibitions are required to prevent worrying developments in society. Rather than imaginatively constructing a theoretical world or character (as Habermas, Rawls and Dworkin do), Part 3 examines the way in which imagination works in both literature and moral and legal discourse to generate fear and anxiety.

The eight chapters of this book are grouped into three parts. Part 1 (Memory, or Ghosts of Violence Past) contains the first two chapters, which focus on the role of memory in legal and moral critique. The 'remembering' of things for legal historians is very often motivated by a desire to tell a story about the emergence of legal cultures and practices in terms of the political and social processes that formed them. Revolutions and struggles for independence provide the historical narrative for the legal codes of nations, and in common law jurisdictions the gradual evolution of legal principles provides its own fascinating historical narrative. In his book on the history of the defence of provocation, Jeremy Horder (1992) uses his historical analysis to trace law's changing attitudes towards lethal violence used in response to provocative behaviour. He describes how the history of homicide in English law moved from a concession to heated blood, to satisfactions of honour, the duties of courage and then psychological frailty. Implied in Horder's work is a narrative about memory itself: the reader is told how the laws of the past ought to remembered, and what this particular form of remembering says about the defence that has survived to the present day. As one of the members of the Law Commission (2006) charged with publishing recommendations for reform of the homicide laws in England and Wales, Horder's historical analysis, like the theoretical arguments of Rawls and Habermas, takes on a practical purpose, and the interpretation of the relationship between law and society in the past becomes pertinent to push the reader (in this case the Government, which in response to the Law Commission's recommendations has proposed to abolish the provocation defence) towards a certain conclusion about the evolving relationship between law and morality. Making up the first third of this book, Part 1 considers the moral and legal significance of 'looking back', of remembering a past wrong. It takes a 'long view' on the question of the way we respond to retaliations for a wrong, comparing modern laws relating to homicide and punishment to the depictions of retaliatory and retributive violence in Shakespeare, Kafka and Euripides.

Memory and imagination are therefore very much part of a legal scholar's toolbox. What I have tried to do in this book is to put the focus onto those faculties of imagination and memory themselves as catalysts of moral and legal critique. I examine the way in which the experience of remembering – of calling past events to mind either by persons or by the law itself – might be significant for ideas of justice. I consider also the significance of the fact that we have the ability to imagine alternative worlds for our moral ideas and the formulation of laws for things not yet possible – the stuff of literary imagination. The eventually cheery conclusion of the Christmas ghosts' horrifying revelations of past, present and future in Dickens' story is underpinned by a metaphysics of moral certainties that is literally the difference between life and death for the innocent Tiny Tim: we must be kind, caring, forgiving, generous, not mean, selfish or cruel. A naïve interpretation of Habermas or Rawls would involve doing the liberal democratic equivalent of the Christmas ghosts' work; that is, to reveal the positive values necessary for a liberal democratic idea of justice. However, if literature and art is to be used to reflect critically on legal and moral issues, then it is the 'moral of the story' itself, where it comes from, and how it is constructed in public discourse, that must be subjected to scrutiny. The authority of a literary text to lay down a law of critique must be questioned, which means that the solid moral foundations that we are required to assume when reading *A Christmas Carol* becomes problematic.

2. What is Imagined, and What is Remembered?

There are a few interlinking themes that appear repeatedly in the chapters of this book and inform its overall concern with memory and the imagination. First, the question of violence – how we respond to it or ought to respond to it – is a central problematic. The terrors and the thrills of this unruly, dangerous and ever troubling aspect of human society that both connects us to our brutal and animalistic past and also radically separates us from it, is at the heart of much of literature and art. As a question for legal and moral critique, the problem of violence is posed in various forms: the violence that one person commits against a fellow human being; the violence inflicted on the bodies of subjects of the criminal justice system; the violence that is experienced as a side-effect of our own ideals and aspirations. Let me explain each of these three aspects of the problem of violence. The chapters in Parts 1 and 2 examine aspects of the most obvious example of violence – the physical infliction of bodily harm by one person against another. Responses to and explanations of inter-personal violence are strongly bound up with questions of class and gender. The struggle for material equality and political emancipation is of course littered with corpses, be they those of working class protesters crushed under the hooves of the Tsar's cavalry, or the middle class victims of Mao's Cultural Revolution, or whatever. In Part 1, Chapters 1 and 2 are concerned with the moral and legal dynamics of provoked killing, that is, killings carried out for personal reasons in hot-blooded or otherwise uncontrolled retaliation to the behaviour of another. On this subject, Chapters 1 and 2 consider the moral status of what are sometimes called heat of passion killings that cannot be fully justified but might (depending on one's perspective) be excused. On what basis do we say that a person's intentional use of lethal violence is to be utterly condemned, and when ought it to avoid the harshest condemnation? As a concession to the frailty of humans and their occasional susceptibility to irrational violent outbursts, there is a question, posed in Chapter 1, as to the emotional basis of any provocation defence: should any extreme emotion provide a basis for a defence or are there some particular sorts of extreme emotions to which we ought not to be at all sympathetic? Personal violence is dealt with also in Chapter 6, where I discuss the divisive topic of violence against children and responses to it. Although public concern for the welfare of children in western society has apparently become an acute anxiety, children are the only members of society that may still be lawfully assaulted. Chapter 6, part of the middle section (Part 2 'Childhood Innocence, or the Frozen Present') considers the discourse of violence against children with regard to moral and legal distinctions between violence that is defended as conducive to preserving an ordered society on the one hand, and violence that is condemned as pathological and disruptive on the other.

Secondly, there is the violence justified by the fact that it is inflicted on the body of a person by the criminal justice system itself. Although the infliction of physical harm is now limited by international legal norms, the state's control over the body of the prisoner through imprisonment is a particular kind of violence that is the subject of critique in Chapter 3. Part of the discussion of memory, Chapter 3 considers the symbolic meaning of the whole life term of imprisonment for murder in English law in terms of the relationship between the offender's wrong and the persistence of the punishment that constitutes a form of institutional remembering. If there is any significance in moral theories that justify punishment according to its rehabilitative or communicative (retributive) effects, then the death of the prisoner would appear to signal the end of the punishment. However, Chapter 3 argues that the moral explanation for 'whole life' imprisonment relates not to the progress of the prisoner towards repentance and reform, but to the seriousness of the crime itself and the consequent length of time for which it must be 'remembered'. Therefore, rather than bringing punishment to an end, I argue in this chapter that there is reason to regard punishment as sometimes continuing beyond the prisoner's death in a symbolic sense. Foucault (1991) argued that the shift from the gruesome spectacle of the scaffold to the prison signalled a symbolic shift from the punishment of the body to a punishment of the soul, since from the beginning of the nineteenth century, prison has functioned not merely to incarcerate but to understand the prisoner, to mould and to discipline them. But Foucault's interpretation of the history of punishment does not take into consideration the significance of the religious dimension of body and soul. Drawing comparisons between the horrors of early modern executions and modern whole life imprisonment through the lens of Kafka's *In the Penal Colony* (also known as *In the Penal Settlement*), I propose an alternative view of the symbolic aspect of punishment that outlives the prisoner.

Central to our fascination with the capacity to hurt others and for we ourselves to be hurt is the idea of taboo, and this is another major theme of this book. The connection between taboo and the wider concerns of memory and imagination are intuitively fairly clear. When we describe a certain moral or legal prohibition as 'taboo' we are first of all making an explicit appeal to memory. Freud (1950) and Bataille (1962) argued that taboos first came into existence in primitive societies to prevent some terrible consequence of extreme primal passion. The observance of taboo also requires imagination: it is crucial to the continued effectiveness of a taboo that those required to respect it believe in the malevolent forces that enforce its unapproachable nature without too much question as to its origin. Central to Freud's notion of the taboo over and above prohibitions of other kinds is the role of desire, or more precisely the unconscious temptation to violate that which is protected by taboo. The existence of a taboo is always a reminder of human beings' primal capacity for dangerous passion – passion so potentially threatening that it explains the original need for the taboo. For this reason, taboo and the ambivalence between respect and desire for transgression that it continues to provoke is discussed in Part 2 (Childhood Innocence, or the Frozen Present) as a whole. This middle section of the book is a group of three chapters that considers the critical significance for legal and moral discourse of fairytales and folk tales, published in the well-known collections of the Brothers Grimm and Charles Perrault. Chapter 4 examines the various versions of the tale of *Little Red Riding Hood*: a much more interesting starting point for a politics of childhood than it is often given credit for, particularly by feminists (for example, Aristodemou 2000). I approach the tale from the perspective of George Bataille's arguments about the erotic appeal of the taboo surrounding death, and violent death in particular. I read Red Riding Hood's sudden confrontation with death, both in the form of the discovery of the murder of her grandmother and her realization that her own death may be near, as an experience so out of the ordinary that, as Bataille argues, it may be experienced as a violation of taboo and hence as an experience evoking both dread and desire. Chapter 5 considers the taboo of childhood with regards to the difficult social anxieties concerning the sexuality and innocence of children in the controversial photographic images of Tierney Gearon. A case-study of the ambivalence between the dread and desire associated with taboo, the ferocious public discourse about the exposure of children to the imagined stalking paedophile that met Gearon's 2001 exhibition is considered here. We are appalled by the thought of a child being hurt or abused and disgusted by the exposure of children to paedophilic desire. However, as discussed in Chapter 5, the cultural anxiety over the uses and abuses of children's bodies in visual culture accords those bodies the very qualities of a taboo, which of course only further implicates the child's body with illicit sexuality, adding to our disquiet. I return to taboo again in Part 3. Chapter 7 considers the way in which conservative critics of the scientific drive to 'play God' (in developing genetic enhancements and other ways of improving human nature) attempt to wield taboo for their own critical purposes. That chapter considers the success with which conservative critics of potentially amazing scientific advances present the 'natural' qualities of human nature as taboo in their own right, that is, as sacred principles that must remain untouched by science or utilitarian logic.

Perhaps as an extension of this concern for taboo, a further overarching and interlinking theme is that of the ideals that are constructed in public discourse as a means of guiding legal and moral activity. I have written already in this introduction about the idealizations of some of the modern liberal jurisprudes whose arguments hinge on convincing the reader to accept a certain construction of justice and its necessary preconditions. The creation of ideals in discourse is approached in Parts 2 and 3, dealing with the ideal of childhood innocence and of natural 'humanness' (or humanity) respectively. Ideals are ostensibly about imagination (recall the Utopia theorists) but also they relate to memory, since many formulations of the ideals discussed here are also *nostalgic*. 'Innocence' and 'humanness' may not be the most accurate labels for the themes I refer to here, but for me they vividly describe the notions discussed in Parts 2 and 3, in which an aspect of life is transformed in (or by) discourse from being a mundane fact into a sacred moral principle, never to be violated or even questioned. I have already described how in this way innocence comes to form a 'frozen present', a desire to believe that a section of society is free from the corruptions and vices and compromises that mar the rest of society. Likewise, in Part 3 the conservative valorization of naked humanity – that is, human life that is not altered or enhanced by artificial or technological means – seeks to isolate our species as a morally superior entity in itself. Both kinds of ideal are related to violence: those who worry about preserving the innocence of childhood unwittingly cause harm by encouraging the child to remain in a defenceless state of ignorance, passivity and silence. Those that worry that biotechnology is compromising the moral life of human society oppose scientific advances that could, if allowed to flourish, bring great benefits to humankind.

3. Justice and the Intersections of Law and Literature

I am aware that I have so far neglected the third central theme alluded to in the title of this book, namely justice. Writers have in the past expressed both joy and anxiety about the coupling of the disciplines of law and literature in approaching justice, probably because those that come to the subject are often lawyers by training, schooled in serious jurisprudential questions as to the binding authority of law, and thus are conditioned to be suspicious of the frivolous imaginings of poets, dramatists and novelists. The coupling of the two disciplines brings value to legal scholarship by its interdisciplinary nature and consequently it embraces a wide range of voices and stories that may have previously been excluded from more traditional jurisprudence. The journey towards scholarly respectability has been a slow and tortuous one and, to many jurisprudes, the expression 'law and literature' is still something of an 'illegitimate touching' (to borrow an expression from Alison Young (2005)) owing to the apparent chasm between the authority of law and the free-play of literature. But for others this flight from authority also gives the discipline of law and literature its critical import. For, if modern law's authority derives from a commitment to universal principles derived democratically, then the use of literature to draw attention to experiences of injustice under the law opens up a critique of its authority. It is for this reason that feminist scholars have seen in 'law and literature' an opportunity to uncover marginalized stories of feminine experience in order to turn the eye of critique on the gendered 'universalism' of modern law as a patriarchal construct that prioritizes masculine experience (Rackley 2006, Williams 2002, Aristodemou 2000). However, as various others have noted, embracing forms of expression traditionally thought to pertain merely to the private (feminine) realm of fantasy and the imagination brings its own risks. To align oneself with law and literature as a discipline risks implying a sort of 'pick 'n' mix' critique for which 'anything goes' if it makes for an amusing diversion, and thereby inviting the kind of scholarly disdain that is often levelled at postmodernism and cultural studies (Norris 1990). This in turn may imply an *acceptance* of marginalization by a lack of seriousness or 'relevance', a rejection of authority and weak theoretical grounding.

In this book I have tried to draw attention to the creative aspect of justice: how, despite the obvious differences between law and literature, we might nevertheless make use of the literary imagination and its capacity to provide narratives of justice that might otherwise remain outside the normal jurisdiction of legal thought. As a discussion of taboos and ideals and the process of their construction in discourse, the question of what it means to offer a just response is an overriding concern throughout the book. In addition, justice is also itself more directly addressed. For example Chapter 2 (Part 1 'Memory, or Ghosts of Violence Past') discusses the ancient notion of justice as the seeking of repayment of a debt, building on Ian Miller's (2006) writings on the same topic, through references to a diverse range of literature including Dante, Shakespeare and the Bible. The chapter itself focuses on the question as to whether there can ever be a just cause for a provoked of hot-blooded killing and uses the dramas of *Hamlet* and *Electra* to explore the hopelessly fine line between lofty justice and mere revenge, where to use violence to restore the scales of justice merely threatens to upset them still further. Secondly, Chapter 7 (Part 3 'Imagination, or Ghosts of Violence Yet to Come', together with Chapter 8), offers a critique of the idea of justice grounded not in a theoretical abstraction, but in the much more immediate metaphor of terror at the prospect of bodily violation. As outlined above, the final two chapters of the book are a critique of philosophers and commentators who morally condemn the possibility that human life might be radically altered by technologies for artificial enhancement. Chapter 7 deals with a view of the nature of justice upon which this condemnation is built, namely the association of justice with bodily integrity and injustice with bodily hurt, disconnection and dismemberment. I draw connections between, on the one hand, modern science-fiction novels by Margaret Atwood and Kazuo Ishiguro as well as Huxley's classic science-fiction dystopia *Brave New World*, and the bloody chaos that Shakespeare imagines engulfing Rome in his early play *Titus Andronicus*. The connection between these ostensibly very different literary sources, and indeed between them and the philosophical condemnations of biotechnology, is the image of the vulnerable human body – its capacity to be broken, bruised and battered – as a metaphor for the vulnerability of justice itself. In its relation to the taboos of human life introduced above and nostalgia for a more innocent time of moral certainties (Chapter 8), the physical human body is a conservative metaphor for universal justice. Less conservative commentators such as Erika Rackley (2006) celebrate the image of Hercules, Dworkin's very picture of integrity (both in body and as a judge), not only as denuded of his judge's wig and gown, but also *skinned* in order to allow him to take on new identities, poetically undermining Dworkin's own idea of justice as unified integrity.

In what follows then, there is no unified theory of justice, law or morality, but nonetheless these ideas are theorized through evoking the creative effects of the intersections between law and literature. Ideas of what it means to be just, to do justice and to represent justice are considered and critiqued by drawing on literature from ancient times to the modern day. In appealing to the literary imagination in this way to reflect on legal and moral issues I hope to have raised some provocative questions for further debate and discussion.

PART 1
Memory, or Ghosts of Violence Past

Chapter 1

'My thoughts be bloody, or be nothing worth!' *Hamlet*, Hot Blood and Malice Aforethought

In the melancholic, brooding young Hamlet, Shakespeare invites us to reflect on the way we respond or ought to respond legally and morally to acts of violence. When do we, and when ought we to, attach the damning label of 'murderer' to someone who has killed intentionally and subject them to the harshest punishment, and when do we feel that such a judgment is too much? *Hamlet* is of course recognized both as more than a revenge play inasmuch as it offers a more satisfying account of the character of the affected avenger than Kyd's *The Spanish Tragedy* or Middleton's *The Revenger's Tragedy*, and also as less than a revenge play: after all, for reasons much debated over the centuries Hamlet arguably never actually gets around to avenging the death of his father at all. Apart from what critics have tended to regard as the 'central question' of Hamlet's hesitation, there is the portrayal of violence itself and responses to it as a moral issue. In this chapter I want to examine this portrayal in *Hamlet* against the legal context of early modern English criminal law into which the play first emerged, as a means of approaching the distinctions in our own moral and legal thinking between 'hot' and 'cold'-blooded killing. The metaphor of the heating of a killer's blood permeates both the play and the development of the laws of intentional homicide since early modern times, and in particular the emergence of the provocation defence. In the play, a Ghost claiming to be that of Hamlet's murdered father and the former king of Denmark, commands the young man to avenge his untimely death. Along the way he also commits a number of acts of hot-blooded killing in response to perceived and actual threats, affronts and outrages. I hope to show in this chapter and the next that what emerges from an analysis of dramatic representations of killing is a critical perspective on the moral and legal understanding of murder (an intentional killing with malice aforethought) and provoked manslaughter (intentional killing that lacks malice aforethought). The evolution of the meaning of the expression 'malice aforethought' is central to my discussion, and in particular to the significance for modern understandings of intentional homicide of the early sixteenth century understanding of murder as only those killings that involved actual premeditation. In both this chapter and the next, this analysis of the meaning of 'malice' as an indicator of murder (as opposed to mere manslaughter) in early modern law leads on to dealing with the central analysis of current criminal legal formulations of voluntary manslaughter: intentional killings that lack malice that are, at the time of writing, represented in English and US law by the defence of provocation. In the UK, the Government has announced that it intends to abolish the provocation defence during the next Parliamentary session and so in these two chapters I also examine the Ministry of Justice's (2008, 2) proposals for two new partial defences to replace provocation: the (not very) elegantly named 'killing in response to a fear of serious violence' and 'killing in response to words or conduct which caused the defendant to have a justifiable sense of being wronged'. In this chapter I focus specifically on the historical idea of *malice aforethought* as the absence of hot blood that would excuse a killing and save a defendant from the gallows in early modern England, and compare two inheritors of this distinction, namely the provocation defence in modern English and US criminal law. I argue here that, unlike the much more general formulation of the 'emotional' aspect of the defence in America as any kind of extreme heated passion, the requirement in English law (and to be preserved in an altered form according to the reform proposals) for a defendant to have at the material time suffered a 'loss of self control' in response to a particular kind of triggering behaviour on the part of the victim, is unduly narrow. I shall argue here that the narrowness of this formal requirement of the English defence seems to be out of step with the way juries apply the defence to excuse any defendant *who simply seems not to have killed with malice sufficient for murder*. What this curious jury behaviour means is that, like the audiences of Shakespeare's plays who are invited to watch and judge the violence represented on stage, juries seem to look not for a specific set of excusing criteria in murder cases, but rather at the moral character of the events as a whole.

1. 'Loss of Self-control' and 'Heat of Passion': The Emotional Basis for a Defence for Provoked Homicide

It is the case in the modern law of murder both in England and the US that the prosecution must show that the defendant killed with 'malice aforethought'. In early modern England, malice aforethought could be found in two ways, as the seventeenth century Chief Justice Edward Coke (1797, 47) stipulated, 'either expressed by the party, or implied by law'.[1] In other words, murder was a killing that involved premeditation (express malice), and if evidence of premeditation were lacking but the defendant had demonstrated wanton cruelty or undue preparedness to use lethal violence, then they could be treated *as if* this violence was premeditated (implied malice). Although the expression 'malice aforethought' has survived into modern times, it is now understood in English law to mean simply 'intention' to kill to or to inflict serious bodily harm, no matter what the motives or level of planning, and so on. In fact it does not intend to imply any prior thought or premeditation at all, ensuring that both planned and spontaneous

---

1 First published in 1641.

killing is treated as murder if it is carried out intentionally, whether by specific intent (purposeful, deliberate) or oblique intent (foresight of death or serious injury as a virtual certainty) (*R v Woollin, R v Matthews and Alleyne*). Since 1965 all murders (as opposed to manslaughters) are punished by the mandatory life sentence and premeditation is relevant only in deciding the meaning of 'life' imprisonment for particular cases. According to the Criminal Justice Act 2003, a murder committed with 'a significant degree of planning or premeditation' is the first aggravating factor for judges to consider in deciding the minimum term of imprisonment before parole may be considered.[2] The same legislation stipulates that where a defendant has been found guilty of murdering two or more persons with 'a substantial degree of premeditation or planning' then it is to be considered to be 'exceptionally serious' and hence worthy of a whole life order without any chance of parole.[3] In contrast, whereas English law has levelled the distinction between premeditated and spontaneous intentional killings, other jurisdictions that inherited the English common law system (and hence share the archaic expression 'malice aforethought' used by Coke CJ (1797, 47)) continue to show strong traces of the early modern significance accorded to premeditation. For example, in the US, premeditation and deliberation are together the distinguishing features of first-degree murder (*State v Texierira*). Most state criminal codes therefore define first-degree murder as requiring evidence of planning or reflection before carrying out the act. This is described in the codes as, for example, 'wilful, deliberate, and premeditated killing' (Virginia), 'deliberately premeditated malice aforethought, or with extreme atrocity or cruelty ...' (Massachusetts), 'killing by means of poison, or by lying in wait, or by any other kind of wilful, deliberate and premeditated killing' (Pennsylvania). Generally, though not always, understood to require more than simple intention, US courts have held that premeditation for first-degree murder means that before committing the homicide, the defendant actually formed a plan to kill having had time to reflect and deliberate coolly on it (*Walker v State, State v Morton*).[4] US courts have not been consistent on the length of time necessary for intent to amount to premeditation, and the lack of agreement on this point suggests that the meaning of malice aforethought itself has become obscure. However it seems that generally speaking, where state laws require proof of premeditation before a jury may return a verdict of first-degree murder, the jury need only be satisfied that there is evidence of some prior reflection, no matter how brief (*People v Halvorsen*).

In this section I shall discuss the English and American understandings of malice aforethought, the flesh on the bones of the general legal principles provided by the English case of John Dickie Baillie in the Court of Appeal (*R v Baillie*) and the US case of Eugene Goforth in the Georgia Supreme Court (*Goforth v State*). As

---

2　Schedule 21, 10 (a).
3　Schedule 21, 4. (2) (a) (1).
4　e.g. 'a plan to murder ... formed after the matter had been the subject of deliberation and reflection', *Commonwealth v Burgess* at 432.

I shall argue, our moral and legal responses to the violence used by the defendants in cases turns upon when and why we find a killing to be malicious, or in other words when we believe there are good reasons to find that a killing was committed with malice or not. I shall argue that there are useful lessons to be learned from reflecting early modern approaches to determining malice aforethought: either expressly through finding premeditation and an absence of heated blood, or else by implying it as a proper response to a cruel or patently unnecessary use of violence. In the first section below I argue that in fact, the English criminal courts have already shown themselves to be prepared to treat the legal requirement of a 'loss of self-control' as a fiction in order to allow defendants to use the provocation defence even although, according to the formal requirements of the law, they ought to be convicted of murder. I argue that there is evidence to show that juries are using a broader moral sense to ensure that defendants who they feel have used lethal force out of fear, terror, panic or desperation – none of which is a recognized basis for a provocation defence in English law – are convicted of manslaughter rather than murder.

The Modern Provocation Defence: Premeditated Killing Filtered Out Using the Fictional Device of 'Loss of Self-control'

In most jurisdictions, provocation as a legal category is a partial excuse to murder and thus represents a point halfway between the worst form of killing and full acquittal; a person found to have been provoked into killing is convicted of (voluntary) manslaughter. Under English law, a person cannot be charged directly with voluntary manslaughter; rather, this verdict is returned when, on a charge of murder, the jury finds that the killing was provoked.[5] In the US, the trial judge decides whether or not to put a voluntary manslaughter charge to the jury for consideration, in addition to any other relevant categories of homicide. In both the US and in England, provocation is by definition antithetical to premeditation, and so contains conditions that ensure that, if the defendant laid in wait for his victim or acted with calculated cruelty or a desire for revenge, then the defendant will be found guilty of murder. In the US, the emotional aspect of the provocation defence is based on the finding of 'heated blood' or 'heated passion': an archaic idea, the meaning of which is not very different to the idea of hot blood that in the sixteenth century English common law denoted the absence of malice aforethought expressly formed. In fact, the similarity between the idea of heated blood in the US courts and its meaning in early modern England is striking. For the

---

    5   The trial judge must allow a jury to consider the defence of provocation and thus a verdict of manslaughter by provocation if there is any relevant evidence. I shall not be discussing defences for those who are judged to have been unfit to have their actions judged against the so-called 'reasonable man', and would therefore not have capacity-denying defences such as insanity, diminished responsibility, non-insane automatism, intoxication or infanticide.

US courts, the defendant's heated blood (coupled with a recognized cause for such passion – discussed in the next chapter) marks the distinction between killings that are merely intended and those that are intended *with malice*. A formulation of voluntary manslaughter in the US was provided in this recent judgment in the Supreme Court of South Carolina as ...

> ... the unlawful killing of a human being in the heat of passion upon sufficient legal provocation. Both heat of passion and sufficient provocation must be present at the time of the killing. The provocation must be such as to render the mind of an ordinary person incapable of cool reflection and produce an uncontrollable impulse to do violence. (*State v Cooley* per Toal CJ 67)

In Massachusetts, voluntary manslaughter is defined rather poetically as 'a sudden transport of passion or heat of blood, upon reasonable provocation and without malice, or upon sudden combat' (*Commonwealth v Burgess*, per Crown J, 438). The Official Code of Georgia Annotated requires the defendant to have acted 'solely as the result of a sudden, violent, and irresistible passion ...'. In Arkansas, the criminal law formerly referred to 'sudden heat of passion', until 1975 when the criminal code replaced this with the phrase 'extreme mental or emotional disturbance', though the meaning of the phrases has been held by the Arkansas Supreme Court to be equivalent (MPC s.219.3, *Bankston v State* 129).[6] It has been recognized in various states that the heating of the blood may be caused by intense rage (as in the current English law that the government intends to repeal), but also other extreme emotions such as fear or terror (*Bankston v State* 128). English law stopped referring to the heating of blood in the nineteenth century as the criminal courts sought to distance the defence from older attitudes that regarding the honourable violent response to an affront.[7] Instead of the broad and semi-justificatory archaic idea of heated passion, the current English formulation of the defence of provocation derives from nineteenth century ideas about the mind and so refers to the much narrower requirement of a 'loss of self-control'. This idea that conveys not a general intensifying of emotions but rather an utter loss of normal composure specifically as a result of uncontrollable rage:

> Where on a charge of murder there is evidence on which the jury can find that the person charged was provoked (whether by things done or by things said or by both together) to lose his self-control, the question whether the provocation

---

6 Some critics have argued that this formulation of the emotional requirement of provocation shows that American law is unduly lenient towards abusive men who kill their spouses out of jealous rage, for example Caroline Forell (2006) to whom we return in the next chapter.

7 See *R v Hayward* (1833) per Tindal CJ 159: court should consider whether the defendant had temporarily ceased to be 'master of his own understanding' or whether 'there had been time for the blood to cool and for reason to resume its seat'.

was enough to make a reasonable man do as he did shall be left to be determined by the jury; and in determining that question the jury shall take into account everything both done and said according to the effect which, in their opinion, it would have on a reasonable man. (Homicide Act 1957 s.3)

This formulation needs to be compared to the Government's proposed new partial defence to murder that is intended to replace provocation. Under the new proposals, a defendant (D) will have a partial defence to murder if the following three conditions are met:

Cl. 1 (1) (a) D's acts and omissions in doing or being a party to the killing resulted from D's loss of self-control;

(b) the loss of self-control had a qualifying trigger; and

(c) a person of D's sex and age, with a normal degree of tolerance and self-restraint and in the circumstances of D, might have reacted in the same or in a similar way to D. (Ministry of Justice 2008, 33)

Like the American formulations cited, the English defence thus contains both an emotional requirement and a justificatory/moral one and both differ fairly significantly from the equivalent requirements in the US. On the emotional aspect, the current English requirement of a 'loss of self-control' has been interpreted in the courts as requiring 'sudden and temporary' uncontrolled anger (*R v Duffy*),[8] which is more specific than the American notion of 'heated blood' or 'heated passion'. Under the new proposals this requirement of suddenness will be dropped, but otherwise the 'loss of self control' requirement will be retained as a safeguard against misuse of the defence by those who kill out of considered revenge (Ministry of Justice 2008, 13) The 'trigger' referred to in the new proposals must either be D's 'fear of serious violence from V [victim]' (Cl. 1 (1) (5)) or else words or actions from V that amount to circumstances of an extremely grave character that 'caused D to have a justifiable sense of being seriously wronged' (Cl. 1 (1) (6) Minisrty of Justice 2009, 12). The new proposals for the homicide laws of England and Wales represent a significant cultural and moral shift in terms of legislative attitude towards anger as the emotional basis for a partial defence. If the Government's proposals are passed into law in their current form, it will not be enough that the trigger might be judged sufficient to cause a 'reasonable man' to lose self control with rage. In fact, in restricting the proposed new defence to responses to 'extremely grave' circumstances, the proposed laws effectively aim to *remove*

---

8   Although in recent times the appellate courts have held that the 'slow-burn' psychological effect of the victim's history of provocative behaviour may be also taken into account, the actual requirement for a sudden temporary loss of self-control due to extreme anger as set out in *Duffy* remains a binding authority.

anger as a basis for a defence. Also, where-as the US laws require the victim to have provoked the defendant with violence or an act of witnessed adultery with the defendant's spouse, both the current English defence of provocation and the new proposed one leaves it open to the jury to consider the provocative nature of *any words or actions* on the part of the defendant's victim (*DPP v Camplin*). I want to leave the thorny point about what ought to qualify as recognized grounds for provocation aside for now and in this chapter focus instead on the emotional aspect, in particular on the merits of the English loss of self-control test, and whether justice could be better served by replacing it with a more general requirement of heated blood familiar to the American courts. Why should it be necessary to limit the provocation defence to only those people who lose self-control – whether as result of a sudden uncontrollable rage as in the current law, or as a result of fear of serious violence as in the new proposals, both of which seek to exclude many other forms of passionate or desperate emotion as a basis for a defence? The standard justification for retaining the 'loss of self-control' test is that it is a sure way of ensuring that cases of cold-blooded premeditated revenge are always treated as murder. Secondly, it is a way of getting around the problem that provocation in effect gives a defence of 'reasonableness' (would the reasonable man have acted as the defendant did?) for people whose actions are fundamentally unreasonable. It may be understandable but *never* straightforwardly reasonable to kill someone out of uncontrollable rage. A 'reasonable man' will surely never make a conscious choice to respond to a provocation by killing, but as a concession to the inherent frailty of ordinary humankind, we can sometimes excuse him for momentary lapses and losses of control if the provocation is severe enough in the judgment of the jury. The Court of Appeal describes the balance to be struck between the moral (reasonableness) and emotional (loss of self-control) aspects of partly excusing a person who kills as a response to a provocation:

> … notwithstanding that a man's reason might be unseated on the basis that the reasonable man would have found himself out of control, … there is still in every human being a residual justification for passing a sentence of imprisonment, to recognize that there is still left some degree of culpability, notwithstanding that the jury have found provocation. (*Attorney-General's Reference (Suratan)*, 282)

However there are arguably more effective ways of providing a morally coherent defence for reasonable people who in the heat of the moment respond unreasonably to provocative, threatening or bullying behaviour without excluding deserving cases. The Law Commission had recommended the removal of the positive requirement of loss of self-control, stating as its reason for recommending the dropping of the requirement that it is 'undesirable' since it 'has been widely criticized as privileging men's typical reactions to provocation over women's typical reactions' (Law Commission 2006, 81) and unnecessary' because if its central aim is to exclude cold blooded and premeditated killings, these can be achieved by simply denying the defence where the provocation was self-induced or where 'the defendant acted in considered revenge' (Law Commission 2006, 81). This recommendation has not been followed in the Government's 2008 proposals for a revised defence, which retain the requirement alongside a different emotional basis that excludes all but the most extreme and exceptional triggers for a violent response in anger at being wronged, but includes uncontrolled killings from fear of serious violence. However, while the current law arguably discriminates against those who kill out of fear or desperation, the new proposed defence, which will retain the loss of self-control test, risks being morally incoherent and legally unrealistic.

Let us consider the following scenario, cited by the Law Commission (2006, 93):

> An Asian woman returned home to find two white men attempting to rape her 15 year old daughter. She got a knife from the kitchen. The men shouted racist abuse at her and started to run away. She chased after them and stabbed one of them several times in the back.

The facts presented in this way preclude all current defences known to English law: the force used is not 'necessary' or reasonable as required for self-defence since the woman understands that the men are retreating; she has no mental abnormality that would qualify her for a defence of diminished responsibility; and although acting in a moment of extreme heated passion, it is not clear that she has lost self control as a result of anger, as required for provocation. She seems therefore to have committed murder according to the English definition of murder as intentional killing without excuse and as such serve the mandatory life sentence, but of those who responded to The Law Commission's scenario, 70 per cent felt she should serve no more than five years in jail for her actions. Furthermore, of all respondents 40 per cent said that she should receive a non-custodial sentence or no prosecution at all (Law Commission 2006, 93–4). One way to explain these responses as compatible with the current English understanding of provocation would be to say that a jury would probably find that, in such a grossly provoking situation, an ordinary person would lose self-control due to extreme anger. If such a case was tried under the Government's new proposed defence, she would escape a murder conviction if the jury can be sure that she lost self-control in response to 'extremely grave' circumstances that caused in the woman 'a justifiable sense of being wronged' (Ministry of Justice 2008, Cl. 1 (1) (6)). However, I would argue that loss of self-control really has very little to do with it; if a jury is satisfied that the rape is exceptionally provocative causing overwhelming anger, then the requirement of loss of self-control is unnecessary and would be treated by the jury as a given. In other words, the woman should have a defence to murder because the conditions of the scenario show that she acted in the heat of passion and killed suddenly without expressly formed malice aforethought and that there is no compelling reason why malice need be implied. Her lethally violent response to her daughter's rapist seems to qualify as what the American lawyers would describe as heated passion or heated blood and she certainly has cause for a justifiable sense of being wronged. Thus, it is not because of a loss of self-control that we offer a partial defence, but because of a belief that there is a tolerably clear culturally and socially constructed understanding of the correct *moral* response on the part of a detached observer to an act of violence committed genuinely from outrage, fear, panic or desperation. For this reason I think that, despite being correct to extend a partial defence to those who kill from fear of violence, in retaining the loss of self-control test, the new proposed partial defence approaches the reform of the defence in the wrong way.

More challenging cases are those involving killings in anger where the trigger for the anger was less than 'exceptional', where a reasonable person *might* be provoked to lose their self-control (and in which case may be able to use the current provocation defence), but it could not be said that the victim's behaviour goes 'far beyond what anyone could reasonably be expected to deal appropriately', thus denying them a defence under the new proposed laws (Ministry of Justice 2008, 11). At what point is it appropriate to allow a defence to murder for intentional killing in anger? Compare the fictional case of the Asian mother with the appeals of John Dickie Baillie in the English Court of Appeal and also that of Eugene Goforth in the Supreme Court of Georgia US, both of which involved a man convicted of murder and appealing on grounds of provocation in anger. In *Baillie*, the defendant had been told by one of his sons that a local drug dealer called McCubbin had made some vague and unspecific physical threats against him. McCubbin was afraid that the boys were planning to buy their drugs directly from his own supplier and had warned them not to cut him out of a deal. Upon hearing the report, the enraged and drunk Mr Baillie drove off to find McCubbin, taking with him a cut-throat razor and a sawn-off shotgun which he kept in his attic. There ensued a confrontation during which Baillie cut McCubbin very badly with the razor. The stricken drug dealer tried to escape through the back of his house, but Baillie pursued him and shot him dead as he fled. At his trial, Baillie relied upon the defence of provocation, but was convicted of murder. At his appeal, the Court of Appeal held that the trial judge had usurped the role of the jury by strongly suggesting that in her opinion, when Baillie killed McCubbin, he was not suffering from a sudden temporary lost his self-control but rather that:

> … there was time for reflection and time for cooling off, because on any view of the evidence what happens is that he goes to the attic, collects the gun, he brings that down and places it in the car, the car is driven from his house a distance of some two miles via a petrol filling station to the place where these events occurred and there is then a walking, albeit of a short distance, from a place where the car is to the house. That seems to me to be evidence which takes this case outside the sudden and temporary loss of self-control so as to make the accused not for the moment mast of his mind.[9]

---

9   The reasoning of the Court of Appeal has subsequently been applied to the opposite effect in *R v Khan*, in which, despite having previously been told by the victim that he intended to kill him and rape his sister and niece, the trial judge was right not to leave

Notwithstanding the usurpation of the jury's role, the trial judge's comments here are a perfectly reasonable interpretation of the *Duffy* requirement of a sudden and temporary loss of self-control. It is more than likely that events intervening between hearing about the threats made against his sons and the killing of McCubbin – which in addition to those listed by the trial judge also included a minor road accident due to his drunkenness – Baillie would have had time for reflection and cooling off. Similarly, it is unlikely that having arrived at the house doubly armed and accompanied by his teenage sons, McCubbin attempting to wrest the shotgun from his hands would be sufficiently grave provocation for a reasonable man not only to cause those 'terrible injuries' with the razor, but also to chase him outside to finish him off.[10] Taken as a whole, Baillie's actions were almost certainly the result of malice expressly formed to kill McCubbin at his home as revenge for the threats issued to his sons. However, because the current legal formulation of the provocation defence requires that the question of the possibility of a loss of self-control at the crucial time be left to the jury, his conviction for murder was quashed and a retrial ordered. But is this the best way to distinguish killings with malice aforethought and killings without? Under the newly proposed partial defence, a jury would still have to consider whether Baillie lost self control, but also whether that was based on 'extremely grave' circumstances, which no-one could be expected to 'deal with appropriately' (Ministry of Justice 2008, 11). In my view, the question as to whether or not Baillie committed murder or manslaughter should not depend upon a finding of loss of self-control, since this diverts attention away from the overall moral character of the event. We simply have no way of knowing whether the requirement was fulfilled and neither does a jury (beyond the wholly meaningless testimony from Baillie himself that he did). American laws, generally formulated at state level, tend to refer not to a loss of self-control but rather to the archaic notion of heated blood, which is far broader that the English mechanism. In *Goforth v State*, the defendant, heard that his former lover was spending the evening with her husband with whom she had begun reconciliation since her relationship with Goforth. Goforth armed himself and drove to the man's house. He spied on the couple for some hours until they began having sexual intercourse, at which point Goforth fired at them through the window, killing the man. On appeal against his murder conviction, the court held that the jury were entitled to find, as they did, that Goforth's preparation and lying in wait indicated that the killing had not in truth been provoked in the spirit of the

---

the question of provocation open to the jury since there was no evidence of a sudden and temporary loss of self-control at the relevant moment.

10   The authority relied upon by the Court of Appeal to show that the victim's attempt to wrestle the gun from Baillie might be sufficient provocation was *Edwards*, in which it was held that even a blackmailer might be able to rely on the defence if the person being blackmailed went to 'extreme lengths'. See 'Provocation   Homicide Act 1957, s.3 – Defence of Provocation' (1995, 739–40).

Georgia criminal code,[11] but rather had sought to take revenge on the couple for their reconciliation. Had this been an English case under present homicide laws, the trial jury would have been instructed to return a verdict of murder *unless* there was reasonable doubt inasmuch as he might have been provoked to the point of a losing self-control at the sight of the sexual activity between the victim and his wife. Such an instruction would surely be to divert attention away from a balanced and holistic assessment of a person's use of violence, as I believe is the effect of the Court of Appeal's approach in *Baillie*. What separates both Baillie and Goforth from the Law Commission's fictional Asian mother character described above, is that taken as a whole, the Asian woman's violence, whether committed out of outrage, desperation, shame, fear, or a combination of those feelings, seems *genuinely to stem from her heated passion, directly induced by the provocation* whilst the violence of Baillie and Goforth seem to have been motivated instead by their own attitudes towards the acceptability of using violence to settle a score. Under the new Government proposals for the English law on homicide, a killing committed as a result of anger in sexual jealousy would be automatically denied a partial defence for the reason that discovery of unfaithfulness is not a recognized trigger for loss of self-control (Ministry of Justice 2008, 11). Therefore as a matter of legal principle, a case such as Goforth's would be denied a defence even if there were a loss of self-control. In Baillie's case, a court operating under the new proposed law would have to consider whether his killing of McCubbin could be interpreted as being committed as a result of a loss of self control due either to fear that McCubbin would actually carry out his threats against his sons, or else that those threats were in themselves so exceptional as to give Baillie a justifiable sense of being wronged, as judged according to the standards of a person of his own age and sex, with 'normal degree of tolerance and self-restraint' in those circumstances. It seems that the day of the 'reasonable man' of the nineteenth and twentieth centuries, who is moved to uncontrollable rage, has at last passed: whereas under the present laws, a jury is directed specifically to assess the reasonableness of an uncontrolled *angry* reaction, the new proposals completely undercut this approach to the emotional aspect of the defence. Killings committed as a result of anger will, if the proposals become law as the Government intends, generally be treated as murder, not manslaughter. Fear, and not anger, is now to be the understandable emotional extreme of modern British society. Whether or not it is wise to restrict the recognition of anger as the 'trigger' in this way, I believe that to require a court to look specifically for a loss of self-control in anger is an unnecessary hurdle in finding that a killing was genuinely provoked and thus properly to be regarded as manslaughter rather than murder. The cooler and determined responses of Baillie and Goforth look more like the actions of men for whom violence is a natural method of settling disputes; lacking a heated or passionate response, we regard their killings as murder.

---

11   The Georgia code requires the defendant to have acted from an 'irresistible passion', OCGA s.16–5–2(a).

There are some very clear indications that the old understanding of provoked violence as a sudden act of violence immediately upon and insult or affront is now merely an historical one. The Government is correct to signal a desire to drop the requirement of 'sudden and temporary' rage from the partial defence in its 2008 proposals, but it is wrong to retain the subsequently half-baked requirement of loss of self-control shorn of the suddenness requirement. The Sentencing Guidelines Council (2005, 5) currently advises sentencing judges effectively to ignore the *Duffy* requirements of a sudden temporary loss of self-control when a defendant seems to have responded in fear or desperation to a 'slow-burn' provocation. The Sentencing Guidelines Council advises that, if the defendant is weak or vulnerable compared to the defendant or has been the victim of domestic abuse, then a lack of evidence of a sudden burst of anger should not count against them. If, instead of reacting suddenly to a provocation, such a person takes advantage of a 'favourable situation' before killing the victim, for example, by waiting until the victim fall asleep, then this should not deny them the defence of provocation. *Charlton* is an interesting case because it further demonstrates not only the inadequacy of the loss of self-control requirement but also that the courts are willing to overcome that inadequacy by taking a broad view on what constitutes a provoked killing. Ms Charlton killed her partner because he had threatened to kill her and that he intended to have intercourse with and then kill her daughter also. Thinking that Ms Charlton wanted to engage in S&M, he allowed himself to be handcuffed, blindfolded and gagged, before she killed him with an axe, which curiously was to hand. Ms Charlton was convicted of manslaughter and sentenced to five years. On appeal, her sentence was reduced to three and a half years to take into consideration the context of her partner's controlling manner, his jealousy and previous sexual abuse of the defendant. The only possible evidence of a loss of self-control specifically was that the defendant's actions were quite out of character with her usual 'happy-go-lucky' personality, that she used only the weapon that was to hand at the time, and that she seems to have suffered amnesia after the event. The reasoning of the Court of Appeal, however, makes it clear that it was the gravity of the provocation itself, creating a very understandable fear and desperation in the defendant that was important. In other words, the reason why Ms Charlton's plea succeeded was because the courts recognize that violent actions stemming from desperation and fear do warrant a defence, whether or not self-control is lost. It is very likely that it is cases like this that motivated the newly proposed reforms to the partial defence to murder. In the 2008 consultation paper, the Government underlines the impression that the traditional requirement of a 'sudden and temporary' reaction in extreme anger does not reflect current attitudes towards the need to provide a defence for people who kill because they are terrified of their abusers. The paper argues that 'it is not helpful for killings which are triggered primarily by fear to be shoehorned into a partial defence which is aimed at killings triggered by anger, and we agree that a tailored partial defence is needed' (Ministry of Justice 2008, 10). The proposals are correct therefore to include fear of serious violence as a basis for a defence rather than 'shoe-horn' such cases into a defence designed for angry responses, but they are wrong to nevertheless continue to insist on the requirement of 'loss of self-control' instead of the broader requirement of heated passion used in the US.

The reason why I think homicide could manage without the loss of self-control test is because there is evidence that it is treated as a fiction by juries in England and Wales, who seem instead to apply a wider test to determine whether the killing should be regarded as murder or manslaughter. Since it resides in the realm of fact, the requirement of loss of self-control is treated as proved once the jury returns a verdict of manslaughter by reason of provocation. This is so even if the evidence for loss of self-control is very thin. In *Suratan*, the Court of Appeal gave judgement on a number of appeals involving men who had been convicted of manslaughter after killing their female partners. The legal point at issue was whether the trial judge had been too lenient in his sentencing. The Court of Appeal made it clear that the question as to whether the defendant had lost self control was to be treated beyond question. This is all very well, but since juries do not have to provide any explanation for their verdicts, it is unclear whether loss of self-control was *actually* found or whether the defence succeeded on broader grounds. Evidence of the manner of the killing and the defendant's own answers in police questioning may provide some help, and in *Suratan* itself Wilkinson reported that he 'just boiled over'. However, this is not always the case. Research by Mitchell and Cunningham for the Law Commission's 2006 report indicated that juries are willing to return a verdict of manslaughter by provocation in the absence of *any* evidence that the defendant actually lost self-control. An act of lethal violence committed out of outrage or ferocious anger immediately or very soon after a gross offence or otherwise trying circumstances will generally suffice, and juries often seem not to trouble themselves with the question of self-control where the provocation was sufficiently gross as to make an angry reaction understandable. In a homicide case described in the research report only as 'case 79', the defendant pleaded both provocation and self-defence together. He had killed the victim who had, together with a number of friends, encircled the defendant threateningly. The defendant reported feeling 'angry and frightened' – the jury spared him the mandatory life sentence and convicted him of manslaughter (Mitchell and Cunningham 2006, 188). On such evidence, surely no reasonable jury could be satisfied that the defendant acted in response to a provocation as set out in the Homicide Act. In returning the manslaughter verdict the jury is surely responding to a perceived shortcoming of the formal law: that the loss of self-control test, excusing as it does only violence committed from uncontrollable anger, offers no partial defence for lethal violence committed out of fear, panic, or other forms of desperation. This is one type of case that the new proposed partial defence to murder, which excuses killings committed out of 'fear of serious violence by V', will make a positive contribution, even although it will continue to insist on what I believe to be an unnecessary finding of loss of self-control. Under the new proposals, evidence such as found in 'case 79' that suggested violence used in fear would be sufficient to provide a partial defence, as long as the jury would be happy, as they seem to be, to assume loss of self-control.

When faced with a malicious provocation involving violence, humiliation, serious bullying or sexual assault, a defendant's angry or frightened reaction will seem to a jury to be the kind of homicide that warrants an excuse, providing that the evidence indicates that the violence used by the defendant was used in heated passion, as a direct result of the victim's grossly provocative behaviour. From what we already know about the Law Commission's fictional Asian woman who stabs her daughter's would-be rapist to death, we can say that evidence points in this direction and a finding of a loss of self-control would probably not be necessary to convince a jury that a partial defence to murder is warranted. Would the killing become any more excusable if the last line was edited to read: 'Suffering a sudden and temporary loss of self-control, she chased after them and stabbed one of them several times in the back'? I submit that it would not. Would Baillie's killing of the drug dealer be more deserving of a defence if there were evidence that he had in fact suddenly lost his self-control in response to McCubbin repeating his threats to Baillie himself at the door? If the evidence showed, as it did at his trial, that Baillie had gone to McCubbin's house having already decided to exact revenge for the threats made against his sons then I don't see that this should alter our understanding of his violence as premeditated murder. In both cases, the addition of the loss of self-control test is an addition of nothing. I am not suggesting that we should simply allow for whatever prejudices juries might display towards violence they happen to sympathize with. After all, we must be aware that for one reason or another juries might be drawn into returning a verdict of manslaughter by provocation in instances that do seem to involve premeditation. For instance, in a case reported by Mitchell and Cunningham as 'case 175', the defendant had been heard to say that he intended to hurt the victim. There was witness testimony that the defendant had accordingly approached and shot the victim. On those facts the inference of premeditation seems fairly clear, but the jury found him guilty only of manslaughter by provocation (he had changed his story at trial from accident to one in which the victim had attacked him with a knife) (Mitchell and Cunningham 2006, 188). In *Latham Attorney General's Reference No. 33* the defendant showed readiness to use violence by carrying a weapon to the scene of an incident and then used it to kill the victim. In both cases, the Court of Appeal increased the defendant's sentence in order to reflect this. However, if the purpose of a partial defence is to excuse killings that lack malice aforethought due to extreme emotional disturbance, then a requirement of loss of self-control surely only detracts from the broader moral question of how best to respond to fatal violence. The new proposals for reform of the English law are a step in the right direction in broadening the emotional basis of the partial defence to 'fear of serious violence' since it acknowledges that anger is not the only response – and indeed not at all the most sympathetic response – that warrants a defence to murder. In going further in excluding anger from the defence in all but 'extremely grave' circumstances, the proposed defence makes a bold claim about changes in social and moral attitudes towards violence. As I have argued, the continued insistence on a formal loss of self-control test is unfortunate in determining whether the killing actually stemmed from the danger, affront (manslaughter) or else from the defendant's own violent temperament (murder). Furthermore, it remains to be seen whether the requirement in the new proposals for juries to consider precisely *how grave* the victim's words or conduct were in provoking the defendant to an angry response will, like the requirement of a loss of self-control itself, be treated by juries as a fiction to be ignored if the jury simply decide that the facts suggest that a murder conviction is too harsh.

2. Historical and Dramatic Perspectives on Malice Aforethought: Hot and Cold-blooded Killing in Shakespeare's England

Given that the loss of self-control requirement in English law seems to be both undesirably narrow and also arguably already treated as a fiction by English juries, the provocation defence seems to be ripe for rethinking in terms of alternative ways of responding morally and legally to killings committed out of extreme passion or heated blood, and therefore to the way we distinguish between murder as killing with malice aforethought and manslaughter as killing that lacks malice. Therefore this section turns to the emotional aspect of provocation from an historical and dramatic perspective. The following discussion examines the emergence of the legal distinction between murder and manslaughter and the way in which this is reflected in Shakespeare's *Hamlet*. In both cases the central question is how to distinguish killings which we can regard as having been committed in such heat of passion that we can regard them as merely manslaughter from those with malice expressly formed, or as the medieval and early modern lawyers would have said, 'pre-pensed'. From Saxon times until the twelfth century, premeditated murder was the only capital homicide offence, which meant a killing committed by stealth, in secret and at night.[12] The reforms of Henry II in the twelfth century effectively removed the legal distinction between murder and other homicides. Through an innovation credited with the creation of the English common law itself, Henry II brought homicide under the new capital offence of felonious homicide, which included all intentional killing whether premeditated or not, for which the penalty was death by hanging (Green 1976, 418). Killing by accident and self-defence were reclassified as non-felonious homicide, for which the accused could expect a royal pardon as a matter of course (*de cursu*) (Green 1972, 669; Hanawalt

---

12   A distinction preserved for their own ends by the Norman invaders in the form of the 'murdrum' community penalty to protect themselves from Saxons (Sayer 1932, 995). In *Mawgridge* Holt CJ explains how William the Conqueror's 'murdrum' was a revival of a much older law introduced by the Danish King Canute to protect his Danish brethren from Saxons who desired to seek revenge against the Danes.

1976, 297–320; Horder 1992, 6; Law Commission 2004, 289–90).[13] According to the formal law of the medieval period therefore, there was no distinction drawn between what we might call murder and manslaughter and so courts did not trouble themselves to distinguish killings carried out with malice 'pre-pensed' (also called malice aforethought) and those without. Other than receiving a royal pardon for killings in self-defence, a man accused of murder could escape the hanging noose by claiming the defence of 'benefit of clergy'. The traditional independence of canon law from royal law meant that members of the clergy who were convicted of a felony could be handed over unpunished to the church for a retrial. Punishments meted out by church courts were considerably more lenient than those imposed by the royal courts, very rarely if ever involving execution even for the worst crimes. Those found guilty under canon law were most often sentenced to branding, short-term imprisonment and penance (Green 1976, 474–5). The benefit seems to have been interpreted increasingly leniently and by the end of the fifteenth century its use had spread well beyond the clergy itself; anyone who could demonstrate a modest level of literacy, for example by reading a few lines from the Bible, would qualify for a canon law retrial and thus avoid the death penalty. It was becoming clear that the widespread use of clergy rights was making a mockery of the royal jurisdiction over felonious homicide, so to reassert its own political power against the church, Parliament sought to restrict the 'benefit of clergy' so that those accused of the very worst kinds of homicide – that is, killed having previously formed the malice – could not avail themselves of the benefit of a clergy retrial and thus would have to face the death penalty. In the Tudor statutes of the sixteenth century then, 'murder' once again became a distinct legal concept in distinguishing killings committed with malice pre-pensed or malice aforethought from those committed as a result of spontaneous violence erupting from a chance dispute, or 'chance medley' (Green 1976, 473; Sayre 1932, 996).[14] Murder regained is special legal meaning, according to *The Boke of Justyces of Peas* of 1510 as applying to homicides 'where a man by malice pre-pensed lies in wait to slay man and according to that malicious intent and purpose he slays him so that he who is slain makes no defence' (Law Commission 2004, 294). By contrast, manslaughter emerged as a legal concept and an offence separate from murder, defined as applying 'where two men or more meet and by chance medley they fall at affray so that of them slays the other'. It is clear therefore that premeditation and its absence are crucial here in distinguishing, not simply between two aspects of felonious homicide as had previously been the case, but between two separate

---

13 To be pardoned was considerably less favourable than an acquittal. Although by the end of the thirteenth century pardons for self-defence and accident had become a matter of course ('*de cursu*'), the accused had to remain in gaol for many months waiting for the pardon to be granted and (from the 1340s) the forfeiture of all of the accused person's property (Green 1976, 425–6).

14 The relevant statutes were those of 1496 (Henry VII), 1512 and 1531 (Henry VIII), 1547 (Edward VI).

offences. The practical difference was one of life and death for the accused (Horder 1992, 12–4, Kaye 1967, 569–601). The expression 'chance medley' applied to all felonious homicides lacking malice aforethought. Thus the expression included clergiable felonious homicide and also excusable non-felonious homicides for self defence or accident for which the defendant could obtain a pardon *de cursu* (Green 1976, 482).

In legislating to restrict the right to retrial under canon law to cases of chance-medley, Parliament was reflecting a moral distinction between premeditated and hot-blooded killing which probably had persevered in English common culture despite the medieval effacement of any formal legal distinction under Henry II's reforms. If this is so, the Tudor statutes restricting the benefit of clergy brought the law into greater harmony with the common belief that a man who 'lies in wait to slay a man' committed a crime of a different moral order to the one who spontaneously became involved in an affray and ended up killing his assailant. The prevalence of knife carrying, a lack of any kind of policing and the ineffectiveness of medical care all conspired to increase the risk that a violent dispute would become fatal, which probably accounts for the social tolerance of chance medley killing in the period. For a discussion on this point in the context of a slightly earlier period see Hanawalt (1976). Chance-medley or chance affray as a basis for voluntary manslaughter is now unknown in English law: it died out along with references to 'heated blood' and 'heated passion' when the law moved towards the idea of a reasonable 'loss of self-control' in the nineteenth century. For instance, in *Welsh* (at 339), Keating J referred to the necessity for a provocation sufficiently grave as to 'cause an ordinary and reasonable minded man to lose his self-control'. However, in the US where pre-meditation – that is, malice aforethought in its old literal sense – continues to form a constitutive element of first-degree murder, a form of the old chance-medley defence remains a living legal concept. First, since premeditation and deliberation are constituent elements of first-degree murder, such a verdict is ruled out if a jury finds that the defendant's violence was sudden, rash or spontaneous so that they did not have time to think through their actions (*State v McGhee*). But more than this, courts have also held that 'mutual quarrel or combat' is an explicitly recognized basis on which juries may return a verdict of manslaughter (*State v Chevalier*). It has also been recognized that the 'sudden transport of passion or heat of blood' necessary to establish a lack of malice may be caused by defendant becoming involved in 'sudden combat' and 'excessive use of force in self-defence' (*Comm. v Burgess, Comm. v Peters*). No such thing exists in English law now, but for the early-modern courts, as in the relevant modern state laws of voluntary manslaughter in the US, the question as to whether the defendant's killing was committed in hot blood arising from a chance affray was a question of evidence for the finders of fact. The earliest case to record a verdict of manslaughter was *Salisbury's Case* of 1553, which involved a servant who, upon seeing his master involved in an affray, spontaneously joined in and killed an assailant. It was clear that the defendant in this case had acted 'in hot blood' in the sense that his violence stemmed not from any actual malice towards the deceased but from the impact of the situation had upon his senses.

It was into the midst of these important legal developments that *Hamlet* appears at the beginning of the seventeenth century.[15] As well as the central narrative of Hamlet's anguished brooding on the Ghost's command to him to exact revenge on Claudius (Hamlet's uncle and Old Hamlet's murderer), Hamlet commits a number of sudden and spontaneous killings that are all notable inasmuch as they pass without much moral concern at all. In III, iv, Hamlet goes to his mother's chamber to remonstrate with her about her 'adulterous' relationship with Claudius, and as Gertrude becomes increasingly terrified by Hamlet's hectoring and violent temperament, they are disturbed by a noise from behind an arras: it is Polonius, Claudius' minister and spy eavesdropping on them. Hamlet dispatches the old man immediately by stabbing him through the arras (Foakes 2003, 126):

> Gertrude: "What wilt thou do? Thou wilt not murder me?"

> "Help, help, ho!"

> Polonius: *behind the arras* "What ho! Help!"

> Hamlet: "How now? A rat! Dead for a ducat, dead." *Thrusts his rapier through the arras.* (III, iv, 21–23)

Hamlet reacts, not like a hesitant intellectual, but more like a trigger-happy gunslinger of a western, and neither does he show much remorse for what he has done. Discovering Polonius's corpse, Hamlet is full of contempt ('Thou wretched, rash, intruding fool, farewell./ I took thee for thy better' (III, iv, 31–2)). At the end of the scene Hamlet seems equally unmoved by his actions. Arden informs us that his sardonic announcement that he will 'lug the guts into the neighbouring room' (III, iv, 214) is Shakespeare's reference to an earlier play in which a body is cut into pieces and fed to pigs (Jenkins 1982, 332). Likewise the other hot-blooded killings that Hamlet commits – those of Rosencrantz and Guildenstern and finally of Claudius himself – are barely commented on as moral issues. Committed as they are in hot-blooded self-defence (Rosencrantz and Guildenstern) and spontaneous rage (Claudius) viewers are left with the impression that Hamlet sees no complication there.[16] There has been some discussion amongst critics as to whether these killings really are committed in hot blood or not. Prosser (1971, 194–5) has

---

15   The Second Quarto, from which most of the references to the play in this chapter and the next are drawn, appeared in 1604.

16   Forcing Claudius to drink the poisoned cup, Hamlet cries: 'Here thou incestuous, murdrous,/ Damned Dane,/ Drinke off this Potion' (V, ii, 277–8). Of the deaths of Rosencrantz and Guildenstern, Hamlet's lack of concern is shown by his remark that 'they are not near my heart' (V, ii, 58, *Folio*).

argued that the killings of Polonius and also of Rosencrantz and Guildenstern are actually instances of premeditated murder that illustrate Hamlet's 'descent into evil'. Prosser argues that Hamlet had already formed the intention to kill Claudius when he entered Gertrude's chamber, and the fact that his intention leads him to kill the 'innocent' Polonius by mistake, whose eavesdropping could not amount to a gross provocation anyhow, cannot exculpate him (Prosser 1971, 194–5). In the case of Rosencrantz and Guildenstern, Prosser claims that Hamlet declares his intention to kill them both before he or they discover that Claudius wants them to kill Hamlet in England, and thus Claudius's attempt to use them to kill Hamlet does not exculpate Hamlet's own malice aforethought regarding their killing. However, I think that Prosser is wrong on both points, and that the explanation of Hamlet's and also most audiences' lack of moral concern for the dispatching of Polonius, Rosencrantz or Guildenstern is explained by the distinction which was recognized to exist between hot blooded and cold blooded killing in early modern times. It is unlikely that Hamlet entered Gertrude's bedchamber with an intention to kill. In this scene he has just left Claudius praying in another room and in any case his fury is directed at Gertrude whom he wants to reform, not kill. Afterwards he declares that he 'knows not' what he has done (III, iv, 24), which we should interpret as a denial of premeditation, not simply of a mistake of identity. Elizabethan and Jacobean political and public life was marked by spying, intrigue and religious strife. England's recent painful conversion to Protestantism and the resentment this continued to cause for Catholics meant that harassment from the authorities was a real fear. Shakespeare's audience would have perceived the discovery by Hamlet of the King's spy in his mother's chamber as evidence that Hamlet probably did kill Polonius in hot blood. After all, the scene unfolding is one in which Hamlet works himself into a frenzy of moral indignation at what he feels is his mother's betrayal of her former husband.[17] His words and actions are illustrative of a man acting in hot blood, in response to a provocative situation. As for Rosencrantz and Guildenstern, in claiming that their killing by Hamlet is also premeditated murder, Prosser (1971, 204) is simply making too much of ambiguously threatening remarks.

In relation to the play's central moral question – whether and how Hamlet should obey the command issued to him by Old Hamlet's Ghost to kill his uncle Claudius – much of the agony we perceive in Hamlet relates to the fact that for Hamlet it is much more difficult to interpret it as a hot blooded killing. In various passages we find Hamlet trying to reason himself into summoning the necessary boiling passion which would allow him to regard himself as an honourable avenger and not a cold blooded murderer according to Elizabethan and Jacobean moral and legal standards. For example, at the staging of *The Murder of Gonzago*, the play within the play, Hamlet reflects on the normal and natural passionate response to

---

17 'Repent what's past, avoid what is to come/ And do not spread the compost o'er the weeds/ To make them ranker' (III, iv, 141–3).

having received news of a father's murder, contrasting it with his own inability to display evidence of such heated passion:

> He would drown the stage with tears,
> And cleave the general ear with horrid speech
> Make mad the guilty, and appal the free,
> Confound the ignorant, and amaze indeed
> The very faculties of eyes and ears. (II, ii, 556–60)

Despite showing himself quite decisive and ready to use lethal violence against Polonius behind the arras and then eventually against Claudius, to obey the Ghost's command would require either becoming so enraged by the news that the killing could be manslaughter by heated blood, or else it would be murder. For a sensitive and thoughtful man, the appreciation of such a choice may have in itself been enough to chill the blood. In that case, the Romantic reading of the character of Hamlet, unfashionable now, as being simply too sensitive and too thoughtful to commit premeditated murder may be correct. He cannot summon up the requisite passionate motivation (Miller 2006, 146). His conscience and thoughtfulness prevents him from taking decisive action – whether to kill Claudius or himself, which he laments as turning him into a coward in this very well-known part of his speech from Act III:

> Thus conscience does make cowards,
> And thus the nature hiew of resolution
> Is sickled ore with the pale cast of thought,
> And enterprises of great pitch and moment,
> With this regard their currents turn awry,
> And lose the name of action. (III, i, 91–5)[18]

It is possible that it is the way in which Hamlet becomes aware of Claudius's crime through the testimony of a Ghost 'of questionable shape' that explains Hamlet's difficulties in summoning up the necessary passion to kill without being a murderer. As we have seen, the provocation that the trial judge in the modern English case of *R v Baillie* identified was the news that Mr Baillie received concerning the threats aimed at his sons. In *Hamlet*, it is the report of Old Hamlet's murder that first inspires the young Hamlet with thoughts of revenge. But is the report of the murder of one's kin sufficient provocation to cause the heating of one's blood? In Baillie's case, the trial judge's assertion that the lengthy car journey to McCubbin's house after hearing the news that so enraged him in all likelihood provided sufficient time to cool off. In the Court of Appeal, it was only

---

18   Ian Miller (2006, 155) suggests that far from showing cowardice, Hamlet's inaction is itself the most effective revenge, since, in deterring bloody revenge he 'succeeds in making Claudius a nervous wreck'.

the possibility of a face-to-face provocation at McCubbin's doorstep that raised the possibility of a loss of his self-control and therefore a verdict of manslaughter by provocation. In the US it is regarded that a killing committed in the absence of a face-to-face provocation in the form of *actions* can never amount to a sufficient heating of the blood. O'Neal Farr of Alabama, who shot dead his teenage wife after finding her naked in a motel room with another man, *would* have had a defence of provocation had he shot her in the instant that he found her since actually catching one's spouse in an act of adultery is formally recognized in the US as a basis for heated passion. However, he was instead convicted of murder (and his appeal dismissed) because he chose instead to make her dress, to drive her back home to his trailer and execute her there in the presence of a neighbour (*Farr v State*). Likewise, when Maurice Chevalier of Illinois shot and killed his wife in a jealous rage, his defence of provocation failed because it was held that simply hearing about a wife's adultery – in this case the woman confessed to him – necessarily fails as a basis for finding heated passion as a matter of law (*State v Chevalier*). I think that it is legitimate to question the logic of holding that no matter what the circumstances, hearing of, say, the rape or murder of a loved one is any less harrowing than a face-to-face provocation. The appeals of O'Neal Farr and Maurice Chevalier failed because their violence was too far removed from the provocation itself (in their cases, their wives' adultery). In *Hamlet*, on the central question of whether Hamlet should avenge his father's murder as the Ghost commands him, we and Hamlet are likewise removed from the crucial provocative event: the murder of Old Hamlet occurs off-stage and we only hear about it through the Ghost's testimony and Claudius' own overheard confession in the prayer scene ('O! My offence is rank, it smells to heaven', III, iii, 36). Shakespeare forces Hamlet and the viewer of the play to reflect seriously on the reliability of third party testimony and the extent to which news of an appalling event can stir our passions to the extent that it could serve as the basis for a defence to murder. Various critics have pointed out that Shakespeare gives us plenty of reasons to doubt the Ghost, not perhaps as to the veracity of his words, but certainly as to the purpose for which he conveys them to the much-affected Hamlet. For instance, consider the effect of the Ghost's message that Claudius murdered Old Hamlet, 'With juice of cursed hebenon in a vial [which] in the porches of my ear did pour' (I, v, 22–23). In reporting the act, what is this Ghost doing – partial and full of hatred as it is – if not pouring poison into Hamlet's ears? (Ratcliffe 1998, 131). Irrespective of whether Claudius is 'really' guilty or not – and for the sake of argument we should assume that he is – the audience and Hamlet alike are presented with a murder performed by *words* – existing in our ears rather than in front of our eyes. What is important here is what we are supposed to make of the poisonous effect of the Ghost's words, both for Hamlet's own mental health and for the course of events in the doomed Danish court (Ratcliffe 1998, 133–4).

To understand how Shakespeare's audience would have viewed the provocative potential of the Ghost's command to seek vengeance we need to consider the religious context of the character of the Ghost. First, because of prevailing theological attitudes of the time, very few members of an Elizabethan or Jacobean audience would have believed that the Ghost was actually Old Hamlet's spirit returned from the dead. Both Catholics and Protestants in Elizabethan times believed that no soul could return to Earth from either Heaven or Hell. Escape from purgatory was a theoretical possibility for Catholics, but even then the chances of it being malignant were very high, especially if its message contradicted scripture (Prosser 1971, 103–5). Protestants, believing that entry to Heaven was secured by grace alone, dismissed purgatory as a papist lie and believed that ghosts were generally devils who preyed on melancholics to do Satan's work. Notably therefore, the Ghost does claim to have come from purgatory, since he speaks of being 'confin'd to fast in fires; Till the foul crimes done in my days of nature; Are burnt and purg'd away' (I, v, 11–3). If this is supposed to confirm that the Ghost is indeed Old Hamlet's spirit returned, this is contradicted by Hamlet's own apparently Protestant frame of reference, since he asks whether the Ghost brings 'airs from heaven or blasts of hell' (I, iv, 41) and thus does not recognize the existence of purgatory (Edger 1986, 12–14; Foakes 2004, 119; Prosser 1971, 104).[19] As Prosser (1971, 118) puts it, 'the play frankly invited both Protestants and Catholics to test the Ghost according to their religious beliefs and then presented them with recognizable warnings of danger.' The danger of the Ghost was not that what he tells Hamlet may be untrue, but that the truth is told for an evil purpose. E. Edger (1986, 9–12) argues that there is no doubt that Shakespeare intended the Ghost to be understood as a 'masquerading devil', and she is certainly not alone in this. On first sight, the Ghost disappears, apparently offended, at Horatio's mention of heaven, and after leaving the audience's sight, the Ghost *'Cries under the stage'* (I, v, 157), suggesting that it resides in hell. This is one of many clues to suggest that the Ghost is the Devil or evil spirit sent to trick Hamlet, since contemporary accounts indicate that the Devil was known to taken the shape of miners underground (Jenkins 1982, 458). Indeed, Hamlet refers to the Ghost now apparently under the stage as an 'old mole' and a 'worthy pioneer', and marvels at the way it seems to 'work i' th' earth so fast' (I, v, 170–1). The guard Marcellus notes that 'It faded on the crowing of the cock' (I, i, 162), a time for evil spirits to seek underground shelter since, as Shakespeare's audience would have been well aware, the crowing cock symbolized the voice of grace that banishes sin (Prosser 1971, 122). Hamlet and Horatio are themselves clearly not ignorant of this possibility. Horatio tries in vain to dissuade Hamlet

---

19   In support of the Protestant belief that devils were sent to spread papist lies such as that of purgatory, Jenkins (1982, 483), Edger and Prosser all cite a number of such sources including the treatise on witchcraft by James VI of Scotland (later James I of England), *Demonology* [1576] and the sixteenth century poet Thomas Nashe, *The Terrors of the Night* [1594], which all testify to this belief (p.483). In making the same point, Edger also cites the scholar Andrew Willet, *Hexapla in Exodum* [1608], Robert Burton's science/philosophy on human cognition, *The Anatomy of Melancholy* [1621] and the treatise on science and religion by the physician Sir Thomas Browne, *Religio Medici* [1643].

from speaking to the Ghost at all, in case it 'tempt you toward the flood, my lord; Or to the dreadful summit of the cliff' (I, iv, 69–70). Although, as noted above, Hamlet decides that the Ghost is indeed that of his dead father, his very first fears that it may possibly be a 'goblin damn'd' (I, iv, 40) return in the next Act:

> The spirit I have seen
> May be a devil, and the devil hath power
> T'assume a pleasing shape. (II, ii, 594–6)

If the Ghost really is a devil, then his purpose may be to spread poison, in particular in the form of a provocative dilemma for Hamlet between obeying the law and fulfilling filial obligations. The Ghost's insinuation that Gertrude had been guilty of actual adultery before Old Hamlet's death contributes to Hamlet's increasing disgust at the physical world in general and women particularly (Bradley 1952, 117–8). It is surely no coincidence then that Gertrude, Claudius, Laertes and Hamlet himself all become victims of a poisoning plot gone very wrong: the poison cannot be contained. Once unleashed into the world it destroys indiscriminately. As the foundations for action therefore, the Ghost is not only a portent of evil: it is actually the source of the evil. As G. Wilson Knight (1989, 38) argues, Hamlet may have been told the truth about the corrupt world, but since its effect can only be destructive 'the truth is evil' and can have no application to justice.

We will leave the question of the relevance of ideas of 'justice' to the recognition of manslaughter by provocation. But the possibility that the Ghost might be a symbol of *false knowledge* goes right to the heart of our concern for the recognition of a defendant's claim to have acted in hot blood. For, if the provocative act in question is not actually witnessed, can we ever be sure that a person responding to a mere report is really acting in hot blood or cold blooded revenge? This view of the morally ambiguous Ghost as a warning about the danger of recognizing killings committed on the basis of news is supported by allusions in the text to an unwholesome comparison between the appearance of the Ghost and the birth of Christ. At the Ghost's first appearance the guard Barnardo refers to the appearance of a star, but whereas the star that appeared to announce Christ's birth had been seen in the east, this one is seen in the western sky (I, i, 39). Cherrell Guilfoyle's (1990, 21–4) work on English folk traditions has shown that Shakespeare's audience will almost certainly have been reminded of traditional pageant performances of the nativity that had been a popular annual event in English towns since the Middle Ages. They would have therefore been sensitive to the incongruity between the initial appearance of the Ghost to Marcellus and Barnardo and that of the Angel's appearance to the shepherds. For instance, Marcellus and Barnardo do not guard symbols of peace (sheep) but war (castle); the apparition is clothed not in radiance but full armour; it appears not from 'above', but from 'below'; although it has a message to relate, it does not come to spread news but rather insists that the witnesses swear not to tell of what they have seen (I, v, 189); it speaks of Gertrude as if a queen of whores (I, v, 47, 54–6), whereas the medieval Nativity pageants celebrated Mary as the queen of virgins; finally, its message is one of hatred and revenge, whereas the Angel's is one of universal love and forgiveness (Guilfoyle 1990, 31). Even if we discard most of these apparent clues as a coincidence, the undeniable sense of foreboding created by the appearance of the Ghost makes it tempting to agree with Landau (2001, 223) that the Ghost appears to be 'a grotesque, parodic version of Christ resurrected'. The direct contradiction of the Ghost's vengeful message to Christian teachings of forgiveness and forbearance is a clear sign that it must not be trusted, and this impression is only reinforced by its finally counselling mercy towards Gertrude (I, v, 85–6; Prosser 1971, 111, 136). Far from providing a justification for positive action the Ghost has made Hamlet into a representative of Death itself, whose role is simply to remind humans of their inescapable mortality. As Belsey notes, a scene in which Hamlet is comfortable and good humoured is the graveyard scene in which he jokes at the mortality of the lawyer and Yorick and indeed all of mankind, just as Death himself is believed to do in the traditional dance of death, depicted in sixteenth century art (Belsey 1999, 156). As a play about the moral dynamics of revenge, *Hamlet* therefore provides a great deal of material for reflection on the dangers of taking provocative news at face value. Through the doubts about the Ghost's identity, the purpose and meaning of his message and its effects on Hamlet and those around him, Shakespeare's play urges us to be reflective about our responses to apparently hot blooded violence. In order for Hamlet to carry out the killing of his uncle with any degree of moral propriety he must do it in hot blood; but Hamlet's justified doubts about the identity and the message of the Ghost force him (and the viewer of the play) to be constantly reflective about the task in hand, contradicting and stymieing the heating of the blood.

Conclusion

Hamlet continually reminds us of the special moral status of premeditation as the antithesis of heated passion. If Hamlet had killed Claudius when he was presented with the perfect opportunity – in the prayer scene (III, iii) in which Claudius is found praying, unaware of Hamlet's presence in the room – this would have been understood by Shakespeare's Jacobean audience as murder. However, his professed reason for not killing Claudius in the prayer scene is even worse: he wants to wait until Claudius is 'about some act/ That has no relish of salvation in't' in order to ensure that he not only kills Claudius but also damns his soul to hell (II, iii, 91–2). Far from suggesting that such complete revenge is to be admired or required by honour, the scene would be naturally regarded by contemporary audiences as 'morally reprehensible and emotionally horrifying' (Prosser 1971, 191), and reinforces the malign influence of the Ghost and his dreadful command (Prosser 1971, 188). Contrast this with what we may imagine to be an audience's reaction to Hamlet's unhesitating dispatch of Claudius at the very end of the play, having seen his mother mistakenly poisoned and realizing that he is himself doomed.

Just as the Court of Appeal held that a final provocative 'trigger' from McCubbin on the doorstep was needed to regard Baillie's violence as manslaughter and the American cases that insist that the victim's provocative act must be actually witnessed by the defendant, so Shakespeare does not allow Hamlet to kill Claudius until he is faced with an overwhelmingly provocative act that takes place before his own eyes, which even the most guarded of audience members would regard as making a hot-blooded response irresistible. Likewise, it is this concern that the law should not permit just *any* trigger for a loss of self-control that has prompted the Government's proposal to limit the availability of a partial defence for killings out of anger to those rare and exceptional cases which go well beyond experiences that can be borne 'appropriately'. In *Hamlet* the death of Claudius is not at all the satisfying revenge that the Ghost urged him to take on Old Hamlet's behalf, but a spontaneous, hot-blooded reflex in the face of the gross provocation of seeing his mother poisoned, and thus a very different kind of killing (Miller 2006, 146). Shakespeare forces us to consider what kinds of trigger should be regarded as an adequate basis for claiming heated passion or a loss of self-control. In a final sign of anxiety that even his hot-blooded killing of Claudius may be open to moral question, the dying Hamlet commands Horatio to 'report me and my causes aright/ To the unsatisfied' (V, ii, 291–2); whether or not a killing really does come from heated blood is, after all, a question for a jury, who will look for evidence that the violence in question arose in truth from spontaneous passion rather than malice.

Chapter 2

'She has her just deserts by your unjust act': Electra, Revenge and the (Im)possibility of a Just Cause

In neither US nor English law may a person lacking a recognized mental abnormality base a defence to murder simply upon having experienced a moment of extreme emotional turmoil or loss of control. Legal excuses for intentional killing also insist that the defendant's extreme reaction be based on a recognizable cause. In this chapter I want to move on from the emotional aspect of provoked killings to explore the moral aspect of provocation, namely the defendant's claim that their violence was in some way understandable in the circumstances. English law currently prioritizes anger over other sorts of extreme emotional outburst, and where there is evidence that the defendant might have lost self-control, the jury must consider whether the victim behaved in such a way that might have caused a 'reasonable man' to become enraged to the point of killing (Homicide Act 1957, s.3). But if the Government's new proposals for the reform of homicide in England and Wales become law in their current form, English law will see a shift away from anger and towards fear: recognizing only 'extremely grave' rather than 'reasonable' bases for a partial defence to murder and the explicit removal of a partner's infidelity from the definition of 'extremely grave' (Ministry of Justice 2009, 12). This move away from provocation primarily as a concession to uncontrolled reactions in anger and towards a concession to reactions in fear, which as we saw in the previous chapter is already discernable in jury behaviour and sentencing, seems to represent a further distancing of law from its historic associations with honour and revenge and the inevitability of 'reasonable' people doing 'unreasonable' things due to a privately perceived intolerable sense of injustice. In this chapter I explore the moral compromise involved in the provocation defence, the possible relevance of ancient attitudes towards revenge and the awkward relationship between law and retaliatory killing. Dramatic representations of revenge provide a way of reflecting on this relationship and the impossibility of converting any sympathy that we might feel for the wronged avenger into a justificatory defence to murder. However, the recognition of a defence of provocation has its ancestry in ancient notions of justice as repayment, or in other words, justice as exacting revenge and thus restoring the balance between parties. Therefore I begin this chapter by considering some of the historical and dramatic dimensions of this idea of justice as repayment or rebalance, considering in particular Euripides and

Shakespeare. I argue in the first section that although previous societies may have
held very different attitudes towards vengeful killing that were often reflected in
revenge dramas, Euripides' *Electra* and Shakespeare's *Hamlet* provide much food
for thought on the possibility or otherwise of a 'just' cause for seeking revenge
and the possibility or otherwise of revenge being just. By portraying the constant
danger that revenge will exceed the requirements of justice and become merely a
further injustice, and also the fixation of the avenger on the personal dimension
of revenge – effectively eclipsing any wider claim to justice – these plays offer a
way of reflecting critically on the ambiguities and tensions inherent in provoked
violence and in particular in the requirement of a normative aspect. The discussion
of those plays then leads us on to examining this ambiguity in specific legal
contexts in the final section. I trace the emergence of 'implied malice' in early
modern English law as a device for ensuring that spontaneous but nonetheless
brutal killings could not take advantage of the leniency afforded to chance-medley
manslaughter. In that final section I also consider the moral content of the modern
provocation defence, namely the standard of the 'reasonable man' in English law,
and the limited set of legally recognized provocations in US laws of homicide.

1. Justice as Repayment in Revenge Literature: Revenge and Justice

a) Justice in Literature: Balance and Imbalance

Violence that is supposed to be understood to be justified, reasonable punishment
for a wrong is depicted in fiction and drama as a reflection and a natural
consequence of the villain's own culpability. However, to exact private revenge
was treated as morally problematic both by Shakespeare and Euripides, giving
us an interesting way to reflect on the moral ambiguities of the provocation
defence. Revenge tragedy relies for its dramatic impact on the play of balance
and imbalance in which villains and heroes (which are not always clearly distinct
roles) inflict harm on each other in order to respond to a perceived upset of the
natural balance of justice which must be restored through exacting payment in
blood. There is often a poetic equivalence between a villain's wrongdoing and his
final end and depictions of justice in Western culture in general very much reflect
this idea of justice as a reflection between right and wrong. For example, in his
book on this subject, Ian Miller (2006, 5) gives an historical account of the familiar
metaphor of the 'scales of justice': originating in ancient times from the language
of commerce. A fair price had to be paid for goods/liberties/life taken. The Old
Testament demand for 'life for life, eye for eye, tooth for tooth, hand for hand,
foot for foot, burn for burn, wound for wound, stripe for stripe' (*Exodus* 21, 23–5)
provided the dramatic imagery of justice as equivalence, whilst in legal culture
equivalences were worked out in a less bloody form (Miller 2006). A particularly
vibrant example of justice as poetic equivalence/reflection is the fairytale form,
discussed elsewhere in this book. When the girl in Angela Carter's retelling of

the Little Red Riding Hood tale discovers her grandmother's true identity as a werewolf, she screams for her neighbours: 'they drove the old woman, in her shift as she was, out into the snow with sticks, beating her old carcass as far as the edge of the forest, and pelted her with stones until she fell dead' (Carter 1996, 211). Such an end might seem excessively cruel for a lonely old woman, but the form of the Grandmother's punishment in Carter's story follows fairytale convention inasmuch as it observes the tradition that punishment reflects the villain's own crime. In the guise of a wolf, the Grandmother had attacked the girl in the forest and had retreated there when the girl managed to fight her off. According to the logic of fairytale justice it is therefore appropriate that the old woman – after all a dangerous liminal creature who is both human and beast – meets her end at 'the edge of the forest', that is, between human civilization and wild nature. As well as physically reflecting her attack in the forest, her death in this manner represents her dual nature – both human and beast. In threatening the integrity of the family, she dies homeless: in the last line of Carter's story we learn that her Granddaughter has taken over her cottage and that there 'she prospered' (Carter 1996, 211). In Grimm's nineteenth century version of the tale, the wolf is repaid for his voracious appetite by having his belly filled up with heavy stones by the helpful woodcutter. The beauty-obsessed stepmother queen in the story of *Snow White* is disposed of by being made to 'dance' on red-hot iron shoes for the amusement of the guests at the royal wedding (Grimm 1993, 224). As a queen, she must have owned some pretty 'hot' shoes for dancing and other social occasions and no doubt the wedding guests would have appreciated the comic irony that she is therefore killed by a thing she loves. Similarly, the queen whose heart burns with jealousy for her husband's lover in Basile's Italian variation on the Sleeping Beauty story *Sun, Moon and Talia* is burned in the fire that she prepared for her victim. Grimm's tale *The Almond Tree* is an archetypal example of a villainous stepmother who brings punishment upon herself through her violation of the natural cycle of life and the bourgeois commitment to productivity within the family. Like *Snow White*, *The Almond Tree* involves the creation of a child that similarly reflects the purity of nature. During wintertime, a childless woman cuts her finger while standing under her almond tree. Watching the drops fall on the snow she says: 'if only I could have a child as red as blood, and as white as snow' (Grimm 1993, 186). The natural environment and childbirth are presented as unified in the shedding of blood and the passing of the months, during which the tree bears its fruit and the woman bears the child she desires. A boy-child is born with skin as white as snow and when his mother dies he is brought up by his doting father and predictably wicked stepmother. The stepmother murders the boy by slamming a chest-lid down on his neck and thereby beheading him. She cooks the body for her husband's dinner and afterwards his bones are laid under the almond tree. The actions of the stepmother are clearly representative of imbalance and excess. Not only has she created a situation requiring that her foul deed must be paid back (the scales of justice are unbalanced), but furthermore the cannibalistic device connects the story to others in which injustice is figured by the eating of one's own. In *The Almond Tree*, the stepmother's excessive act and the imbalance she has created are both nullified through the magic powers of the tree. As a confirmation of the irrepressibility of natural life, the magic tree has the boy resurrected as a beautiful bird that finally takes its revenge on the stepmother. It is no coincidence that he chooses to do so by dropping a millstone on her, physically reflecting and hence balancing the injustice done to him and restoring the natural moral order (Grimm 1993, 195). In Basile's fairytale *Sun, Moon and Talia*, a variant of the Sleeping Beauty story, a jealous queen orders the cook to have her husband's children (Sun and Moon, whom he had fathered with the sleeping beauty Talia of another kingdom) killed and served to him as kid meat. For the heroes of those stories simply to forgive the villains would be unsatisfying, leaving the reader with the feeling that moral imbalance has not been restored (Tatar 1987, 181).

This idea of justice as striving towards balance is deeply ingrained in western culture, embodied perhaps most recognizably in the figure of the blindfolded lady justice, depicted in art and sculpture most often with her scales balanced, signifying reciprocity, evenness, the price for a wrong done having been extracted and the account settled (Miller 2006, 10). In terms of public justice as criminal punishment, the idea of the punishment 'fitting' the crime predates the liberal retributivist concern to punish the offender to the correct extent. The torments and mutilations inflicted on offenders' bodies in medieval and early modern times involved a concern for equivalence not in terms of limiting the pain to reflect the seriousness of the crime, but rather for the symbolic reflection of the nature of the crime in the punishment. In his fourteenth century poem *Inferno*, Dante employs the device in his graphic and dramatic depictions of the nine circles of hell: each circle offering more terrible punishments than the last but all poetically reflecting the sinners' life choices. In the second circle of hell, Dante (2003, 110) finds adulterers ceaselessly and aimlessly buffeted and blown about by an 'infernal storm, eternal in its rage' since in life they had allowed themselves to be driven by lust and made 'reason slave to appetite'. In the third circle of Dante's (2003, 121) hell we find the gluttonous being made to lie submerged in 'dirty water mixed with snow', representing the waste that they made of their lives (canto 6). Languishing deep down within the eighth circle of hell, Dante tells of those who, because in life they created discord and division, are punished by having their own bodies eternally divided. Dante meets a man 'ripped open from his chin to where we fart', who informs him:

> The souls that you see passing in this ditch
> were sowers of scandal and schism in life,
> and so in death you see them torn asunder. (Dante 2003, 326)

Amongst some very famous figures of history apparently condemned for creating schism, Dante meets Mohammad and Ali, regarded as founders of the great schism between Christians and Muslims, and also Bertran de Born who had supported the failed rebellion of young Prince Henry against his father Henry II of England. Having thus turned the royal family against itself, Bertran de Born is himself doomed to remain close to the centre of hell carrying his severed head like a lantern:

> Because I cut the bonds of those so joined,
> I bear my head cut off from its life-source,
> which is back there, alas, within its trunk,
> In me you see the perfect *contrapasso*. (Dante 2003, 329)

In his lifetime, Bertran de Born had boasted that he had more intelligence than he needed. In death therefore, it is poetically fitting that his brain is physically separated from his body (Dante 2003, 333). The *contrapasso* or 'law of counter penalty' informs what Dante and his contemporaries regarded as the nature of justice itself, in which those who committed wrongs brought punishment upon themselves. A person who did wrong must be made to pay for it, and we see this monetary metaphor repeated vividly also in biblical accounts of wrongs punished. It is no accident for instance that the divine writing that Belshazzar the 'proud, injurious king' of Babylon is astonished to see written on the wall at the feast before his fall to the Persians ('Mene, Mene, Tekel, Uparsin', *Daniel* 5, 25) literally translates rather mundanely into references to weights and measures. 'Mene' as an Aramaic noun meaning 50 shekels (a weight of about one and one quarter pounds and is related to the verb menah, 'to number'. Likewise, 'tekel' is a noun that refers to a shekel (two fifths of an ounce) and derives from the verb teqal, 'to weigh'. 'Parsin' is a noun meaning a half-mina (25 shekels, about two thirds of a pound) and derives from the verb peras, 'to divide.' In reading it as 'peres', Daniel is making a pun that signifies the role of Persia in the downfall of Babylon. The 'U' before 'parsin' simply means 'and' (Dolphin 2004; Kemp 2008, 5). However, as the Prophet Daniel explains, these are metaphors for justice, which is about to be meted out on Belshazzar:

> So from his presence the hand was sent and this writing was inscribed. And this is the writing that was inscribed: MENE, MENE, TEKEL, and PARSIN. This is the interpretation of the matter: MENE, God has numbered the days of your kingdom and brought it to an end; TEKEL, you have been weighed on the scales and found wanting; PERES, your kingdom is divided and given to the Medes and Persians. (*Daniel* 5, 24–28)

Injustice is signified by the imbalance of the measures that Daniel refers to. The invasion of Babylon by the Persians and the consequent freedom of the Israelites from captivity, brings the scales back to an even balance. Justice described through metaphors of equivalence and exchange has an aesthetic appeal that is relied upon to foreground a general principle of justice both in legal and religious codes such as the Old Testament demand for an 'eye for an eye', but also for the great revenge sagas of Greek drama (Miller 2006, 28).

Of course, as a way of reflecting on modern approaches to justice and the defence of provocation in particular, this talionic notion of eye for eye and blood for blood needs to be approached with caution. On a surface level, the poetic conceptions explored above would seem to present a now outmoded view of justice as violently restored balance that has little in common with modern attitudes towards punishment or private revenge. After all, human rights instruments prevent the infliction of bodily hurt on offenders that physically reflect the latter's wrongdoing and private revenge killings usurp the authority of the law and its own commitment to measured justice, and thus cannot be legally justified. As Peter Fitzpatrick argues, law's violence is generally perceived to be legitimized by its being proportionate, necessary and in accordance with pre-determined parameters – in opposition to the uncontrolled 'savagery' of illegitimate violence of which we might say private revenge is paradigmatic (Fitzpatrick 1992, 81). However, this dramatic notion of justice is not and never has been a simple matter of insisting that wrongs be paid for. While some dramatic sources, notably fairytales, tend to depict justice and injustice as clearly distinct ideas (and thus just and proportionate retaliation clearly defined from cruel and excessive revenge) the great revenge dramas discussed below problematize this distinction. 'Just revenge' is shown to always be in danger of spilling over into excess, into imbalance and hence injustice, and far from glorifying revenge, provides warnings that if justice means restoring an upset balance, seeking justice through blood might be counter-productive. Since balance means achieving peace and an end to hostility and a cycle of violence, to do justice means seeking to curtail bloodshed rather than blindly seeking it in return for earlier hurt (Miller 2006, 29–30). Seneca's revenge tragedies might be read as being concerned chiefly with this theme. In Seneca's *Thyestes*, King Atreus of Mycenae tricks his twin brother Thyestes into eating the flesh of his own sons as punishment for Thyestes's adulterous relationship with Atreus's wife Aerope. As in Shakespeare's *Titus Andronicus*, one act of revenge does not settle the matter. Atreus is killed by Thyestes's son Aigisthos, who later also murders Atreus's son Agamemnon, assisted by Agamemnon's unfaithful wife Clytemnestra. The final murders of the tragic cycle are those of Aigisthos and Clytemnestra by the children of Agamemnon and Clytemnestra: Electra and Orestes, the story that I return to in the next section. Shakespeare's *Titus Andronicus*, arguably inspired by Seneca, is another example of the dramatic tension between justice and injustice in revenge drama. Titus Andronicus tends to be cast as a sympathetic character. He is the heroic war general who returns home having expended all his energy and having lost twenty sons fighting for Rome against the Goths. Audiences sympathize with him as he buries his heroic sons and then suffers one tragedy after another at the hands of Tamora, her husband Saturninus and her sons Chiron and Demetrius. However, our sympathy is tested, arguably beyond any bearable limit, by witnessing the lengths to which Titus goes to avenge the deaths of his sons, the rape and mutilation of his daughter and the loss of his own hand by tricking the wicked Tamora into eating the flesh of her own sons (Prosser 1971, 88). In one of

Shakespeare's most bloodcurdling dramatic speeches, Titus explains to Tamora's two young sons how he means to use them to take revenge on their mother:

> Hark, villains! I will grind your bones to dust
> And with your blood and it I'll make a paste,
> And of the paste a coffin I will rear
> And make two pasties of your shameful heads,
> And bid that strumpet, your unhallow'd dam,
> Like to the earth swallow her own increase.
>
> This is the feast that I have bid her to,
> And this the banquet she shall surfeit on;
> For worse than Philomel you used my daughter,
> And worse than Progne I will be revenged:
> And now prepare your throats. (V, ii, 185–95)

Like the wicked stepmother of Grimm's *The Almond Tree*, Titus was of course acting to restore the balance that he perceived as having been tipped against him. We might at least partly sympathize with the poor father driven to such murderous excess by preceding events, but of course his own act of revenge – in tipping the balance of justice too far – leads to Titus himself being killed by Tamora's husband after he triumphantly announces to her what she has eaten. To make one's enemy 'swallow her own increase' signifies an excessive form of revenge and thus an extraction of too much payment that leads not to peace but to further extraction in response. Prosser has argued that the excessive nature of this act of revenge (and also the cruelty he arguably shows in killing his own daughter in the final Act 'and thy shame with thee' (V, iii, 45) and his son Mutius at the beginning for blocking his way) demonstrates that, *Titus Andronicus* does not in any way condone blood revenge, let alone depict it as demanded by honour. Rather, *Titus Andronicus* shares the overriding theme with *Hamlet* as a play about the control and release of extreme emotion. Titus' brother Marcus seems to function in the play as a commentator on the unfolding tragedy, the significance of the action (for example, his speech on the significance of the rape and mutilation of Lavinia, discussed elsewhere in this book) and on the relationship between the proper emotional response to tragedy. After Titus lops off his own hand as what he soon discovers is futile payment to Emperor Saturninus for his sons freedom, Marcus counsels him: 'But yet let reason govern thy lament' (III, i, 217). However, when, in return, his sons' severed heads are delivered to him, Marcus gives up on trying to temper Titus' grief: 'Rend off thy silver hair, and thy other hand/ Gnawing with thy teeth' (III, i, 259). The theme of the instability of bloody revenge – its failure to settle matters and the tendency for it to instead simply incite yet further acts of bloody counter-revenge – is of course a familiar one also in Greek drama, which provided inspiration for Shakespeare's own plots, and I shall discuss an example of that later in the chapter.

Ian Miller (2006, 15) may be correct to point out that 'the English word *peace*, coming via Latin *pax* from *pancare*, derives from the idea of paying', but this certainly does not mean that a wrong paid for in blood through revenge is guaranteed to be a just rebalancing of accounts. Since violence of this nature is inextricably bound up in passions that are difficult (impossible?) to contain within reasonable limits, blood payment tends to be an overpayment and thus not one that can readily be accommodated by law. Miller (2006, 30) suggests that 'some of the evocative brilliance of the biblical talion's eye/tooth formulation [may] lie in the suggestion of just how fine the line is between talionic equivalence and balance, on the one hand, and reciprocity gone mad'. Danielle S. Allen (2001, 205) agrees that the purpose of justice is to seek peace – to 'restore' rather than simply to 'satisfy'. If, as Allen (2001, 195) argues, the anger that drives wronged parties to seek revenge is a 'disease' that infects all parties to revenge and must be cured before we can say that scores have been settled once and for all, it would seem that there can be no place for blood revenge as such in a theory of justice. As I discuss below, the idea of 'reciprocity gone mad' is very subtly presented in Euripides' *Electra*, Euripides' version of the story of the revenge of Oresetes and Electra against their mother Clytemnestra and her husband Aigisthos for the murder of Agamemnon, and by Shakespeare in *Hamlet*.

b) Private Revenge and Christian Morals in Hamlet

It is possible to understand why a Jacobean audience might have regarded the demands of Old Hamlet's Ghost as morally compelling without inferring a revenge culture that contradicted Christian orthodoxy. It is this tension between accounting for our sympathy for an action that must also be condemned and the relationship between the emotional and moral aspects of this issue that helps us to formulate a critical perspective on legal responses to provoked killings. Shakespeare was not the first to invoke the voice of the dead as a cry for justice. In Genesis (4.10), God heeds the call of the slain Abel – 'Listen; your brother's blood is crying out to me from the ground!' – by banishing Cain from the land and sending Seth as a replacement (Miller 2006, 93).[1] The ideas of brotherly rivalry and the use of violence to achieve power in this simple biblical story may have influenced Shakespeare, particularly in his History plays (Foakes 2003, 27). However, the important theme for our discussion here is that of the relationship between justice and revenge: on the one hand *Hamlet* invites audiences to sympathize with the Ghost's call from beyond the grave for young Hamlet to seek revenge and yet because of the possibility that the Ghost may be a 'goblin damn'd' (discussed in the previous chapter) and Hamlet's own awareness of the troubling ethical nature of revenge itself in a Christian context, this sympathy may not convert to a straightforward approval of the Ghost's proposed action. Hamlet is very much

---

1   Miller interprets 'Seth' to mean 'substitute' or 'replacement', hence a settling of the debt.

aware of the personal, as opposed to the public or universal, nature of the Ghost's command to revenge Old Hamlet's untimely death. 'Remember me!' (I, v, 91); 'Revenge his foul and most unnatural murder' (I, v, 25); these terrible commands are aimed primarily to appeal to Hamlet's sense of filial solidarity rather than a wider sense of justice. The Ghost tries to get Hamlet to grieve for the murdered man's eternal soul languishing in purgatory or possibly hell itself, as it reports of being 'confin'd to fast in fires; Till the foul crimes done in my days of nature; Are burnt and purg'd away' (I, v, 11–3). It also complains of being 'Cut off even in the blossoms of my sin; Unhousel'd, disappointed, unanel'd' (I, v, 76–7), indicating that he had not had an opportunity to confess or receive holy rites which a Catholic would believe would enable them to save their soul (Hoff 1990, 52). As Miller puts it, the Ghost is saying that Old Hamlet must not be 'mis-remembered'; young Hamlet must exact repayment to settle the old king's blood-debt and therefore bring peace to his soul (Miller 2006, 101). The dilemma is that Hamlet is being asked to remember his filial obligations in the face of the moral and legal condemnation of premeditated, vengeful killing. The Ghost's command offers a terrible moral conflict between committing a heinous premeditated murder while at the same time appealing to Hamlet's sense of loyalty. It prompts Catherine Belsey (1999, 160) to ask: 'What kind of father would expose his son to the possibility of damnation?' The question of how to respond both honourably and morally to the revealed murder of his Father was a tension between 'the early modern' law of homicide and social attitudes with which Jacobean audiences would have been familiar.

The Ghost exploits Hamlet's fragile self-regard as a man. From the way Hamlet speaks about his dead Father we know that, whilst Hamlet is himself a scholar, he reveres his dead Father's reputation as a warrior king who fought terrible wars for honour:

> He was a man, take him for all in all
> I shall not look upon his like againe. (II, ii, 376–7, *First folio*)

> An eye like Mars, to threaten or command
> A station like the herald of Mercury
> New lighted on a heaven-kissing hill. (III, iv, 56–7)

The Ghost plays on the younger man's reverence for his war-like father and manipulates Hamlet by encouraging him to feel that in failing to be moved to violent revenge, he will show himself to be less than a true man and less than a true son:

> If thou didst ever thy dear Father love ... (I, v, 24)

> And duller shoudst thou be than the fat weed
> That rots itself with ease on Lethe wharf
> If thou wouldst not stir in this ... (I, v, 32–4)

> If thou hast nature in thee, bear it not. (I, v, 81)

The appeal to Hamlet's manhood cuts deeply and would have been keenly felt by Jacobean audiences also. Hamlet is clearly affected by this personal appeal to him as a 'true man and a true son' when he considers whether his delay makes him a coward:

> Am I a coward?
> Who calls me villain, breaks my pate across,
> Plucks off my beard and blows it in my face,
> Tweaks me by the nose, gives me the lie i'th'throat
> As deep as to the lungs – who does me this? (II, ii, 565–70)

As discussed in the previous chapter, *Hamlet* was written and first performed against the background of a society that drew a clear distinction between premeditated killing and sudden, hot-blooded ones. Like the juries of both centuries earlier and centuries later, the Jacobean theatre-goers would be prepared to take a broad view of what constituted excusable (or clergiable) homicide, but only if they could be convinced that there was a good reason to interpret it as hot blooded retaliation rather than calculated revenge. In order to be convinced, they would look for a *cause* for allowing one's blood to become so heated that one commits an intentional killing. In the last section of this chapter I discuss what these reasons were in early modern England. Similarly, modern audiences, whilst not being concerned with the provocation defence as such, also judge Hamlet's actions according to familiar attitudes towards violence. Thus the moral problem posed in the play is whether or not there is good cause to regard Hamlet's use of violence as hot blooded retaliation or as calculated revenge. For both Shakespeare's audiences and modern ones, the longer a person waits before striking, the less likely it is that the violence can be read sympathetically. It is significant that Hamlet uses a theatrical metaphor when he bemoans his lack of genuinely murderous rage, comparing himself to a tragic hero who with grief 'would drown the stage with tears' (II, ii, 556).[2] For a theatrical production of *Hamlet* to be successful, it is important that the audience cares about the play's central character and feels the crushing weight of his dilemma. In both the theatre and the criminal court, a judging audience/jury must watch the accused, consider their actions as laid out in the performance/trial in order to decide whether they really did act in response to a sufficiently serious provocation.

We saw in the previous chapter how Hamlet finds he is unable to summon the necessary hot-blooded passion to carry out the Ghost's commands immediately. For this he chastises himself for cowardice and hence of moral failure. As he admits, 'Swounds, I should not take it: for it cannot be/ But I am pigeon-liver'd

---

2   Laertes is just such a character, who does not hesitate to formulate a plot to avenge Polonius' death on Hamlet.

and lack gall' (II, ii, 572–3). In other words, Hamlet wants his hot-blooded rage to overcome his reasoned awareness of the wrongness of premeditated killing; he knows that in failing to do so, avenging his father's death will be acting in cold blood and thus be a murder. Witnessing the march of 2,000 Norwegian troops to fight the Poles over 'a little patch of ground/ That hath no profit in it but the name' (IV, iv, 18–9), Hamlet reflects that his own cause is much the greater. He acknowledges that 'Rightly, to be great ... [is] to find quarrel in a straw/ When honour's at stake' (IV, iv, 53–6). This being so, Hamlet resolves: 'O, from this time forth,/ My thoughts be bloody or nothing worth' (65–6). His anguished reflections on what he supposes a passionate man who truly loved his father would do when faced with such a stirring of filial loyalties go to the heart of Hamlet's dilemma. Instead of making him jump to taking hot-blooded violent revenge, his predicament makes him sick and depressed. It is the Ghost who, in reminding him that his first duty is towards his murdered father, causes the most anguish in Hamlet.

Despite the terrible authority with which the Ghost commands Hamlet to direct his thoughts and actions towards bloody revenge, *Hamlet* does not necessarily mean to imply that Hamlet should as a matter of right take revenge. The first signs of what later became recognizable as a provocation defence in the early modern period was, as we have seen from the cases, based on discovering whether there were good grounds to regard a killing as having been committed in hot blood. Although A.C. Bradley (1952, 99–100) and Haydn (1950, 555–98) were confident that Elizabethan and Jacobean audiences would have fully approved of and in fact *demanded* blood revenge in a situation analogous to Hamlet's as a matter of honour, Prosser (1971, 23–4) and Foakes (2003, 108) have more recently argued that the orthodox condemnation of revenge and the honour-revenge culture that apparently existed in continental Europe at the time would have been shared by the majority of audiences as well. Prosser (1971, 32–4) argues that the natural sympathy that audiences tend to have for Hamlet's cause, the regular violation of the ideal of Christian forbearance amongst Elizabethans and Jacobeans and their enjoyment of other revenge tragedies, should not be interpreted as approval of revenge, but rather merely of sympathy for a man caught in an understandable ethical bind. On this view, the conflict experienced by Hamlet should probably not be regarded as between two binding codes (those of law [forbearance] and honour [revenge]) but an ethical dilemma between the duty under both religious and secular moral codes (Prosser 1971, 6–7) and a *personal* cause. This view is supported by the insistence of the early modern courts that only killings that were a spontaneous hot-blooded response to an immediate provocation (that is, stemming from a genuinely internal conflict, not one carried out from a felt duty towards an externally imposed honour code) could avoid being classified as premeditated murder. It is for that reason that Hamlet is so often seen chastising himself.

c) Revenge and Justice in Greek Drama: Euripides' Electra

Of the three best known dramatizations of the curse of the house of Atreus –
Aeschylus, Sophocles and Euripides all wrote variations on the tragedy – all focus
on the blood-debt that must be exacted by the victim's kin. The final part – the
story of how Electra and her brother Orestes murder their mother Clytemnestra in
solidarity with their murdered father Agamemnon – has interested legal theorists,
psychoanalysts and feminists and is interesting also for my own concern for the
relationship between blood-debt and justice. As narrated in Euripides' *Electra*,
Aeschylus's *The Oresteia* and also Sophocles' *Electra*, the Atreus myth ends
with Agamemnon's children Electra and Orestes completing their revenge on
their mother Clytemnestra and her husband Aigisthos and atoning for their own
killings by Electra's banishment and Orestes standing trial and being acquitted
by a court at Athens.[3] The Furies, who would have otherwise pursued Orestes
until his death, are banished by Apollo to Hades. To James Boyd White (1985,
180) the fact that the cycle of blood letting is ended by a legal trial shows that
the story represents the triumph of justice as court procedure over ancient ideas
of blood revenge, represented by the finally defeated and banished Furies.[4] On
the other hand, feminists have argued that the story is about gender inequality:
why do Electra and Orestes regard their dead father as a hero and their mother
a traitor and a slut when both their parents had been guilty of killing their kin
and adultery? (Agamemnon himself had killed their sister (and Clytemnestra's
daughter) Iphigenia and had taken Cassandra back from Troy to Mycenae as his
lover.) For Lacan, a girl's natural lack of a physical means of identifying with her
phallic father means that her full entry into the patriarchal adult realm of language
and symbolic order is blocked and so she must be content to identify instead with
'the castrated mother, the powerless mother who has submitted to and acts as a
representative of the phallic father' (Barnett 1998, 152). This inequality is arguably
narrated by the story of Orestes and Electra: since it is only Orestes who has *his*
guilt removed by Apollo and the Athenian court while his sister Electra by contrast
must continue to bear hers in exile, only he can fully overcome his crime and
re-enter society. In other words only he, as a man, is fully equipped to associate
with the phallic realm of the authoritative father, unlike Electra who despite a
very active role in Clytemnestra's death, must remain subordinate. Furthermore,
for Aristodemou (2000, 69), Apollo's banishment of the Furies in order to lift
the curse – an act that represents the fading significance of private blood ties

---

3   References to the text of these Greek dramas will be to page numbers. Translators'
and editors' introduction and notes are referred to separately (for example, Janet Lembke
and Kenneth J. Reckford's translation of Euripides' *Electra* is cited as Euripides 1994, and
own their introduction and notes are cited separately as Lembke and Reckford 1994).

4   Boyd White also notes that the earliest of the three versions of Electra and Orestes
– Aeschylus' *The Oresteia* – was written shortly after the creation of the first court in Athens
to hear homicide cases.

and the rise of a more civilized culture of legal procedure, rhetoric, persuasion and argument – represents the subordination of the feminine by the masculine. In these ways, many feminists regard the myth as the 'founding moment of patriarchy' (Barnett 1998, 153).

From a feminist perspective then, the lifting of the curse of Atreus is a story of how the primitive and unruly world of blood-debts (that is, the feminine) was replaced by the emerging civilized one of public justice as legality (that is, the masculine). However, unlike the audiences of early modern England with their Christian moral influences, audiences of fifth century BCE Athens would probably have seen little ethical objection to the surviving children of a wronged heroic ruler fulfilling their filial duty by exacting bloody revenge on Agamemnon's murderers. As asserted by Lembke and Reckford (1994, 4), 'To Euripides' audience the rightness of revenge at Argos must have seemed self-evident. ... Few Greeks can have doubted that Orestes' revenge, albeit painful, was finally necessary and right.' But this does not mean that the writers of the plays simply gave their audiences what they wanted. However remote the moral attitudes of the ancient Greeks to our own views about revenge, coloured like those of the early moderns by Christianity, it is significant that the Greek revenge tragedies appeal to moral sense through the careful deployment of balance and exchange as a dramatic device. This is important for us here in reflecting on the moral ambiguities of revenge as a personal compulsion that contradicts with public justice and the possibility of there ever being a truly 'just' cause to kill in response to a previous wrong.

In Euripides' *Electra*, the young avengers Orestes and his sister Electra repeatedly speak in terms of the duty to repay a debt and the rhetoric of the chorus and other characters echo this. Unlike Hamlet, Electra herself does not agonize about carrying out the revenge. It has been foretold by Apollo that Aigisthos and Clytemnestra will pay for their crimes against the house of Atreus and so once the hated spouses are within their sights, the siblings act decisively to fulfil the prophecy. In a scene that in some respects mirrors the prayer scene in *Hamlet*, Orestes finds that his opportunity to kill Aigisthos comes when he finds the usurper at the temple about to sacrifice an animal. Like the 'smiling villain' that is Claudius, Aigisthos proves to be charming and hospitable and, not recognizing Orestes (the latter was a baby when he and his sister Electra were sent away from Mycenae after Agamemnon's death), invites the youth to join him (Lembke and Reckford 1994, 9). Aigisthos hands Orestes a cleaver to open up the sacrificial animal and when Aigisthos bends down to inspect the entrails Orestes uses it to smash Aigisthos's spine and decapitates him. The messenger jubilantly reports: 'Yes, blood for blood, his bitter loan came due. He paid with death.' Picking up and addressing Aigisthos's freshly severed head, Electra cries (Euripides 1994, 56): 'Be damned! I regret you cannot know how you have paid at last a just price.' In this horrific exchange, the avenger plays the role of debt-collector; the person being avenged is the creditor and the person revenged upon the debtor. When Electra confronts her mother Clytemnestra she states that she (Electra) owes it to her murdered father Agamemnon to collect payment for his death and that it is through the spilling of Clytemnestra's blood that the debt must be paid (Euripides 1994, 61–2): 'If blood calls for blood in the name of Justice, then I will kill you – I and your son Orestes – to avenge our father.' Dramatic equivalence between misdeed and grisly fate tends to connote a deserved, proportionate punishment: Just as Agamemnon was killed by a man and a woman plotting together, so they are themselves murdered by a man and a woman together. In Euripides it is clear that for the killing of Clytemnestra at least, it is only Electra's determination that ensures that Clytemnestra is killed, since Orestes becomes horrified at the prospect of killing his own mother. Likewise at the start of the play we learn it was Clytemnestra, not Aigisthos, who was the decisive party to Agamemnon's murder – 'he was killed by Clytemnestra's treachery' (Euripides 1994, 21). In his own, possibly earlier version of the story, Aeschylus presents the killing of the pair by Orestes as the necessary resetting of the disturbed scales of justice. Having been ordained by Apollo and demanded by the debt of blood to Agamemnon, the chorus approvingly comments that 'his hand was steered in open fight by god's true daughter, Right, Right we call her' (Aeschylus 1977, 220; see also Lembke and Reckford 1994, 6).

In murdering Agamemnon the noble king of Mycenae, worthy son of the wronged Atreus and the heroic destroyer of Troy, Aigisthos (son of Atreus' brother Thyestes by an incestuous match) and Clytemnestra are the villains of all the dramatic versions of the story, whose death is the deserved self-inflicted destruction for treachery. Clytemnestra and Aigisthos are marked as villains by being depicted in all accounts of the myth as the opposite to the Greek sexual ideal. Aigisthos is a cowardly man, preening and effete, relying on a woman (a sure sign of weakness in Greek drama) to realize his own ambitions. In the scene in which Electra addresses his severed head we learn that unlike her father Agamemnon, Aigisthos did not fight in the Trojan war, instead staying at home to seduce the king's wife and turn her to treachery against her heroic husband after the war (Aristodemou 2000, 67; Euripides 1994, 55). Clytemnestra herself is dismissed by her daughter Electra as 'a slut' (Euripides 1994, 58) for her adultery with the unworthy Aigisthos, incapable of regaining the 'chastity she has already flouted' (1994, 55) by her betrayal of her husband Agamemnon and tainted by Aigisthos's wickedness (Aristodemou 2000, 67–8; Euripides 1994, 56). Electra, by contrast, is a model of sexual purity and fraternal loyalty. Despite having been married off by her mother and Aigisthos to a poor farmer in order to ensure that she has no highborn offspring who might help her to seek revenge, she has managed to remain a virgin. Furthermore she is unwavering in her commitment to the memory of her father and in her eagerness for the eventual return of her exiled brother Orestes who she believes will help her, Electra shows no fear despite the dangers. The chorus echoes Electra's judgment of Clytemnestra's bloody deed of all those years previous: 'But, blood for blood, you paid the just price' (Euripides 1994, 65).

Although Euripides' audiences would have found no difficulty in relating to this notion of justice as revenge, nevertheless it is wrong to read the play as condoning such a view. I have already noted the interpretation by legal theorists on the resolution of the curse by a legally constituted court and the banishment of the symbols of blood revenge, the Furies, common to all versions of the myth. Furthermore, as in *Titus Andronicus*, Euripides' play itself implies that although justice does require a price to be paid, it is almost impossible for an avenger to avoid going too far in pursuing a just cause and exacting too high a price, compromising the moral high ground claimed and causing fresh injustice. Justice, although often invoked by the siblings, is an ambiguous, slippery character for Euripides, and he often seems to invert the notion of justice as balance by invoking themes of poetic reflection between wrongdoing and revenge to connote the *absence* of justice. For instance, the young avengers and their deeds often grotesquely mirror those of the previous generation whom they strive so hard to destroy. Clytemnestra was single-minded and wilful in her pursuit of Agamemnon's death, whom she could never forgive for having sacrificed their daughter Iphigenia prior to the Trojan War. And according to Euripides it was foremost Clytemnestra's own 'treachery', for which the 'hand' of Aigisthos was merely a tool, which brought about Agamemnon's death. In his earlier play, Aeschylus had more clearly distinguished the characters of Clytemnestra and Electra in terms of the degree of sympathy they respectively demanded from audiences. But Euripides's Electra is unreflective in her fixation with seeking revenge. She is unself-conscious about her own hate as Clytemnestra herself was, and in this regard is much closer to Shakespeare's rash and impulsive Laertes than the brooding and reflective Hamlet. As a character, Euripides' Electra is also closer to Sophocles' morally compromised and unreflective Electra than Aeschylus' more sympathetic depiction. Sophocles goes further than Euripides in showing the moral degradation that vengefulness brings: his Electra urges Orestes to leave Aigisthos' body unburied for the animals to eat. In Greek culture to fail to bury the dead was a heinous blasphemy. Sophocles was well aware of this as we know from his account of the downfall of King Creon at Thebes, who refused to allow the burial of the body of his nephew and enemy Polynices in the tragedy *Antigone* (Gurnham 2004). Sensing that Orestes is perhaps not the brave warrior she imagined him to be, Euripides' Electra urges her brother to 'Be the man you need to be' for if he fails to kill him, she threatens: 'My hand would drive a sword right through my heart' (Euripides 1994, 47). She bullies the reluctant Orestes into overcoming his squeamishness at turning the blade on their own mother, using arguments chillingly similar to those we saw being used by the Ghost to manipulate and provoke Hamlet: 'Let no coward's thoughts topple your manhood, but bring to this task the same guile our mother used to kill her lord and husband with Aigisthos' help' (Euripides 1994, 58). It is difficult to resist the implication here that in this moment Euripides is inviting us to think that Electra actually becomes Clytemnestra in moral terms. Like the killing of Agamemnon, it is clearly Electra's own forceful determination that will ensure that the debt is paid. However, until the revenge is completed, Electra herself shows no awareness of the irony of her condemning the 'shameful' way in which Aigisthos allowed himself to be led by his wife's designs. Although Euripides does not show us the earlier murder by Clytemnestra we come to suspect that she is probably very much 'the domineering daughter of a domineering mother' (Lembke and Reckford 1994, 84).

In contrast, Euripides' Orestes is thoughtful, hesitant and not at all the enthusiastic avenger that Electra wants him to be. He is wracked by doubts about the morality of killing his own mother despite the command coming from Apollo and has to be cajoled into the final violent act (Electra: 'If even Apollo's judgment fails, is anyone wise?' ... Orestes: 'Kill my mother – his voice should not have told me that' (Euripides 1994, 57)). Like Hamlet, Orestes suspects that the voice he hears urging him on to bloody revenge may be evil – 'did some demon of vengeance speak in your voice?' he says to Electra – and his eventual agreement is more of a resignation to the cruelty of his fate than an acceptance that the course of action Electra urges is right: 'I start on a course I dread. I'll do the things I dread. If that please the gods, so be it. For me this sport is bitter, not sweet' (Euripides 1994, 58). In the scene in which Clytemnestra is finally slain, Euripides seems to parody Aeschylus' depiction of a decisive achievement of justice. For, in Euripides' version, Orestes does not approach Clytemnestra alone to carry out the deed (underlining that he is not the independent avenging hero acclaimed in Greek revenge culture), and it is not 'justice' that is reported to have guided Orestes' hand. Rather, Orestes and Electra go into the tent together and it is Electra herself who guides her brother's hand, since he cannot bear to look at what he is doing. Her involvement is as critical to the death of Clytemnestra as Clytemnestra's was to that of Agamemnon, and thus the disparaging judgment on the older woman's domination of the usurper king both by Electra – 'He lets her have her way in everything' (Euripides 1994, 56) and the chorus – 'killed by Clytemnestra's treachery and the hand of the son of Thyestes' (Euripides 1994, 21) – could just as easily apply to the dominant Electra and reluctant Orestes. Even in her absolute sexual virtue, Electra's difference from her mother's oft-mentioned adultery is not quite so straightforward since, and again *Electra* parallels *Hamlet* in this regard, Electra proves to be utterly obsessed with her mother's sex-life, recalling her sexual relationship with Aigisthos as much as her involvement in the murder. In the scene in Gertrude's chamber in *Hamlet*, we begin to wonder if Hamlet is losing touch with reality when, having slain the unfortunate Polonius, he ignores the presence of the corpse and continues to lecture his mother on sexual morality and speaks of her marital bed as a 'enseaméd', a 'nasty sty' and 'stewed in corruption' (III, iv, 82–4). Likewise, Electra constantly returns to this theme in her speeches, invoking vivid sexual imagery such as that of Aigisthos and Clytemnestra 'fouling my father's bed' (Euripides 1994, 55), Clytemnestra as 'designing the crime that she helped Aigisthos commit so he'd lie in her bed' (Euripides 1994, 26), and the couples' marital home as a 'murder-bloodied bed' (Euripides 1994, 28). Disgust at her mother's sexuality dominates Electra's thoughts, and she describes her and her beautiful sister Helen as 'rotten with lust' (Euripides 1994, 61). Electra's fixation with her mother's sexuality implies not a rational moral judgment against her mother but a mind driven to extremes by grief and rage. In contrast to Electra's own passionate excess, Clytemnestra is lucid in her defence. Clytemnestra tells

Electra that her murder of Agamemnon was not motivated simply by adulterous lust for Aigisthos but by despair at Agamemnon for having killed her daughter as a sacrifice to the gods before the Trojan War and for then reigniting her passion by returning to Mycenae with Cassandra as his mistress.

After the killing of Clytemnestra, the initial elation of having successfully completed the appointed task is very quickly replaced with regret, uncertainty and fear, and we may interpret Euripides here as casting doubt on the very idea of blood revenge despite its evident acceptability to his contemporary audience. The killing is remarked upon ambiguously by the chorus: 'Savage your death, poor creature, but savage the death you devised' (Euripides 1994, 65). However, the chorus leader is more clearly regretful when he declares:

> I want to run
> from such unhappy proof of sacrifice.
> No family and its many generations
> have been more their own victim. (Euripides 1994, 65)

With Clytemnestra dead, Electra can at last allow herself to be philosophical about what has happened, and quickly comes to regret so forcefully compelling Orestes to kill ('The rush of tears – oh brother mine the guilt and shame' (Euripides 1994, 65) and then soon after, 'Of most dreadful suffering I am the cause' (Euripides 1994, 67)). Orestes remembers his initial horror of the notion and in a speech that denies that the final blood revenge really is the 'just payment' that Electra and the chorus placed so much emphasis on until this final scene, cries out in anguish to Zeus:

> look now on the blood
> That defiles me – two bodies struck to the ground by my hand
> As poor reparation
> For wrongs I have suffered. (Euripides 1994, 65)

Not even Castor, son of Zeus and brother of Clytemnestra, who descends from mount Olympus at the close of the play to declare an end to the curse of the house of Atreus, can make much moral sense of what has happened. Of Clytemnestra he condemns both her own misdeeds and those of her avengers: 'She has her *just* deserts by your *unjust* act' (Euripides 1994, 67, emphasis added). When Orestes asks Castor the pointed question – 'Why, as gods and brothers to her did you not keep the Death Spirits away?', Castor can only suggest that 'fate and the unwise cry of Apollo' determined it (Euripides, 1994, 69). It is clear that Euripides' treatment of revenge is very much more complex than a satisfying end to a family's troubles; that blood revenge leads not to final satisfaction but rather further bloodshed, chiefly owing to the strong sense of justice in the form of a debt of loyalty owed to the dead. Electra's hope that Clytemnestra's death might be 'an end of great woe for our house' (Euripides 1994, 67) therefore rings hollow as an assessment of the siblings' achievement, and we are again reminded of her earlier lack of self-awareness. As mortals, Orestes and Electra cannot justly resolve the injustices they have suffered, they can only seek satisfaction. They are themselves infected by what Allen (1999, 195) describing the murder of Agamemnon, calls a 'festering wound' that 'symbolizes the idea that no party to the experience of wrongdoing is exempt from the trouble it introduces to the community'.[5] Like the poison that is poured into Old Hamlet's ear infecting also young Hamlet and the whole Danish court, thanks to the Ghost's testimony, just deserts exacted through revenge will always be *unjustly* brought. In an admission that revenge does not resolve but only adds to evil, Euripides' *Electra* ends with Apollo taking Orestes' blood-guilt upon himself, and as I have already mentioned, some legal theorists have interpreted the trial of Orestes in Athens and the banishment of the Furies as celebrating the supplanting of private revenge by legalistic justice. The ending of Euripides' play is hardly happy: neither Electra nor Orestes may inherit the crown of Mycenae and they are forced to part forever: 'we're torn – cursed by a mother's murder – apart' (Euripides 1994, 70). It seems that Euripides presents killing from vengeance as both right and wrong simultaneously; that a murderer is himself unworthy of a happy end, but nonetheless that the person who exacts revenge on him will also become tainted with murder; that the sin of one person in bringing down his enemy does not exculpate the repeat of the same sin perpetrated by the kin of the original victim. For both Euripides and Shakespeare, all who bring themselves within this sorry chain of violence are damned and if their violence is in any way excused, it is not because they chose right (remember that Castor in Euripides' *Electra* describes revenge as an 'unjust act') but because the emotional pressure of being presented with the ethical dilemma of whether to be damned by avenging or mis-remembering one's own kin by declining to do so is too much for a person to bear. It is from this conclusion that I proceed to discuss the recognition of this dilemma in the form of the distinction between murder and manslaughter and the emergence of the provocation defence and the legal insistence on a recognizable *cause* for the defendant's recourse to intentional killing.

2. The Cause for a Provoked Killing in Modern and Early Modern Law

Hamlet interpreted as a straightforward conflict between law and the early modern honour codes, or *Electra* as the inevitable fulfilment of the duty to revenge the murder of kin in ancient Greece, are of limited interest for anyone wishing to reflect on the ethics of provoked killing today. However, interpreting them as narrating a conflict between the need for peace and healing on the one hand, and on the other understandable hot-blooded, internal filial loyalty which makes observance

---

5   Underlining her argument about the poisonous effects of murderous anger, Allen notes that the Greek word for 'glare' comes from a word meaning 'snake' (196).

of the law too much to bear, the plays offer the reader important insights into the laws and ethics of interpreting violence. In any case, even if *Hamlet* does imply the existence of a code of honour that contradicted the Christian condemnation of calculated revenge, this is clearly not intended to be presented as a *living* code: the only representative of it in the play is the Ghost of the Old warrior-king Hamlet whose warlike manner is an echo of an older time – possibly harking back to the pre-Christian classical revenge ethos of Seneca's tragedies (Foakes 2003). But as we have seen, Shakespeare's terrifying Ghost is one of ambiguous identity and questionable veracity and he invites audiences to be suspicious of it on theological grounds; in the same way the play should be viewed through the ethical lens of Christianity and the human difficulties in meeting its demands. As R.A. Foakes (2003, 130) argues, 'the central issue of the play' is not revenge as such, but rather 'the control or release of instinctual drives to violence'.

a) Early Modern English Criminal Law Revisited:
The Emergence of 'Implied Malice' and Holt CJ's Four Grounds for Provocation

The courts of early modern England developed a doctrine of *implied* malice to ensure that people who were quick to erupt into lethal rage could not use their own propensity to sudden violence to take advantage of the legal distinction between premeditated murder (capital offence) and spontaneous 'chance-medley' manslaughter, for which defendants could claim the benefit of clergy and be retried under the much more lenient canon law. Although Kaye (1967) has argued that the murder verdicts recorded and unavailability of clergy and chance medley defences in the sixteenth century are explained simply by finding a lack of hot blood or passionate outrage on the part of the accused (Kaye 1967) records of homicide cases in this period show convictions for murder despite being seemingly committed spontaneously and without any evidence of malice expressly premeditated. As Jeremy Horder (1992, 14) has pointed out, the facts of, say, *Herbert's Case* (1558), *Emerie's Case* (1585) and *Dorest Hunter* (1584), *Watts v Brains* (1600) all involved intentional homicides in circumstances in which the courts felt that there was just cause to *imply* that malice aforethought existed even though it probably did not. In those cases, the accused could not claim to have acted in chance-medley, because, although the killing was committed suddenly, there was no good reason to categorize it as an act of passion or heated blood. The fact that the defendant's violence stemmed from his own violent temperament meant that it was held to be morally equivalent to premeditated murder rather than to chance medley manslaughter, meaning that the defendant found guilty might face the gallows in circumstances that would previously have allowed the possibility of a re-trial under canon law. Thus the courts of the sixteenth and seventeenth centuries seem to have been becoming increasingly interested, not simply in whether a killing was a sudden outburst in hot blood or else premeditated, but also in the *reasons why* a person's blood had become heated to such an extent that it caused him to kill; and where no there was no good reason for the outburst the apparently absent malice aforethought could simply be implied.

This analysis of the cases raises some thorny legal-historical questions. For example, if it is true that courts had become used to implying malice aforethought by the time of *Hamlet*, why did Parliament feel it necessary to enact the 'Statute of Stabbing' in 1604, which expressly removed the benefit of clergy from all cases involving little or no provocation?[6] Horder argues that the 1604 statute was simply unnecessary, since the courts had indeed begun to adopt implied malice as a common law doctrine and thus to treat unprovoked homicides as murder (Horder 1992, 30–1, 18–9). Certainly by the middle of the seventeenth century it is clear that the courts were looking for a specific provocation before allowing defendants to escape the death penalty through clergy. For instance *The Protector and Buckner* is a case that specifically relates to the interpretation of the Statute of Stabbing. The defendant had killed a man who had tried to hold him prisoner in his own house. The defendant argued successfully that he should avoid the effects of the 1604 Statute (and thereby 'have his clergy') because the deceased's violation of his liberty was a sufficient provocation. Although by the mid-seventeenth century a charge of murder could be made out on the basis of either expressed or implied malice, the moral benchmark of the most heinous kind of homicide was the premeditated one, carried out in secret and at night. Malice was only implied in cases in which the violence used was so shocking and lacking in any grounding whatsoever that not to treat it as murder would be an injustice in itself. The understanding of murder that had prevailed in the first half of the sixteenth century continued to exert a powerful influence: the very fact that the two types of malice existed means that it was felt to be important that the moral basis of distinguishing murder from manslaughter must be respected. Even if express malice could not be found, the court would have to satisfy itself that the crime in question was serious enough to treat it as if it were. In other words, the calculated exaction of blood revenge such as urged by the Ghost of *Hamlet* was, if carried out according to plan and not simply the outcome of a chance melee, the archetype of capital murder with malice aforethought.

The effect of the early modern cases was that over time a certain number of provocative actions or circumstances would be regarded as sufficient for a court to go on to examine whether the killing was committed in hot blood. A little over a century after *Hamlet* and the distinguishing of murder and manslaughter by the formal removal of the benefit of clergy from the former type of case by the Statute of Stabbing, there were four recognized grounds for provocation, set out famously by Holt CJ in *Mawgridge* (1707) and explained here by Lord Hoffman:

> The first was the quarrel which escalated from words to physical assault ("by pulling him by the nose, or filliping upon the forehead"). If the assaulted party

---

6   1604 incidentally being the year of the Second Quarto of *Hamlet*, the text of which this chapter draws its extracts from the play.

drew his sword and immediately slew the other, it would be "but manslaughter". The second was a quarrel in which a friend of the person assaulted joined in and gave the deadly blow. The third was where someone took the part of a fellow-citizen who was being "injuriously treated" and the fourth was killing a man in the act of adultery with one's wife ("for jealousy is the rage of man and adultery is the highest invasion of property"). (*R v Smith (Morgan)*, 160)

Holt CJ's 'four categories' formalizes the movement of the courts over the preceding century towards implying malice aforethought in the absence of a recognized cause for the heating of the defendant's blood. By restricting the list of recognized provocations to these four Holt CJ recognizes only those causes regarded by gentlemen of his day as the worst kinds of interference – that is, with a man's bodily integrity, with his sense of loyalty to friend and fellow citizen and with his sexual privacy. An incursion into a man's own private sphere of the nature described here by Holt CJ was recognized not only as provocative but furthermore as an *injustice* of such a distressing nature as to lead to a feeling that its immediate punishment was warranted in restoring the perceived imbalance. The interpretation of Holt CJ's judgment has caused some disagreement amongst commentators: for Ashworth (1976, 293–4) it is important that all four of the provocative acts described by Holt CJ share the quality of illegality (whether by criminal or canon law); for Horder (1992, 25) the significance of the four grounds lies in the fact that they were all affronts to honour, in response to which a virtuous man would be expected to be moved to lethal violence. In any case, to admit of specific conditions such as these in which intentional killing naturally could be regarded as something less than murder, poses a moral and legal difficulty since, as an intentional killing carried out not in self-defence but by the defendant himself exacting punishment (and thus assuming a role reserved only for the law), the retaliation cannot be justified. The use of violence to exact private revenge cannot be authorized because to do so would require the law to legislate for its own private usurpation. Therefore the distinction between murder and hot blooded manslaughter is used to excuse the retaliation only partially, thus also partially *condemning* both the provoker and the provoked. The killing of a person who offered a defendant such galling affronts as those listed by Holt CJ had committed a wrong, and even though to respond to any one of them by killing the wrongdoer would also be a wrong, there could be no denying that the provoker thereby paid a price, not entirely just perhaps, but certainly not unwarranted. Therefore, in Holt CJ's formulation we recall Hamlet's desperate wish for his thoughts to 'be bloody or nothing worth' in order that his desire to kill the uncle that wronged his father might be interpretable as a provoked hot blooded killing, and also Castor's judgment that condemns both Clytemnestra and her avengers: 'She has her just deserts by your unjust act.'

b) The Moral Element of the Modern Provocation Defence

In modern law, the English and US approaches to the moral aspect of the provocation defence are as different as they are in their approaches to the psychological aspect. English law has generalized the justificatory element and since the nineteenth century has required simply that the defendant's reaction showed 'reasonableness'. An early formulation of this requirement is found in the nineteenth century case *R v Kirkham* by Coleridge J at 119: 'though the law condescends to human frailty, it will not indulge human ferocity. It considers man to be a rational being, and requires that he should exercise a reasonable controul [sic] over his passions.'[7] Furthermore, since at least 1957, words as well as actions on the part of the victim may suffice as provocation under English law.[8] However, in the US, 'sufficient' provocation on the part of the victim is substantiated as a matter of law and in many states the formulation of what qualifies as sufficient seems not to have moved on at all from the *Mawgridge* criteria of 1707. For instance, Holt CJ would probably thoroughly approve of the short list of provocations recognized in Illinois in 1989 in *State v Chevalier*, where 'the only categories of serious provocation which have been recognized are: substantial physical injury or assault, mutual quarrel or combat, illegal arrest and adultery with the offender's spouse' (at 71). The reasons for the different ways in which the English and the US legal systems have evolved from their early modern roots are beyond the scope or purpose of this chapter. The reason why the justificatory element is so limited, however, is more transparent. Given that in the US *any* form of extreme heated passion or heated blood will suffice to establish the defendant's emotional state, there is clearly a need for a degree of tightening as to the recognized reasons for it. Until the law in England and Wales is reformed as promised, the far broader scope of the English justificatory requirement of 'reasonableness' under the Homicide Act 1957 is narrowed by the further requirement of a loss of self-control, discussed in the previous chapter. Under the proposed reforms of English law the reasonableness test will be replaced with a requirement that the defendant was confronted with a situation of such danger or grave insult that it might be sufficient to make a 'normal' person in the defendant's circumstances act as they did. The restrictions on what is meant by 'extremely grave' circumstances in those proposals, like the narrow justificatory element in the American provocation defence, means that juries will be required to scrutinize the moral character of the defendant's action more closely in the light of modern expectations of restraint and self-control.

---

7   By the time of *R v Welsh* (1869), provocation was being described in a way very familiar to a modern English lawyer (Keating J at 339): the provoking behaviour must be 'something which might naturally cause an ordinary and reasonably minded man to lose his self-control and commit such an act'.

8   The Homicide Act s.3 only requires that the defendant is provoked 'by things done or by things said or by both together'. The new proposed partial defence designed to replace provocation in English law will not change this.

Narrowing the justificatory element to 'extreme' conduct or words in this way will have the effect of removing the defence from many types of spontaneous or hot-blooded killings that under the 1957 statute would currently avoid a murder conviction. The defence in the US adheres closely to Holt CJ's list in admitting *physical* provocations only, deeming words and gestures as insufficient provocation however extreme or insulting they may be. Some critics have argued that this approach is to be commended for guarding against flagrantly odious uses of the defence, such as by homophobes who claim that their killing was driven by their passionate disgust at a homosexual advance (*State v Volk*). For this reason, Martha C. Nussbaum (1999, 38) praises the American law as being 'rational and consistent, [offering] perfectly clear reasons why some emotional reactions are relevant to mitigation, while others are not.' Nussbaum is surely correct that a homosexual advance could not rightfully be brought within any of the stipulated bases for the provocation defence no matter how disgusting this is felt to be by a defendant, although she may be guilty of a selective reading of the cases given that even according to her own references, the narrow justificatory basis under the US laws has not always prevented homophobic killings from using the defence (*Schick v State*, Nussbaum 1999, 37). However, unlike the English law, the defence in the US explicitly preserves not only the seventeenth century bias towards violence as grounds for provocation but also the special significance of marital infidelity. Since the defence is otherwise formulated so tightly, the inclusion of this non-violent provocation sticks out somewhat awkwardly.

Let us therefore consider the *Baillie*-type modern provocation case, introduced in the last chapter, as an example of violence used in response to a threat of violence issued towards a loved one. If the facts of *Baillie* – upon hearing that his son had been threatened by a local drug dealer, a father drove across town and shot the man dead at his home – had come before the criminal courts in the seventeenth century, Baillie would have sought to show that his violence ought to be treated as a killing in defence of one's kin and treated as 'clergiable' manslaughter. Of course it is rather pointless to speculate on whether this argument would have convinced an early modern court that there was sufficient provocation for the benefit of clergy to be applicable. What is more important is the notion that in addition to 'hot blood' – a very broad emotional basis for finding a lack of malice – the early modern legal mind looked for a sufficiently weighty cause on which to base the defence. Baillie clearly had a cause to feel upset, aggrieved and fearful when his boys told him they had been threatened. However, rather than asking whether or not such news would cause a reasonable man to lose self-control and do what Baillie did (and in finding that he would not have so acted, consider the patently fictional notion that a reasonable loss of self-control might have occurred on McCubbin's doorstep) the early modern court would have simply made an assessment of the defendant's actions in the light of contemporary attitudes towards violence in the face of a provocation. In the sixteenth century decision *Salisbury's Case* outlined above, it was considered to be mere manslaughter where a man witnesses his master (or other kin) involved in affray and he intervenes with lethal effect. While this case on its own may simply indicate (as Kaye argues) that killing in hot-blood would be treated as manslaughter (and as we have seen, the Statute of Stabbing seems to confirm that this was so), the later famous case of *R v Mawgridge* interprets *Salisbury* as an example of one of the four recognized provocations. In this case, Holt CJ held the second of his 'four categories' thus: 'If two be fighting together, and a friend of the one takes up a bowl on a sudden, and with it break the skull of his friend's adversary, of which he died, that is no more than manslaughter' (136). Therefore in *Royley's Case* decided almost a century earlier, a father who, upon finding that his son had been wounded by another boy's father, had walked a mile to find the man and beat him to death with a cudgel, was also found guilty only of manslaughter on the same reasoning. The cases do not seem to provide a sufficiently clear distinction between hot-blooded provoked homicide and premeditated murder. The question is one of degree to be decided on the facts.

Consideration of the rightful role of a moral or justificatory element in the defence of provocation (or whatever we call it) provides a similar tension today, even if we have long since stopped talking about 'honour'. Is it possible, or even meaningful, to stipulate the behaviour on the part of the victim that would suffice to allow for a manslaughter verdict? As we have seen, the approach in the US is to do precisely this, and so the provocation defence in its various guises in the US states that lethal force used in heated passion in response to violence, the threat of violence or the witnessed infidelity of a spouse, may be manslaughter rather than murder. In England and Wales until now, the 'reasonableness' requirement alone has provided the 'cause' for provoked killing. According to the proposed new partial defence in England and Wales, the cause is defined negatively: partner infidelity is never grounds for the defence (Cl. 1 (1) (9)), but otherwise it must simply amount to 'extremely grave' circumstances for the defendant (Ministry of Justice 2009, 12). This approach is a helpful on the one hand, since if a fear of violence is not in evidence then the requirement for an extremely grave trigger and its effect of a 'normal' person ought to focus the jury's attention on the necessity for a moral relationship between victim's behaviour and defendant's reaction presently lacking in the English defence of provocation. However if the requirement is interpreted too literally by the courts, then it will probably remove the defence from far too many defendants who should be permitted to avoid a murder conviction. What is to be regarded as sufficient provocation is too much bound up in cultural relativism for a clear or unequivocal answer to be rendered, and this is perhaps why English law has until now simply left it as a question for the jury to compare the defendant's actions against those of a theoretical 'reasonable man'. As Windeyer J of the Australian Court of Criminal Appeal said of the history of provocation rulings in *Parker*: '[they] show how different in weight and character are the things that matter in one age from those which matter in another.' As we have seen, Holt CJ included the killing of another man 'taken in adultery' with the defendant's wife as one of just four sufficiently grave provocations, on the basis that 'jealousy is the rage of a man, and adultery is the highest invasion of property'

(*R v Mawgridge* 137). Although the current formulation of the defence in English is no longer formally gendered in its language, many critics have argued that to kill out of jealousy is a particularly male phenomenon. The requirement of a reasonable relation between provocation and response in both the English and American criminal laws continue (at least for the time being) to prioritize anger over fear or desperation, arguably the more common emotional state of women who kill abusive partners. Caroline Forell (2006, 44) describes the reference in the American Model Penal Code to excusing a defendant's 'extreme mental or emotional disturbance' as allowing for a 'firmly entrenched' male-bias, providing a defence for 'men who kill women who seek to exercise their autonomy through infidelity or leaving.' As a general statement about American law Forell has misinterpreted US law here, since the courts have consistently held that the heating of blood alone is insufficient for a defence unless it is accompanied by a legally recognized provocation. However, statistics are clear on both sides of the Atlantic that the hot-blooded killing of an unfaithful spouse is far more likely to be committed by a man than a woman, just as men are more likely than women to be the aggressors in domestic abuse cases (Forell 2006, 32). Therefore, defending a killing on the basis of a spouse's infidelity is now regarded by many people as tainted by misogyny; the idea that a man's lethally violent reaction to an unfaithful woman should be provided with a defence favouring the male abuser over the female victim of domestic abuse. As Home Office Minister Baroness Scotland of Asthal stated in response to the Law Commission's proposals: 'it may be too easy for a jealous partner to use the partial defence of provocation to escape a murder conviction through blaming the victim's alleged infidelity. Unfaithfulness should not be an excuse for murder' (Lords Hansard 2007, 1 March, Col. 1720). Feminist critics have argued that male sexual jealousy should not be a basis for the provocation defence at all, since it implicitly holds the unfaithful woman to blame for a man's inability to control his violence simply because she exercised lawful sexual autonomy (Forell 2006, 34). In England and Wales, the Government's proposed homicide reforms aims to redress this perceived gender inequality by removing the defence from men who kill their spouse on the basis of the latter's infidelity. The proposals have been welcomed by Women's Aid (*Murder Law Proposals Criticized* 2008): 'The current law allows men to get away with murder and places the blame on victims of domestic violence, rather than the perpetrators.' In response to the Government's proposals the Senior Law Lord, Lord Phillips of Worth Matravers, explained in a recent speech that he is 'uneasy about a law which so diminishes the significance of sexual infidelity as expressly to exclude it from even the possibility of amounting to provocation' (Rosenberg 2008). Lord Phillips' comments have not been well received by women's groups which see the Government's proposal to withdraw the defence from most cases of killing in anger as an overdue correction to law's traditional leniency towards domestic murder. Certainly men should not 'get away with murder' if that is the right way to describe a particular case. However, in my view, simply removing the defence from all cases of domestic killings of the 'unfaithful spouse' draws a line of exclusion which, although may rightly deny a defence to abusive defendants in many cases, is nonetheless a crude and inflexible way to redirect the application of the defence. I argued in the previous chapter that juries currently seem to apply the requirements of section 3 of the Homicide Act 1957 according to their own moral feeling as to when a particular killing ought to be classified as murder and when it ought instead to be regarded merely as manslaughter, and thereby overcome the shortcomings of the current law. There is certainly a need for the defence of provocation to be reformed in order to reflect more truly modern social and moral attitudes towards violence and hence I support the shift in bias towards killings committed out of fear. However, to attempt, as the Government proposes to do, to use legislation to further curtail juries' discretion by excluding particular kinds of killings from the defence risks ensuring that the formal requirements of the law continue to be regarded by juries as a fiction. The feminist position represented here by Caroline Forell and Women's Aid make the same mistake as some interpreters of *Hamlet*: that in their understanding of the reasons for granting a defence to murder, they confuse a condemnable but nevertheless understandable hot-blooded act of violence for an appeal to honour and rightness. As I have argued, *Hamlet* is less about recognizing a morally compelling code of ethics about restoring one's honour through violence than reflecting on the way we respond to those who fail to control what Foakes (2003, 130–1) calls the instinctual drives to violence. Likewise, the current availability of the provocation defence to those who kill their unfaithful spouse is not an endorsement of domestic violence or gendered power structures, and neither is it an assertion that killing in such circumstances has moral integrity. Instead it is a recognition that such a killing *may*, if the facts are regarded by a jury to bear such a view, be a killing that lacks malice aforethought or sufficient cruelty for such malice to be implied if it can be established that a person acted truly out of an understandable failure to exercise restraint when he should have restrained himself.

In stark opposition to the proposed reform to the defence in England and Wales, formulations of the provocation defence in state codes and appeals in the US gives the discovery of one's spouse in the act of adultery pride of place among the shortlist of recognized provocations. Indeed, it is the only circumstance in which a provocation defence to murder will be successful in the absence of violence or the threat of violence on the part of the victim (*State v Cooley*). However, given the empirical evidence of jury behaviour cited earlier in the chapter from the Law Commission's report on partial defences to murder in English criminal courts, it would be wrong to regard the US courts as uniquely gendered. The arguable tendency of juries to return a manslaughter verdict even where the evidence of a loss of self-control is very weak means that the appellate courts in England have been called to make sentencing judgments precisely on the question of what constitutes a severe provocation on the part of the victim, and what a defendant ought to be expected to bear. In fact, in the decided cases, appellate judges have shown themselves to be quite comfortable in setting the determinate sentence for men who are convicted of manslaughter after killing out of jealous rage. For instance in *Light* the Court of Appeal held that seven years imprisonment was appropriate for the provoked killing of an unfaithful spouse. If the victim boasted about it, taunted the defendant for sexual inadequacy, or where the defendant caught them '*in flagrante delicto*', these could all be mitigating factors in sentencing (per Lord Taylor, 827).[9] In its recommendation to the Sentencing Guidelines Council, the Sentencing Advisory Panel (2005, 30)[10] distinguishes 'extreme conduct' by the victim from lesser provocations. It states that, in its opinion, infidelity cannot constitute a high level of provocation. On the other hand, it cites persistent domestic violence as an example of 'extreme conduct' (Sentencing Advisory Panel 2005, 31–2),[11] and violence generally (whether actual or anticipated) as being a higher degree of provocation than abusive or offensive words (SAP 2005, 37). On one end of the scale, in *Byrne* the Court of Appeal held that a sentence of eight years was suitable for a man who had killed the victim after the latter had called him a 'wanker' (SAP 2005, 36). At the other end of the sentencing scale, the Panel recommend that three years or less is appropriate where the victim's provocation involved 'attack, even terror, evoking extreme passion' in the defendant (SAP 2005, 26). Where the victim 'presented a threat not only to the offender but also to children in his or her care' then this will be treated as another aggravating factor (SAP 2005, 31). The Sentencing Guidelines Council incorporated the Panel's views in its publication of instructions for trial judges, and stipulate that killings 'motivated by fear or desperation' will normally be treated as carrying a lower level of culpability than those motivated by 'anger, frustration or a desire for revenge' (SAP 2005, 5). The indications are that for both sentencing and jury attitudes to conviction, affront to honour, violence and the fear of violence all already have their place in the law of provocation even although the Homicide Act 1957 s.3 seems to allow only for homicide in anger to be excused. It would seem that the Government's proposal to replace the current excuse for killing in anger with one that excuses killings from the fear of serious violence is therefore already effectively and substantially part of the law.

Conclusion

The tallionic demand for like repayment, the restoration of balance between aggrieved parties, resetting the upset scales; these are all powerfully dramatic ways of thinking about what people have tried to attain in their pursuit of justice. As metaphors of the struggle towards a just end to problems, they provide a basis from which to view the connections between the symbols of law and literary and poetic traditions that narrate bitter feuds and passionate and violent acts. However,

---

9   Quoted approvingly in *Attorney General's Reference (Suratan)* by Mantell LJ at 279, para. [16].

10   References to Sentencing Advisory Panel (SAP) refer to paragraph numbers.

11   Referred to as SAP hereafter.

if there is anything to be drawn from the representations of the efforts of the families of wronged kin in the works of literature discussed here, it is that even if revenge can bring about brief satisfaction, it cannot of itself bring about resolution or peace. This is why in the categorization of different kinds of intentional killings, laws have tended to recognize that those committed suddenly, without any premeditation and in response to a recognized provocation are condemned, but not as murder. In the previous chapter I discussed the legal requirement in English and US law that a defendant who pleads the defence of provocation be temporarily overtaken by extreme emotion to the extent that in that moment they are incapable of exercising normal self-control. In this chapter I have tried to supplement that discussion by examining the emotional character of the normative aspect of provocation – that in using the defence, the defendants must not rely solely on their loss of self-control or heated passion, but that there was a cause for them to do so that a court can recognize as sufficiently provocative. I have steered away from the discussion of the leading cases familiar to lawyers, presenting instead a view of provocation through the treatment of violence in Shakespeare and Euripides. I have argued that these works help us to understand that the normative basis for the defence also admits an emotional explanation, both for our sympathy for the protagonists of those works who kill in order to remember properly a wronged parent despite the conflict with law and morality that this involves; and furthermore that, understood thus, the dramatic works also provide an approach to understanding violence in our own society and when a killing is to be utterly condemned as murder and when partially excused as voluntary manslaughter.

Chapter 3

'Abandon every hope all you who enter': Punishment, Communication and the Longevity of the Whole Life Sentence

The idea that punishment might continue beyond the death of a condemned person is reasonably regarded as belonging to extinct societies in which the membrane between the world of gods and the world of people was believed to be porous. In Sophocles' *Antigone*, King Creon of Thebes punishes his fallen enemy Polyneices by declaring that his body may not be buried, but instead, 'must be left all ghastly where he fell, a corpse for dogs to maul and vultures pick his bones' (Sophocles 2001, 350). Of course, an offender's eternal soul is beyond the jurisdiction of modern courts, but can it nevertheless make moral or symbolic sense to impose punishment upon an offender knowing that they will not live to experience it in full? In the US, a prisoner who escapes the death penalty may instead be imprisoned for several life sentences without parole and the natural limitations of the human lifespan will mean that in some cases only a fraction of the total punishment will actually be served. In Spain, although offenders may in theory be sentenced to serve many thousands of years, in practice no one may be imprisoned for more than forty. This chapter considers the moral problem presented in jurisdictions in which the death penalty is unavailable and other forms of punishment are prohibited under the United Nations Declaration of Human Rights (1948, art. 5) as being 'cruel, inhuman or degrading', by those rare cases in which a crime committed is so heinous that even lifelong imprisonment does not seem to exact satisfying retribution. We are in the realms here of the moral issues relating to the amount of punishment to be meted out in cases such as that of Myra Hindley who, in the opinion of many people, died in prison long before she had paid for her role in the kidnap, torture and murder of five children near Manchester with her boyfriend Ian Brady in the 1960s. According current retributive theory, it is a moral imperative that punishment can only be justified if it can serve to *communicate censure to the prisoner*: if the prisoner dies then the communicative link is broken and hence the punishment is over. But in 2000, House of Lords ruled in *R v Hindley* (2000, 390) that 'there are cases where the crimes are so wicked that even if the prisoner is detained until he or she dies it will not exhaust the requirements of retribution and deterrence'. Perhaps Lord Steyn intended his remark to be regarded as mere hyperbolae, but whatever else, it is certainly a vivid use of rhetoric that speaks to the heart of our moral and symbolic ideas about punishment. Reading this important moment in English legal history together with

Kafka's short story *In the Penal Settlement*, or *In the Penal Colony* as it is better known, I argue in this chapter that to understand 'whole life' imprisonment in this way as a mere portion of the full punishment lays down a challenge to the way we understand the symbolic meaning of punishing. In characterizing the requirements of retribution and deterrence as exceeding the prisoner's natural death, the state seems to be making a metaphysical claim on the prisoner's soul that invokes pre-Enlightenment ideas. Punishment that purported to exceed a prisoner's death was meaningful to the early moderns, for whom the infliction of pain on the offender was regarded as necessary for negating or expiating the crime itself. The offender's body, whether alive or dead, was considered to be a legitimate medium through which the state could deliver a message of terror and deterrence to the public. I argue in this chapter that the idea of 'whole life' imprisonment has more in common with this early modern spectacle than Enlightenment philosophy since it speaks a message not primarily of censure to the offender, but one of expiation to society as a whole by using the offender's body as a means of communication.

1. The Modern Justification of Punishment as Communicative Retribution

For the sake of argument, I shall assume that whether one proceeds from a deontological or a consequentialist basis, we nevertheless restrict a theory of justified punishment to the punishment of the guilty person for a crime which they actually committed. This rules out the use of punishment *purely* for, say, general deterrence, political expediency, social engineering, population control, incapacitation, terror, and so on, for which the person punished is treated not as having any intrinsic value but simply as a means to an end. It follows from this that punishment only really makes sense if the offender is alive and is mentally competent. In order to accommodate a liberal notion of the individual as a free agent with intrinsic worth, recent academic moral theorizations of just punishment have tended to accept a retributive model of punishment as a moral response to wrongdoing. The insistence by modern theories of punishment as *retribution* that an offender must be respected as a rational person of inherent value leads to the idea that punishment represents not an effort to engineer that prisoner into a better person, but rather a communication of censure that is owed to everyone whom we recognize as a free agent (Duff and Hirsch 1997, 112). Kant (1998, [6:331]) denied that there could be any moral reason for punishing a person other than the fact that they had committed a crime, 'for a human being can never be treated merely as a means to the purposes of another'. The censure communicated by punishment is an extension of the moral blame and criticism that we would direct at anyone who knowingly transgressed society's norms. In order for this to work in practice, it must be possible to imagine that an invisible line of communication connects the offender to the offended society, and that through punishment, the offender learns how and why society as a whole feels hurt by their crime. Retributive theorists seem to agree that even if the amount of punishment for any given offence is in some way arbitrary and relative to changeable political and social conditions (as Hegel argued), it is important to get that amount right in order for the censure to be meaningful. Every day that a person is held in prison is in itself a punishment and thus in order to be morally justified we must be able to believe that the prisoner can 'hear' society's continued reprobation. The body of the prisoner is clearly separated from society by imprisonment since they languish in gaol. However, this very act of separation – and the continuation of this separation – gradually unites the prisoner and society, since the prisoner comes to understand that their actions were wrong and their return to society is thus made possible. In order to allow for the actual reunification of individual and society, Duff implies that in most cases there will eventually come a time when the censure of the offender will be complete and the prisoner released. Punishment therefore works towards an actual (as opposed to a merely metaphysical) reunification of individual and society, however distant that reunification might be. Whereas a purely rehabilitative justification for punishment would seek to keep an offender in prison only as long as (if at all) the state actually needs to change their mind or personality irrespective of the heinousness of their offence, the liberal retributivist calculates punishment according to the moral idea of the extent to which a person should, on principle, suffer to expiate his crime and earn re-admittance to society (Duff 1996, 41–5; Duff 2001, 40–1). Duff (1999, 52) argues that criminal sentences should be proportional to the amount of time we would reasonably consider necessary to make a rational agent repent their actions.

This moral understanding of punishment is based on the liberal notion of a political community of morally autonomous agents who respect themselves as free and competent to make their own decisions and participate discursively in democratic public life and accord the same respect to all others. For example, Rawls (1993) and Habermas (1997) both endorse a framework of human rights and a public life committed to open participatory democracy as the only way of securing what they see as these fundamental aspects of a free society. Modern liberal retributivists retain the sense of desert in the moral relationship between crime and punishment inherited from Kant, but in seeking to move beyond Kantian metaphysics they emphasize the role of punishment as not only an intrinsically right response to a crime but also in helping the offender to find a way to 'work through' their punishment and eventually be reunited with the community from which their crime has cut them off. Of course in a physical sense all punishment might seem to have a divisive as opposed to a re-uniting effect, but in fact it is a central reason *for* punishing prisoners that by virtue of their inalienable status as rational agents, they rationally strive to gain re-admittance to their community. Duff (1999, 69) argues that a wrong is committed against the offender if punishment is not imposed, since this would deny that they are capable of taking responsibility for their actions. Not to punish – or to punish simply to achieve some social purpose such as deterrence, incapacitation or rehabilitation – would be to treat offenders not as 'moral agents', but as 'beasts in a circus'. 'Punishment addresses the wrongdoer as a responsible citizen; it is owed to him, as an honest response to his crime' (Duff 1999, 50). Reflecting the liberal concern for mutuality between individual and society, the 'debt' of punishment is paid both by the offender (by serving time in gaol) and also by the state itself to the offender, as something owed to him in symbolic recognition of his moral character which yearns to be reunited with society. Importantly, this is a *post*-metaphysical understanding both of liberal political theory in general and retributive theory in particular. As Duff (1999, 56) argues, this is an appeal not to a set of rationally given principles, but to 'shared values' and a 'common life'.

The psychological aspect of punishment – the wrongdoer's fall from grace and painful road to repentance – has a certain poetic allure, and is arguably what sustains public interest in punishment generally (Sarat 1999, 171). The theme of the moral sickness of alienation and renewal by expiating one's crime and undergoing the painful, slow process of reconnecting the links between oneself and society is perhaps most famously depicted in Dostoevsky's *Crime and Punishment*. Sentenced to heavy labour in Siberia, we share Raskolnikov's change of aspect on the very last pages of the novel:

> From the other bank, far away, was faintly borne the sound of singing. There, in the immensity of the steppe, flooded with sunlight, the black tents of the nomads were barely visible dots. Freedom was there, there other people lived, so utterly unlike those on this side of the river that it seemed as though with them time had stood still, and the age of Abraham and his flocks was still the present. Raskolnikov sat on and his mind had wandered into day-dreams; he thought of nothing, but an anguished longing disturbed and tormented him. (Dostoyevsky 1998, 525)

Separated from the free world by 'the wide, solitary river', Raskolnikov longs for freedom, not simply out of frustration at being a prisoner, but because he begins to realize that through punishment he can find his way back to society. At this point he has seven years of exile left – 'what unbearable sufferings and infinite happiness those years would hold!' – which means that his renewed life has a definite endpoint to work towards. The alienated Meursault of Camus' *The Outsider* convinces the court at his murder trial that he is guilty because through his failure to show remorse for the killings or to cry at his mother's funeral he demonstrates that he has effectively cut himself off from society (Camus 2000).[1] When Meursault himself understands this, he realizes that he is, like Raskolnikov, on the far side of the river from society: 'And I felt something stirring up the whole room; the first time I realized I was guilty' (Camus 2000, 87). If the idea of punishment as Duff envisages it is ever to be possible on a practical level, true remorse on the part of the offender is a necessary step since it is important that they come to accept responsibility for having committed a crime. However, in

---

1   The unremorseful 'are viewed as if they have offended the community twice [in their] refusal to acknowledge that mores were violated' (Sarat 1999, 170).

order to preserve the moral aspect of punishment as retribution, it is important to maintain the objective aspect of the expiation of crime. Remorse and other feelings are merely subjective matters and as such are not part of the realm of liberal moral theory. Retributivism is not concerned with purely subjective measures but with the objective question of the expiation of the crime. As Theodore Dalrymple (2002) has commented, gaol is not intended to be 'treatment', even if as a consequence of incarceration offenders might also find a way to rehabilitation. 'Punishment' is not therefore dependent on a particular offender's susceptibility to reform.

In the case of punishments that do not demand their death, the prisoner may be entitled to expect that one day they will be judged to have suffered sufficiently to pay for the hurt caused to society. The case of the offender for whom there is no prospect of *ever* returning to society in a physical sense is rather different. For the offender who might otherwise have hoped to complete his punishment and be released, the idea of a whole life term raises questions about what implications this has for morally justifying punishment. With its now seemingly barbaric notions of the uses to which the offender's body could be put as a means for transmitting this message of deterrence, it is early modern public execution and not Enlightenment moral philosophy that elucidates the moral character of the whole life prison term. I shall attempt to identify a common thread that runs between the Myra Hindley appeal, Kafka's depiction of a hideous execution device in his short story *In the Penal Colony* and some of the notions supporting early modern public executions. To reiterate, the link between these apparently diverse case studies rests upon the particular communicative work performed by the punishment in question. Accounts of each of these apparently diverse species of punishment are capable of causing discomfort and upset for the liberal reader, not because they are barbaric or because they fail to communicate any coherent message at all, but because they apparently communicate the *wrong message*, or rather, that the conveyance of censure is misdirected and thus fails to justify itself in liberal moral terms. In the next two sections I would like to set out my arguments on why I believe this to be the case.

2. Kafka's *In the Penal Colony* and Myra Hindley's Whole Life Sentence: Two Stories of Symbolic Miscommunication

In 2000, the House of Lords put an end to Myra Hindley's appeal against the Home Secretary's policy that her life sentence for murder must mean her whole life. At each stage of Hindley's appeal it was accepted by the judges that both as a matter of law and principle, there were exceptionally heinous cases such as this in which the period of a lifer's sentence involving imprisonment (the part that represents the requirement of 'retribution and deterrence') would never be fulfilled in the course of the offender's life. As a matter of statutory interpretation, it was held that in order to respond adequately to such cases, 'imprisonment for life' as it is referred to in the Murder (Abolition of the Death Penalty) Act 1965 must be capable of bearing this literal meaning. In the House of Lords, Lord Steyn declared that he believed Hindley's crime to have been 'uniquely evil' and hence one that fell into the category of cases in which 'life imprisonment' could bear such a meaning (*R v Hindley* 2000, 392). Their Lordships did not merely decide that a punishment might sometimes equate to the whole of a prisoner's natural life, but that their natural life might sometimes represent only a *portion* of the time required to fully pay for the crime:

> But there is nothing logically inconsistent with the concept of a tariff by saying that there are cases where the crimes are so wicked that even if the prisoner is detained until he or she dies it will not exhaust the requirements of retribution and deterrence. (*R v Hindley* 2000, 390)

Lord Steyn seems to be implying that 'life' here means much more than merely a life in the biological sense, for although in practice the punishment suffered by Myra Hindley was simply the whole of her natural life, on a moral and symbolic level, this period '*will not exhaust the requirements of retribution* and deterrence' (my emphasis). This is problematic if we want to justify punishment as a continuing communication of society's censure to the offender as well as signifying due respect for the offender as a rational agent. Is it possible to regard the punishment in this way if it is taken as given that the whole of the prisoner's life might not actually satisfy the requirement of retribution, and that a price greater than that which can physically be paid by the prisoner is owed to expiate the crime? If we think of punishment as involving a gradual process of reconnection between offender and society then the voice that we imagine to be society's censure is surely muted by Lord Steyn's comment. As a further problem for morally justifying the punishment, in Lord Steyn's reference to the punishment in terms of 'retribution and deterrence' simultaneously, he implies that two quite different communicative functions being performed. Retribution is a justificatory narrative that anticipates communication issuing from society (via the state) to the offender. Deterrence, on the other hand, is the communication of a message from the state *to* society at large, in which the prisoner is held up as an example of what becomes of those who transgress the law. Deterrence is therefore a very different kind of communicative function to retribution, involving as it does a line of communication directed not to the prisoner, but rather *through* them. In this respect the power exerted by the state is in speaking its message to its people by silencing the prisoner, or by symbolically turning a prisoner into a puppet or mouthpiece for its own message.

Franz Kafka's *In the Penal Colony* is a short story in which a western explorer is invited to witness the execution of a prisoner in a remote colonial outpost. The unfortunate prisoner had been caught by his captain sleeping at 2am when he should have been on sentry-duty and saluting the captain's door each hour. As the explorer discovers, the condemned man is to be executed by means of an horrifically ingenious battery operated machine which, over a twelve hour period, will gradually inscribe a judgment (in this case 'HONOUR THY SUPERIORS!') deeper and deeper into his body with a harrow until the prisoner dies in agony of his accumulated wounds. The machine is the pride and joy of the presiding officer (who is also the judge) who explains its functioning and his understanding of the legal and political landscape of the colony to the explorer. The explorer for his part looks on, first with boredom, then mild and increasing discomfort and finally horror. The officer wants to impress the foreign explorer with the exquisite intricacy of the machine's operation and its power to bring enlightenment and understanding of the justice being done both to the prisoner and for the sublime education of anyone watching. He believes that the explorer will come to appreciate the amazing transformative powers of the execution device and will consequently use his influence to promote its use to the new commandant of the penal colony, who seems to regard the device as outmoded and barbaric. The explorer refuses to support the officer and so the latter eventually releases the condemned man and instead places his own body under the harrow, instructing the machine to inscribe the command 'BE JUST!' However, the machine quickly begins to malfunction, killing the officer within moments rather than hours and then self-destructing without him enjoying the twelve hour 'enlightenment' that its previous victims had apparently enjoyed. For the officer, the communication of censure and the enlightenment of the prisoner through pain is a central justification for his execution device. The bodily inscription of legal and moral judgment depicted in this story might be read as a literal representation of the cumulative effect of any kind of punishment upon a convicted offender. Reading Myra Hindley's case in the light of Kafka's *In the Penal Colony* brings into relief some specific difficulties of applying a liberal idea of retribution to the whole life minimum term for murder as it is understood by Lord Steyn. It narrates the need for a meaningful relationship between an offender's responsibility for having committed a crime in the first place and the degree or severity of punishment exacted on them and also the ambiguous communicative role that punishment actually serves.

In Kafka's story, the punishment to be inflicted upon the condemned man is comically far in excess of his responsibility for his actions. He is described in the story as a 'stupid-looking wide mouthed creature with bewildered hair and face' who understands nothing, either about his offence or the judgment made against him (Kafka 1961, 169). Since he does not understand French, the condemned man 'could not understand a word' of what the officer says (in French) in his explanation to the explorer about the machine. Nevertheless throughout the officer's explanations he is 'apparently listening with all his ears' (Kafka 1961, 174). The image of a creature attentively listening, paying attention to every sound and movement but without comprehending the words, might remind one of a dog. Kafka (1961, 169) also remarks that the heavy chains around the man's hands and feet were unnecessary, since he 'looked so like a submissive dog that one might have thought he could be left to run free on the surrounding hills and would only need to be whistled for when the execution was due to begin.' Stanley Corngold (2001, 286) suggests that the 'doggishly submissive' character of the condemned man is a metaphor for the 'violent application of political power'. In being denied any chance to answer to his charge, the prisoner is treated like a dog or, as Duff's circus beast. Counsel for Myra Hindley argued that in her case, the whole life tariff failed to recognize the accepted difference between her culpability and that of her accomplice and boyfriend Ian Brady. This was described as an 'irrationality argument'. In the High Court, Lord Bingham acknowledged that it was accepted that there was a distinction to be drawn between Hindley and Brady:

> ... she had been dominated, intimidated, and suborned by her co-defendant Brady, with whom she had at the time been deeply in love. She described how she had been drugged and assaulted by Brady; how she had told a girlfriend of her fear of him; how he had made threats against her and her family; how she had applied for a job in Germany in order to get away from him. This account was accepted by the police as in all essentials correct. (*R v Hindley* 1998, 763)

Soon after her conviction on the charge of the murders of two children and one charge of accessory after the fact for a third, the trial judge wrote to the Home Secretary in May 1966 explaining that, while Brady should never be released, 'I cannot feel the same is necessarily true of Hindley once she is removed from his influence' (*R v Hindley* 1998, 760). It should be conceded that there was a practical difference between the two: whilst Brady remained a deeply disturbed and dangerous person in gaol, Hindley did not. However, counsel for Hindley was also making a moral argument in appealing to the retributivist concern that punishment must fit the responsibility for the crime as well as the crime itself. Since the Home Secretary's policy would apply the same degree of punishment to both the overbearing Brady and the cowed Hindley, there appears to be some mileage in this argument in terms of the moral justification of the sentence. Lord Bingham rightly rejected an argument made out by counsel for Hindley that in order to recognize the difference between the two, a whole life tariff for Brady must mean a determinate number of years for Hindley. As Lord Bingham said, 'If Brady satisfied by a wide margin the criterion for imposing the maximum penalty permitted by law, that does not lead to the conclusion that the applicant did not satisfy it' (*R v Hindley* 1998, 776). However, the difficulty in morally justifying the whole life tariff on this basis is that Lord Bingham seems to want to have his cake and eat it too: there is a moral difference between the two cases, but in effect the same (whole life) prison term will apply to both. It seems that we are being asked to imagine the penalty extending into some indefinite point in the hypothetical future; to imagine that, if the two prisoners were immortal beings we would come to see that the demands of retribution in Hindley's case would be satisfied before the demands in Brady's case. Of course, no judge would admit that the criminal law has any claim on the offender's immortal soul, and indeed the very idea is absurd, not least for theological–jurisdictional reasons. However, such is the nature of punishment as expiation and communication to the public that there is really no necessary limit to its symbolic continuation. The death of the prisoner does not mean the death of the crime: the memory of the murders that Hindley committed or helped to commit has a life independent of Myra Hindley herself. The prisoner is in effect 'lost' in the process that aims at expiating the crime.

The second difficulty narrated by Kafka that we also find troubling the judges in the *R v Hindley* appeal is that of the precise nature of the communicative work done by punishment itself. In both Kafka's story and the appeal there is a troubling conflation of the sentence and the punishment. In *In the Penal Colony* the officer explains to the explorer that, as a matter of course, the condemned man has received no information about the justice process whatsoever. The only information that he is to receive will be provided by experiencing the torture and execution:

> ... the explorer interrupted him: "He doesn't know the sentence that has been passed on him?", "No" – said the officer again, pausing a moment as if to let the explorer elaborate his question, and then said: "There would be no point in telling him. He'll learn it corporally, on his person." (Kafka 1961, 174)

In fact, the condemned man does not even know that he has been sentenced at all. 'My guiding principal is this: Guilt is never to be doubted. ... The captain came to me an hour ago; I wrote down his statement and appended the sentence to it. Then I had the man put in chains' (Kafka 1961, 175). Since the sentence is clearly considered to be none of the prisoner's business it is left to the punishment alone to communicate every aspect of the relationship between him, his crime and the law. The condemned man's guilt and his punishment thus bypass the individual offender himself. The impossibility of the condemned man himself learning his sentence until it is actually carried out means that the offender as a person is morally irrelevant: the only relevant factors are the crime and its expiation through pain. There is therefore a 'semantic collapse' as the critic Andreas Gailus (2001, 297) put it, between accusation and guilt and also between crime and punishment. There is no room in this equation for the prisoner as an individual in a liberal sense. It is significant that the sentence is literally indecipherable until it is carved into the prisoner's flesh. The officer shows the explorer the template for the words to be set into the machine to inscribe them onto the body of the condemned man. '"Read it", said the officer. "I can't", said the explorer. "Yet it is clear enough", said the officer. "It's very ingenious", said the explorer evasively, "but I can't make it out"' (Kafka 1961, 178). The document 'needs to be studied closely', the officer warns, 'I'm quite sure that in the end you would understand it too'. However, the explorer can make out nothing but a confusing mess of black lines. Kafka seems to imply that the only way for anyone to understand the inscription would be to experience the exquisite death offered by the machine for oneself. The indecipherability of the script means that it would be impossible for anyone to understand their sentence until they have it torturously and fatally inscribed on their body, and the fact that this necessarily causes the death of the prisoner shows that the understanding is nothing more than a fantasy. It is precisely this incomprehensibility that, for some theorists, is the very essence of Law. 'Do we', Danilyn Rutherford (2001, 303) rhetorically asks, 'accept authority more readily when its foundations evade our comprehension, when something other than reason encourages us to submit?' In attempting to answer his own question, Rutherford enlists Slavoj Zizek, who has argued that the idea of justice under the law and its acceptability are mutually definitive. There is no need for the system as a whole to make sense; indeed it is Law's very senselessness that lends it the air of mystique necessary for it to gain the respect of a people:

> We obey the Law, not because it is good or beneficial, but simply because it is the Law; rather than its virtues leading to obedience, obedience brings its virtues to light. The incomprehensible, traumatic character of the Law is what sustains its authority. (Rutherford 2001, 305)

It is thus the lack of knowledge rather than its gain that is, on this analysis, crucial in understanding the moral narrative of the sentence.

The theme of knowledge and its concealment is a theme that pervades the *R v Hindley* appeal. Her guilt of course was established in the normal way of a conviction by a jury in the Crown Court. However, the uniqueness of her case at the time and the undimmed monstrosity of her memory in subsequent years posed real problems in determining the meaning of her sentence – 'life imprisonment' – which had never before been used to mean a person's whole life on grounds of retribution. Like Kafka's condemned man, the issue here was the deciphering of her sentence, for it was opaque to everyone involved: between the trial judge, Lord Chief Justice and Home Secretary, no firm decision could be made as to what these requirements entailed. Perhaps it should not be surprising then that Myra Hindley was kept in ignorance of these tariff discussions at crucial points. She was sentenced to serve 'life imprisonment' in 1966 without the trial judge making any further recommendation as to how long this should be. In 1985 the then Home Secretary set the tariff 'provisionally' at 30 years, having received advice from Lord Lane CJ that it should not be less than 25. None of this information was communicated to Myra Hindley herself until 1994 when the House of Lords ruled that it was a legal duty to do so (*Doody*), by which time the provisional 30 year tariff had been replaced by a subsequent Home Secretary (Michael Howard) with the 'whole life' tariff (*R v Hindley* 1998, 765). Hindley's counsel argued that the whole life tariff was inconsistent with existing principles that governed sentencing. This was so, counsel argued, in part because the case of *Pierson* should be interpreted as conferring a 'legitimate expectation of release', thus preventing a tariff from being raised once it has been set, whether or not a finite sentence in terms of years had been communicated to the prisoner. Both of these arguments were rejected. According the later policy announced by a third Home Secretary (Jack Straw) evidence of 'exceptional progress' towards reform could still be considered in Hindley's case from time to time, and for crimes as serious as hers, the requirements of retribution and deterrence were such that there could be no entitlement to an expectation of eventual release. The expectation of release after a certain period of time could only be dependent upon a tariff having been 'fixed' and communicated in the first place. Although it had been held in *Doody* that tariffs did have to be communicated to prisoners, the expectation of release anticipated in *Pierson* depended upon a fixed tariff being communicated. In Hindley's case, the 'provisional' nature of the 30 year tariff which itself was not communicated, meant that *Pierson* did not apply. Perhaps it was considered unnecessary to inform Hindley of her tariff, since, as her imprisonment wore on and on, she would, like Kafka's uncomprehending prisoner, eventually 'learn it corporally, on her person'. This is not so much a point about the lawfulness of imposing a sentence without informing the prisoner as one about the work that we expect the sentence itself to perform. Myra Hindley did not need to be told what her sentence was because the purpose of passing the sentence was simply to convey to her a very strong message of censure – a message that she would presumably understand as the months and the years of her incarceration wore on, as it turned out, until her death. For reasons that are discussed elsewhere, Myra Hindley was no ordinary lifer (Gurnham 2003). The meaning of 'life imprisonment' in her case, involving increasing the tariff and then making it indefinite, conveys nothing more precise than that she is exceptional and that for her sentence to satisfy the mysterious requirements of retribution and deterrence, she would probably have to live several lifetimes. For Rutherford (2001), it is the fact that this way of thinking about the requirements of retribution can make no sense given the shortness of natural lifespan that lends Law its authority of 'foreignness'. It cannot be understood – it is mysterious.

There is a moral distinction to be drawn here between being sentenced to life imprisonment during which the prisoner dies and serving a sentence that is interminable due to the impossibility of satisfying the requirements of retribution and deterrence within one lifetime. Although the men responsible for the Madrid bombings of 2004 were sentenced in 2007 to between 34,000 and 43,000 years each, those sentences are purely symbolic, as life imprisonment literally interpreted as a never-ending term does not exist in Spanish law. The millennia of imprisonment were calculated by combining determinate sentences for each of the 191 people killed and 1856 injured in the explosions and thus represent the court's view of the moral requirements of retribution for the bombers' crimes. The *legal* effect of the punishment is rather different, since according to Spanish law, no one may be kept in gaol for more than forty years. Of course, the prisoner might die before their forty years have expired, but in principle the possibility of working through the punishment is still a theoretical possibility. The millennia of the symbolic sentence expresses the court's view of the actual moral price of their crime, and their view that it is a price too high for any moral reunion between them and civilized society to be possible. However the crucial point here is that the Spanish forty year maximum limit concedes that in fact the actual price exacted through retribution is socially arbitrary, as Hegel and Kant both acknowledged.

Therefore the limit rightly separates morality from law and makes it impossible for the state to claim full control over the body and soul of the offender. In English law by contrast there is no such divorce between the moral and legal aspects of punishment. When the indefinite expression 'life imprisonment' is interpreted to mean a prisoner's whole life, the message is that, as a matter of both law and morality, the requirements of retribution are such that its endpoint is out of sight, and this being so, the death of the prisoner cannot equate to the end of the punishment. Whole life punishment is aimed, therefore, not at appealing to the rational aspect of the offender's will, but rather at extinguishing the crime itself by taking both real and symbolic control over the offender's body. In appealing the point that she should be entitled to a legitimate expectation of release, counsel for Myra Hindley wrongly presumed that *all* punishment was directed at the reintegration as an eventual end. However, as Lords Bingham and Steyn ruled (*R v Hindley* 2000, 392), some crimes are so heinous that the requirements of retribution and deterrence cannot be fulfilled in the time-span of an offender's natural life. It is the seriousness of the crime and not the prisoner that is the target of the punishment and thus it makes sense for punishment to extend beyond the prisoner's life. The violent message of the whole life minimum term is in the excessiveness of the punishment: exceeding the prisoner's own natural life means that the projected date for parole occurs once the prisoner is silent in their grave. For the Madrid bombers, their forty year maximum sentence is certainly a long time (Hindley died after 'just' 37 years in prison) but unlike Hindley, they have an end point to work towards and so the state does not claim full responsibility for ensuring that the moral price of the crime is reflected in punishment.

In *In the Penal Colony*, the officer's explanations of the torture/execution machine never stray from the topic of its power to communicate the prisoner's sentence and it is clear that he believes that prisoners subjected to the machine are brought to a higher state of consciousness as a result. In a state approaching religious fervour, he describes the experience of revelation in the prisoner: 'Enlightenment comes to the most dull witted. It begins around the eyes. From there it radiates ...' (Kafka 1961, 180):

> ... the man only begins to understand the inscription, he purses his mouth as if he were listening. You have seen how difficult it is to decipher the script with one's eyes; but our man deciphers it with his wounds. To be sure, that is a hard task; he needs six hours to accomplish it. By that time the Harrow has pierced him quite through and casts him into the grave, where he pitches down upon the blood and water and the cotton wool.

What sort of enlightenment is the officer referring to here? A prisoner pierced right through by the harrow would be able to experience nothing but an agonizing death. The inscription cannot be read by a prisoner: they only feel the pain of the harrow, and the opening of his mouth is purely reflex. Rather, it is the gathered onlookers, who can see the inscription forming on the prisoner's flesh, who come to see the meaning of justice. Significantly, the communicative power of Kafka's execution machine lies in the play between communication and silence.

> And then the execution began! No discordant sound noise spoilt the working of the machine. Many did not care to watch it but lay with closed eyes in the sand; they all knew; now Justice is being done. In the silence one heard nothing but the condemned man's sighs, half muffled by the felt gag. (Kafka 1961, 184)

The unconvincing fantasy of the transformative power of punishment is supplemented by the apparent profound effects of the ritual upon the onlookers. This is a fantasy that is also narrated through the language of the Court of Appeal and the House of Lords in their Lordships' justifications for the whole life tariff. As noted above, Lord Steyn always referred to 'retribution and deterrence' as if they were part of the same explanation. But of course retribution and deterrence are two very different narratives: retribution in its liberal sense speaks to the responsibility of the offender while deterrence speaks to society at large. In other words, Hindley's whole life punishment spoke both *to* her and *through* her. If her incarceration failed to bring about the desired transformative effect in the prisoner, at least those who took an interest in her punishment could experience the communicative effect of her enforced silence. Myra Hindley was never able to see the inscription carved by the whole life minimum. The writing in her case, as in that of Kafka's condemned man, was intended to be deciphered by others. It is with this point that the next section deals in providing an historical perspective on punishments that outlive the prisoner. In permitting Myra Hindley to be kept in gaol until her death because of the unsatisfied requirements of retributions the House of Lords effectively turn her body – to be kept in perpetual incarceration – into a vehicle for communicating the expiation of the crime. On a symbolic level then, the punishment of Myra Hindley shares this much with that of Kafka's condemned man: the effects of law's power over the offender's body speaks a message of retribution which is heard and interpreted, not by the offender herself, but by society at large. Towards the end of her life, Hindley was vocal about her own understanding of her punishment: she periodically publicly complained that her demonic image was being used by politicians and the media for their own ends and this may well have been true enough (Panorama 1997). However, what is important for the moral significance of her punishment is that it was not her own voice but the indefinite continuity of her imprisonment which expressed itself. Her imprisonment, which would last until her death (upon which, according to the logic of the speeches of Lord Steyn and Lord Bingham would continue indefinitely on a symbolic level), was itself the inscription carved onto or into her body, for others to read and understand.

3. Life Imprisonment and the Horrors of the Early Modern Age:
An Historical Turn

The horrors and excesses of early modern public execution would seem to have little in common with modern punishments tempered and limited by human rights and liberal principles. However, if the retributive requirements of punishment can be understood to outlive an offender then there is a moral dynamic at play that does invoke pre-Enlightenment notions about the body and the soul. There are three aspects of early modern capital punishment that I want to draw out here, all of which offend against the liberal insistence on treating the offender as a being of inherent worth since they involve eclipsing the individual thus understood in order to use the offender's body in order to achieve purposes beneficial for the state and/ or the community as a whole. First, medieval and early modern punishments were sometimes aimed at utterly annihilating the offender in order for a community to disassociate itself from a heinous offence and thus avoid divine vengeance in the form of famine or disease. Second, the body of the offender – particularly its public destruction and humiliating display – was used by the state as a *means through which* to demonstrate its own power and to terrorize the public. Foucault in particular is insistent that the target of the early modern execution was the body itself. Foucault describes the ritualistic torture and slow death inflicted upon serious criminals of the age as 'an art of unbearable sensations' (Foucault 1991, 11). Related to this is a third point, that an offender's punishment was understood to continue beyond death, often for many years, in order to ensure the expiation of the crime. Since there was no notion of the offender being readmitted to society in early modern times, the use of his dead body to communicate the state's terrible message for an indefinite period of time would have seemed appropriate. Both the early modern murderer left hanging on the gallows after his execution for the crows to peck and the prisoner serving a whole life minimum term have been judged to have committed a crime so heinous by the standards of their respective societies that the requirements of pure punishment are greater than that which can be paid in the prisoner's own lifetime. In both cases, since there is no hope of re-admittance to society, the liberal notion of working through the punishment towards redemption is removed and with it the idea of punishment as a recognition of the prisoner's responsibility and intrinsic dignity. A punishment that formally forecloses the possibility of the prisoner actually seeing their punishment through to a rapprochement with society cannot be justified by liberal moral theory and this is why we must look to early modern moral ideas rather than to Enlightenment liberal ones to understand the whole life tariff.

In early modern Europe those convicted of an offence against religion or morality (that is, heresy, witchcraft, adultery, sodomy, infanticide and so on) could be punished by being drowned, burned or buried alive. Since the offender's crime had been against nature, it was thought most appropriate that the elements of nature itself and not a human hand that should be the executioner. The execution by water, fire or earth would leave no trace of the offender, thus effecting a radical separation between them and society. As Richard van Dullmen (1990, 88) writes of the German experience: 'Insofar as their objective was the radical extermination and annihilation of a malefactor of whom no trace – either memory or grave – remain, these forms of execution can be viewed as society's rituals of purification.' For early modern popular society dominated by superstitious beliefs in causal links between impurities in the community and failed harvests, disease and pestilence, mixed with a fear of divine retribution, punishment aimed at the pragmatic wiping out of the wrong committed (Wegert 2003, 27). After Myra Hindley died in 2002 she was cremated and her ashes scattered in a secret location. All trace of her was therefore obliterated. The stated purpose of the secrecy was to avoid controversy as far as possible. It might seem to some people far-fetched to suggest that the disappearance of her mortal remains might bear any relation to her punishment, and I am quite prepared to accept the motivation was indeed simply practical. However, the relevance of early modern purification punishments becomes clear as soon as one reflects upon the impossibility of any existing mortal remains, gravestone or memorial. It is not merely the risk of vandalism or disturbances to public order that preclude such a thing, but the need to bury the memory of Myra Hindley. The purificatory aims of the early modern executions for crimes against morality or religion could not be further removed from modern communicative retributivism. Purification is a principle foreign to liberal communicative retributivism, since a liberal understanding of agency incorporates the capacity to commit wrongs as well as right. For a liberal, punishment addresses the latter and seeks to bring the offender to understand the incompatibility of crime with liberal society based on freedom and equality.

Although drowning, burying alive and burning were all carried out in public, the visual narrative of these punishments was that the offender would be made quite literally to disappear, thus purging the community. For other kinds of offences such as murder, robbery and larceny, punishments had the opposite visual effect. Offenders convicted of these crimes and executed by hanging, breaking on the wheel and later by beheading were generally left there afterwards for public display, exemplifying the power of the state over the body of the individual and as a general deterrent. The moral significance of these punishments is that the body of the offender became an instrument – a sort of macabre loudspeaker – through which the state could directly admonish its subjects to respect the sovereign and the law. The offender's status as an individual in a liberal sense is obliterated and they become instead purely a means for displaying the power of the king relative to the offender and to terrorize the public. The communicative aspect of early modern public execution was also bound up in the coding of power relations, in which the prisoners themselves played their part. Early modern executions marked the body both physically through its excruciating ritual destruction and also morally, indicating the power differential between punisher and punished (Foucault 1991, 29). Foucault (1991, 34) explains:

> Punishment must mark the victim. It is either by the scar it leaves on the body, or by the spectacle that accompanies it, to brand the victim with infamy ... [T]he fact that the guilty man should moan and cry out under the blows is not a shameful side-effect, it is the very ceremonial of justice being *expressed* in all its force.

As in Kafka's *In the Penal Colony*, the body is effectively hollowed out and the individual's own life, vitality and subjectivity are gradually replaced with that of the law. Andreas Gailus (2001, 299) writes of the operation of Kafka's execution machine: 'Thus the radiating image of comprehension on the prisoner's face is the product of a terrifying exchange; it is the chiastic transfer of a meaning whose vitality is brought about through the extraction of life from the body.' This, it should be noted, is the very opposite to the liberal understanding of justified punishment that aims not to annihilate the individual, but send a message the offender a message of censure in recognition of their moral autonomy. This is why it is important for Kafka's story that the execution of the condemned man takes place not in the Western state from which the explorer has travelled, but on a remote penal colony not governed by the principles derived from the Enlightenment that the explorer represents. The setting of the story, taking place as it does under a baking sun, suggests that the explorer has travelled far from civilized Europe to the periphery of the known world and 'a more primitive society' (Gailus 2001, 296). Accounts of early modern executions show that this use of the offender's body meant that the ritual of punishment presented to the public a collection of body parts upon each of which a particular act of violence was performed. Consider, for example, the English Gunpowder Plotters, sentenced to be hanged, drawn and quartered in January 1606 for their failed attempt to blow up the Houses of Parliament and with it the King and most of the Protestant ruling elite of England on 5 November 1605. It was decided that the prisoners should be dragged to their place of execution to indicate that their feet were 'not worthy any more to tread upon the Face of the Earth whereof he was made'. Since God had made a man's head his 'highest and most supreme part', they would be dragged upside-down, not merely because the proximity of their faces to the filthy, hard street will thereby cause them maximum discomfort, but they were thought 'unfit to take benefit of the common Air' (Armitstead 2006). Furthermore, the entire protracted process would be aimed at exacting such pain and humiliation on the bodies of the plotters that those bodies would be reduced to mere symbols of hatred:

> [H]e shall be strangled, being hanged up by the Neck between Heaven and Earth, as deemed unworthy of both, or either; as likewise, that the Eyes of Men may behold, and their Hearts contemn him. Then he is to be cut down alive, and to have his Privy Parts cut off and burnt before his Face, as being unworthily begotten, and unfit to leave any Generation after him. His Bowels and inlay'd Parts taken out and burnt, who inwardly had conceived and harboured in his heart such horrible Treason. After, to have his Head cut off, which had imagined

the Mischief. And lastly, his Body to be quartered, and the Quarters set up in some high and eminent Place, to the View and Detestation of Men, and to become a Prey for the Fowls of the Air. (Armitstead 2006; Sharpe 2005, 76; Ward 2007, 111)

Therefore early modern execution was not only retribution for a past wrong, but a ritualistic destruction of the body as expressive of the crime and communicative of a message to onlookers, expected to marvel in terror at the awesome power of the sovereign to utterly destroy the body of the justly condemned. The destruction of the body of the condemned and its ritualistic dismemberment indicates that the individual human body is nothing in itself but is utterly consumed by the power of the sovereign (Foucault 1991, 58–63).

From early modern times until the nineteenth century crowds gathered at public executions, sometimes in very great numbers, and seemed to play an active role in 'seeing off' the offender. For example, according to Dullmen (1990, 107–8), the entire population of Basle is reported to have attended an execution in 1819. Tulloch (2006, 440–1) states that 'at least 30,000 people' were reported to have gathered to watch an execution in Lincoln in 1849, which if true means that the city's population on that day swelled by a third. The presence of the public at executions was regarded as necessary for both the authorities in ensuring public consent, legal and social legitimacy and the demonstration of state power and also for the offender as a final chance to seek forgiveness for his crime, to say goodbye to family and friends and in many cases for a moving public oration (Dullmen 1990, 107; Werget 2003, 39). When public executions were finally ended in the nineteenth century (for example, in Britain by the Prisons Act 1868) it was because the authorities had become appalled at the utter ineffectuality of the solemn message of deterrence and moral reprobation that it was supposed to convey. Instead of being chastened, the crowds seemed to regard the occasion as mere entertainment (Tulloch 2006, 441). What interested the public most was not so much witnessing the just punishment of a deserving criminal but the behaviour and demeanour of the condemned and the effectiveness of the executioner (Werget 2003, 34–5). Depending on how the offender behaved – and how well or badly the executioner did his job – every public execution carried the risk that the public might become restless or side with the condemned person, which in extreme cases might end in violence against the executioner (Foucault 1991, 63). In the reported cases of mob violence directed against executioners it tended to be that the executioner has failed to kill the accused properly or had refused to honour one of the customs of practice that the public insisted upon, for example that the condemned person should go free if the rope broke. Dullmen (1990, 114–5) tells of how, at a beheading in Weissence in 1601, the headsman failed to cut through the condemned man's neck first time. When he resorted to trying to saw off the man's head on the ground, the crowd became enraged. They stoned the executioner to death and strung his body up. Foucault himself cites in his account of why public execution gave way to the prison in the nineteenth century the realization amongst the authorities that the scaffold's communicative power was so weak. Foucault (1991, 78–80) explains that the difficulty of attempting to exact revenge and deter further crime through the spectacle of public execution was the arbitrariness and irregularity of its application, its consequent mixture of 'weakness and excess' and its symbolic focus on the personal vengeful power of the sovereign. Much more effective was the developing system of prisons, which allowed for controlling and gaining knowledge about the social body, efficiently and systematically punishing, thus inculcating an image of 'continuity and permanence' without the state expending excessive energy on arbitrary spectacles of terror (Foucault 1991, 82–7). Since the public was excluded from executions in the nineteenth century and further removed from punishment after the abolition of the death penalty (e.g. by the Murder (Abolition of the Death Penalty) Act 1965 in Britain) despite consistent public support for its retention/reintroduction, we can only gain glimpses of public involvement through the mediation of the media. But as John Tulloch argues, the Press (invited to observe and report on executions) proved to be no less 'misdirected' in their observations. Like the crowds of early modern public events, the Press tended to focus on what the journalists identified as the character and fortitude of the condemned, rather than the more serious matter of the moral lesson (Tulloch, 2006, 442–446).

The transition from the early modern faith in the communicative power of punishment to the nineteenth century disillusionment in it is evoked also in Kafka's *In the Penal Colony*. The presiding officer of the story is no more realistic in his accounts of the machine's admiring spectators than he is about its power to bring enlightenment to the condemned. He becomes lost in an ecstasy of reminiscence when he recounts how, in the days of the 'former Commandant', executions were attended by 'hundreds of spectators', all desperate to get a good view of the machine 'freshly cleaned and glittering. ... They all knew; now Justice is being done' (Kafka 1961, 184). In the officers' memory, each and every one of the hundreds marvelled at the transformative power of the machine in bringing the prisoner to understand his transgression:

> How different an execution was in the old days! A whole day before the ceremony the valley was packed with people; they all came only to look on; early in the morning the Commandant appeared with his ladies; fanfares roused the whole camp ... Before hundreds of spectators – all of them standing on tip-toe as far as the heights there – the condemned man was laid under the Harrow by the Commandant himself. ... How we all absorbed the look of transfiguration on the face of the sufferer, how we bathed our cheeks in the radiance of that justice, achieved at last and fading so quickly! (Kafka 1961, 183–4)

What is it that the rapt onlookers found so compelling in the execution ritual? If we are to expect them to bear relation to early modern European spectators, they might simply be curious to see the manner in which the condemned approaches death: will they be penitent, obstinate, terrified? However, the scene that Kafka's officer evokes of the old days could not be more different from the desolate environment in which the condemned man of the story is executed: apart from the officer himself, the explorer and a soldier employed to restrain the prisoner, no one else comes to witness the execution. The officer bitterly reports that, now the colony has a new Commandant who does not respect the old traditions, there is no longer sufficient funding to maintain the machine properly and that he has somehow managed to change the minds of the vast hordes of former supporters as well. (Kafka 1961, 184) It seems that in the space of just one generation, the execution machine has altogether ceased to be an expression of the general moral standards of the society. It is clear that the officer regards the lack of public support and the recent poor maintenance of the machine as a sign not that the punishment lacks moral justification,but of the failings of the new Commandant:

> [Y]ou don't even need to mention the lack of public support for the execution, the creaking wheel, the broken strap, the filthy stump of felt, no, I'll take all that upon me, and, believe me, if my indictment doesn't drive him out of the conference hall, it will force him to his knees to make the acknowledgement: "Old Commandant, I humble myself before you". (Kafka 1961, 189–190)

Of course, there is no such acknowledgement since the explorer has no intention of doing as the officer wants or expects. In fact, it turns out that the old Commandant, whom the officer accredits with so much authority, is so reviled that when he died the Priest refused to allow his body to be buried in the graveyard. Instead, his body lies under a table in a teahouse in the nearby town. The failure of communication and moral authority for punishment presented in Kafka's story is what causes the crisis for the officer. In the absence of a living public audience, punishment by the ingenious machine is justified by a few meagre remnants of the old Commandant's former authority: the plans originally drawn up by the old Commandant that the officer keeps in his breast pocket are the written remains of a once living, breathing, and watching (in their hundreds) source of authority. The old Commandant's indecipherable scrawls are the officer's 'most precious possessions' because they are all he has left of defunct authority. Referring once more to the good old days, the officer says: 'the Commandant always used to do the explaining, but the new Commandant shirks his duty' (Kafka 1961, 173). In moral terms, 'explaining' is precisely what the machine itself is supposed to do to the offender regarding his sentence, the explanation witnessed and approved by a marvelling multitude who underline the message. Now the machine is wearing out and breaking down and the multitude have ceased to perform their role too.

I now turn to the third aspect of early modern punishment relevant for our discussion: that the death of the offender did not necessarily bring about the end of the punishment ritual. This made sense for the early moderns since, as I have said, the function of the public execution was not the expiation of the crime as such but the purported terrorizing symbolic value for the assembled public. In fact, not only was death sometimes only the beginning of the process, it occasionally happened well before the commencement of punishment. A person hanged or broken on the wheel (where the offender was tied to a cartwheel and had his limbs crushed) was typically left there for the birds to peck or else buried under the gallows rather than on hallowed ground. Foucault – who argued that early modern punishments aimed only at the *body* of the condemned – should not be read as ruling out the relevance of the soul, at least in the sense of the immortal soul that many of the assembled spectators, as Christians, would have believed was being sent on its way to eternal torture in hell.[2] Therefore, having been denied a Christian burial, it would be expected that a person executed in this way would find that the treatment of their body would have consequences for their immortal soul (Dullmen 1990, 97). Punishment as aiming at eventual reintegration of the offender in to society was unknown to the early moderns, for whom the priority was to expiate the crime itself. This view directly converted into physical punishment of the dead: prisoners who committed suicide whilst awaiting execution were treated as having committed two capital offences, and thus the offender's body might be broken on the wheel after execution by hanging. Dullmen (1990, 103–4) writes that, 'as a rule', the body of a suicide in early modern Germany was burned, 'stuffed into a barrel and thrown into the river or buried beneath the gallows'. Accordingly it made sense not to distinguish between the living and the dead: both had to be punished since the requirements of expiation would not be satisfied merely by causing the offender's death. One notable example of the punishment of the dead from English legal history that brings together the themes discussed above is the posthumous 'execution' of Oliver Cromwell after the restoration of the monarchy. On 10 December 1660, Parliament made the following resolution:

> Ordered, by the Lords and Commons assembled in Parliament, That the Carcasses of Oliver Cromwell, Henry Ireland, John Bradshaw, Thomas Pride, whether buried in Westminster Abbey or elsewhere, be with all Expedition, taken up, and drawn upon a Hurdle to Tyburne, and there hanged up in their Coffins for some time; and after that buried under the Gallows. (*House of Lords Journal* 1660, 204–5; Marks 1980, 191)

As diarist John Evelyn noted, on 30 January 1661, just over two years after former Lord Protector's death, state funeral and burial in Westminster Abbey, and on the day of the twelfth anniversary of the beheading of Charles I, the bodies of Cromwell, Ireland and Bradshaw were exhumed, 'dragged out of their superb tombs in West-minster among the Kings' and publicly hanged for the crime of regicide,

---

2   It is important to remember that Foucault's notion of the 'soul' that he claims became the target of punishment only after the demise of public executions was not the soul in a Christian sense of a 'soul born in sin', but a far more modern creation that emerged in the nineteenth century as the subject of a system of knowledge, 'born ... out of the methods of punishment, supervision and constraint' (Foucault 1991, 29). This distinctly Foucaultian notion of 'soul' is beyond the ambit of this discussion.

still wrapped in their burial sheets, and 'thousands of people who had seen them in all their pride being spectators' (Marks 1980, 192). Having been left hanging until sunset, the regicides' heads were unwrapped and the bodies decapitated. George Wharton, another contemporary, reported that their 'loathsome truncks' were then dumped into a common pit under the gallows (symbolically not hallowed ground) – and their heads set up high on a spike on the roof of Westminster Hall. It is not known what became of the heads of Ireland and Bradshaw, but Cromwell's at least is known to have stayed on the roof of Westminster Hall until it blew down in a gale some twenty years later (Clymer 1999, 91; Marks 1980, 192). As in Germany then, ritual punishment of the dead was consistent with English attitudes towards crime and the body. As in the early modern punishments described above, the moral focus of this symbolic execution is the expiation of the crime rather than the experience of the offender.

Like the condemned man of Kafka's story, Cromwell, Ireland and Bradshaw obviously had no way of presenting a defence for the charges laid and this is consistent with the aspect of early modern punishment discussed above, that the offender as a person is not really relevant to the symbolic significance of the ritual. Law's power reveals itself through writing its judgment on the body. As Kafka's officer put it, 'Guilt is never to be doubted'. Bringing the crime to symmetrical union with the punishment through the public display and annihilation of the body is absolutely the point of Kafka's machine and of the hanging of Cromwell's corpse. As in Kafka, the ambivalence between silence and speech is a theme that informs our reading of the event. Clymer noted this in relation to Cromwell's severed head displayed on Westminster Hall:

> Silenced by death, the bodies now reduced to their heads seemed compelled to speak, as if their status as spectacular fragments must be made verbal. This phenomenon was not lost on contemporary observers. One French travel writer, Charles Pain, recorded his reaction to seeing the regicides' heads in 1671: "One can't view them without blanching and without imagining that they will throw out frightening word, People, Eternity cannot expiate for our crime; learn from our example that the life of kings is inviolable." (Clymer 1999, 28)

Cromwell is silenced by death, and yet passers-by such as Charles Pain nevertheless perceive a message emanating from his lifeless mouth. We might say that the punishment of Cromwell's and the others' corpses has forced them to speak, but not in the way that they would themselves have chosen to do so. In this sense, the posthumous execution ritual is a stark mockery of the very idea of republicanism and regicide, and a reminder that the condemned offender does not have the last word. This was precisely the effect of Kafka's machine, which silences the offender but through inscribing the sentence on his body, makes that body – in fact silent and lifeless – communicate a message to the onlookers. The law speaks through the body and through the desecration of the body; in other words, the body is silenced in order to bring it under the authority of law and then made to speak as the law's puppet. In Kafka's *In the Penal Colony*, the machine's ability to silence both those being executed ('how silent he grows at just about the sixth hour' (Kafka 1961, 180) the awed onlookers ('Many did not care to watch it but lay with closed eyes in the sand', 184) commands respect. Danielle S. Allen (2001, 326) argues that it is therefore the disgusting felt stub that the officer explains is placed in the condemned man's mouth to prevent him screaming that is the 'essential feature' of the machine and not the harrow that actually carves the message into the man's flesh. It is the only part that the officer – his incessant chatter having been reduced to silence by the explorer's adverse judgment on the execution method – briefly resists when he finally subjects himself to the machine's terrible work (Allen 2001, 330).

Conclusion

Of course, the extinction of early modern ideas about the body and the continued punishment of offenders after death mean that as a purely procedural or practical matter, the death of the prisoner brings an end to punishment. Standing between the early modern execution rituals and today's notions of justified punishment is the central place that liberal theory accords the individual offender as a member – or at least a former and potential future member – of a political community of rational agents. However, I think that there is a moral significance of the 'whole life' sentence such as that imposed on Myra Hindley that alludes to the spectre of the hanged corpse and that the sentence is not merely a matter a keeping a person in gaol for the rest of their life but rather that the requirements of retribution and deterrence *exceed* the offender's lifetime. If these requirements are to exceed the prisoner's death, what can we say about the relationship between crime, prisoner and punishment? The macabre display of Cromwell's head was intended to be punishment with no determinate end point–point, and we might imagine punishment continuing through the centuries until it was finally accepted for burial at Sidney Sussex College in 1960. That the requirements of retribution after the offender's death are indeterminate and arbitrary is not in doubt. What is still more problematic for post-mortem punishment is that, since one half of the purported communicative relationship has expired, the moral basis for continued punishment is lost. The impossibility of eventually 'working through' punishment for a crime which an offender accepts responsibility is one central reason for my argument that in cases such as Hindley's the image that the communicative retributivists present of the moral justification of punishment is not convincing. From the kind of modern liberal perspective discussed above, Hindley's sentence cannot be *justified* communicatively, but rather only be thereby *explained*, since it communicates not the gradual return to and re-unification with the society from which her crime originally disconnected her, but rather the eventual crushing of any such hope. This is the danger in the Lords' decision that there are cases for which payment for the crime will take longer than the offender's natural lifespan. For it this were so, we are perhaps supposed to imagine that Myra Hindley's ashes, scattered in a secret location, are in some mysterious and undefined way and for an undefined length of time still subject to the demands of retribution and the process of expiation. Like Kafka's ingenious execution machine, such punishments inscribe law's power into the body of the offender, which is reduced, emptied of his living vitality, for the community itself to see and interpret. To this end it does not matter if the person punished is alive or dead.

PART 2
Childhood Innocence,
or the Frozen Present

'What sharp teeth you have, Grandmother!' Grimm's Tales of Innocence and Experience

The fairytales that we find in the well-known collections of the Brothers Grimm in nineteenth century Germany and Charles Perrault in seventeenth century France are undoubtedly a fertile source of historical information about cultural and social attitudes and ideologies (Aristodemou 1999, 193). However, like all great literature, the themes explored in the various versions of the tales – including the oral folk tales they evolved from – are also important for reflecting on issues relevant to our own moral and legal culture. This chapter is the first of three that argues that the way in which we read these tales, and particularly the characterization of the protagonists in alternative European versions of the tale, for example Christine Schneller's *Little Red Hat* and Achille Millien's *The Grandmother*, provides a basis for engaging with current issues relating to childhood. One theme that ties together all three of these chapters is that of 'innocence': what it means to label someone or something as innocent and what this reveals about our cultural understandings about childhood and the meaning of childhood in modern society. In the next two chapters I shall develop this concern for innocence as a cultural discourse through a discussion of two thorny issues: anxieties about the difference between artistic representation and exploitation of children in visual images in Chapter 5, and then cultural readings of physical violence used against children in Chapter 6. However, the focus of this chapter is predominantly thematic and literary; I examine the story of *Little Red Riding Hood*, and what the differing versions of her journey through the woods and her encounter with danger say about our ideas on childhood and development.

1. Innocence and its Significance

The idea of 'innocence' has received a degree of academic critical attention in recent times in the context of adult attitudes towards children. It is a familiar argument that emphasizing the innocence of the child risks doing more harm than good. Valorizing innocence implies that some children are more deserving of protection from harm than others (Ost 2002, 456–7). Innocence and the cultural baggage attached to it is not only an unreasonable ideal for judging children but, ironically enough, it also sexualizes the child since the greater the societal anxiety about protecting childhood innocence, the greater the emphasis on that very quality believed to arouse the sexual interest of paedophiles (Kitzinger 1988, 79–80). But let us first consider the notion of innocence as it is presented in the fairytales.

a) Innocence and the Fairytale

It is well known that the tales as they existed before Perrault and Grimm appropriated and reworked them to appeal to bourgeois sensibilities were myths told amongst the poorer classes in order to connect their own experiences to the wider world and give them significance. As Aristodemou (1999, 194) puts it:

> Oral folktales often expressed the hopes and aspirations of a peasant class where paupers became princes and virtuous girls princesses. Through such myths a disadvantaged class faced with poverty and sickness could express their dreams for a different, a happier and more just world.

The Grimms saw in these peasant stories an opportunity to promote what they regarded as core values for the bourgeois family: the need for a home, loyalty between family relations, punishment of evil, achievement of contentment through simple hard work and an acceptance of the rule of the Father (Zipes 1988, 37–9). Thus, Grimm's tales are bourgeois patriarchy in which patriarchal family values are mobilized to teach young Prussians right from wrong. Whilst innocence is not fetishized by Grimm to the extent that it is by Perrault (as we shall see in the next section where we compare the two versions of *Little Red Riding Hood*) obedience and acceptance of the rule of the patriarch are fundamental to the Grimm's project. For the Grimms, the promotion of childhood innocence in the context of nineteenth century German culture held a certain political significance. For the seventeenth century French aristocrat Perrault, innocence may not have held the same kind of significance but still figured importantly in his tales in which innocent protagonists suffered all manner of trials at the hands of knowing adults. How is this understanding of 'innocence' evidenced in their tales? It is well known that the bourgeois family and gender values presented in the tales of Grimm and Perrault appeal to an idea of nature and the natural cycle. Birth, marriage and death within the bourgeois family unit are associated with the natural and inevitable cycle of the seasons.[1] Interpreting the tales conservatively, the heroine (who often finds herself cruelly treated before being rescued and finally married) has nowhere to go as such, or if she has she must learn not to deviate from the path assigned to her by someone in authority. For example, in *Little Red Riding Hood*, the girl is instructed to follow the forest path and not deviate from it. In *Snow White*, she is firmly instructed by the dwarves not to open the door to strangers. In *Bluebeard*, a new wife is told by her husband never to use a particular key. In all such tales, the heroine brings about her own ordeal by disobeying these instructions. In other

---

1   The Grimm's *The Almond Tree, Snow White*, and *Sleeping Beauty* are generally regarded as prime examples, which I discuss at a later stage.

words, whereas the heroic prince must journey to far off lands, fight through forests and wild beasts, the heroine by contrast tends to be rooted and passive. Immobility is a key idea in the etymology of innocence. Deriving from the Latin *innocentem* meaning doing no harm, 'innocence' denotes a lack of effective action. In referring to harm as a verb it implies a distinction between acts and omissions in which to do nothing is favoured over action. An 'innocent' is someone who *does* nothing to harm others; to be innocent is not really to be one who achieves their aims through endeavour, but one who is passive. As such, innocence implies both stillness and ignorance. The heroic men of the fairytales who perform the rescue and fight the evil monsters may be good in the sense that they know right from wrong but they are not innocent and nor would they choose to be, since they are by nature active in their pursuit of their goals. Villains and questing heroes are equally active and knowledgeable, which distinguishes them from most of the female protagonists of fairytales. The innocent, in contrast to the experienced, is one who stays at home and does not go adventuring. The idea of the home as a moral concept reflects the rootedness and immobility of such a life and also the simplicity and familiarity associated with it. A person who is yet to leave the safety of home may be an innocent since they are not mobile and generally as yet uneducated – being rooted they are not at liberty to do harm. On this basis the unmarried girl (whom we repeatedly encounter at the beginning of fairytales) is clearly distinguished from, say, the newly-wed woman at the end of the tale and also from the wicked stepmother who comes to live with a hapless widower in order to torment and abuse his children.[2] The innocent is simple in the sense that they have not become morally compromised by the complexities of adult life outside the home. An understanding of the world that one might describe as 'childlike' is both simple and innocent: it is characterized by a straightforward attitude towards, for example, who to trust (one's immediate family and friends) and who to be suspicious of (strangers), as well as 'primitive emotions and values' (Swann Jones 1995, 64–5). The promotion of this idea of innocence as stillness, rootedness and ignorance in the fairytales is not difficult to spot, and both Perrault and Grimm foster a bourgeois idea of innocence and the dangers of its corruption. We are presented with an array of heroines such as Little Red Riding Hood, Snow White, Sleeping Beauty and so on who are young (often children, at least initially), naïve, tending towards the masochistic in their inability to observe critically important instructions, who despite their ineptitude manage to survive adolescence and in many cases win the hand of a charming prince. These heroines are marked by their passivity in the face of danger and heroism and eventual acceptance of their place within the patriarchal order (Swann Jones 1995, 65). Since they take their names from their physical appearance we are reminded that these are characters that *are*, rather than ones that *do*. The names imply not a subjective personality but the objectivizing gaze of someone else, who finds them attractive. Grimm's Little Red Riding Hood and Grandmother both wait patiently inside the belly of the wolf to be

---

2 For example, Grimm's *Hansel and Gretel* and *The Almond Tree*.

rescued by the woodcutter (who keeps a paternalistic eye on events); Snow White finds temporary safety first because of the mercy of the Queen's manservant who cannot bring himself to murder her, and secondly by becoming a live-in maid for the seven dwarves who issue her with strict instructions; Sleeping Beauty attracts the affections of the prince by a combination of the difficulty involved in getting to her (a dense magical forest of lethally sharp thorn bushes that he must fight through is a fitting metaphor for the efforts that a man must go to in order to win a woman's heart in the chivalric ethos) and especially by her passivity and silence in sleep. Snow White and Sleeping Beauty are clear examples of innocence as stillness and passivity: nothing that happens to those two protagonists in Grimm's tales is as a result of any significant decision that they make for themselves. Their beauty is sufficient to rouse the passions of both their enemies and friends, the actions of which provide the respective plots – their suffering and eventual rescue (Aristodemou 1999, 198).[3]

b) What is the Point of Little Red Riding Hood? Innocence and Autonomy

The story of *Little Red Riding Hood* in its various versions provides us with a case study of the ethical and cultural significance of innocence. Unlike other childhood protagonists, Red Riding Hood shows some spirit of adventure by travelling from her home to her grandmother's cottage through the woods. What is in debate here is the extent to which we can and should read her as an 'innocent', and what such a reading means in terms of the way we interpret other texts. On the one hand, some versions of the tale do not give the female protagonist much of a role beyond being the innocent victim of malignant desire, and in this sense do not really move beyond being simple cautionary tales. In other versions, she is given much more of a character and a role in her own rescue and personal development, which makes possible a very different kind of reading.

i. Charles Perrault's 'Little Red Riding Hood' as Innocent Victim and Object of Desire
Perrault's version of this well-known story has been read, particularly by feminists, as clearly heterosexual in focus, and the girl protagonist as an object of the wolf's sexual as well as gastronomic desire (Bacchilega 1997, 57). Her innocence, in terms of her ignorance and lack of a strong personality, means that she is utterly defenceless against being consumed by this desire (Bettelheim 1976, 168). Her being eaten by the wolf is final: there is no escape and no happy ending for Perrault's Red Riding Hood. Perrault seems to portray the girl as an innocent in order to demonstrate most clearly why the wolf is attracted to her. Perrault in fact makes it clear that the 'wolf' really is a smooth-talking seducer who preys on naïve little girls – too obviously so for some commentators to accord the story

---

3   Aristodemou sees fairytales as selling to girls their own subordination in bourgeois society: 'Girls are thus led to believe that meekness, suffering, and self-pity will be rewarded and the greatest reward of all is marriage to a rich man.'

very much significance (Bettelheim 1976, 169). His story even closes by spelling this out:

> Children, especially attractive, well bred young ladies, should never talk to strangers, for if they should do so, they may well provide dinner for a wolf. I say "wolf", but there are various kinds of wolves. There are also those who are charming, quiet, polite, unassuming, complacent, and sweet, who pursue young women at home and in the streets. And unfortunately, it is these gentle wolves who are the most dangerous ones of all. (Perrault 2008)

In other words, Perrault has the girl fatally punished for her failure to recognize the danger she was in. As is typical of Perrault, the sexual theme is aimed at adult readers and designed to escape the notice of his young audience, just as the wolf's intentions escape the notice of Red Riding Hood herself. In a scene which is repeated in various forms across the range of different versions of the story, Perrault (2008) depicts the girl stripping off her clothes, getting into bed with the wolf and initiating the conversation that will eventually lead to her death:

> The wolf, seeing her come in, said to her, hiding himself under the bedclothes, "Put the cake and the little pot of butter upon the stool, and come get into bed with me."

> Little Red Riding Hood took off her clothes and got into bed. She was greatly amazed to see how her grandmother looked in her nightclothes, and said to her, "Grandmother, what big arms you have!"

> "All the better to hug you with, my dear."

Significantly, Perrault's narrative does not at any point give an indication that the girl is aware of the wolf's dangerously close interest in her body or his intention to consume her/it. She shows no inhibitions about removing her clothes, presumably because, as an innocent, she has no reason to suspect that her body could be an object of sexual interest. For this reason Bettelheim (1976, 169) is surely wrong to claim that her readiness to strip for the wolf shows that she 'nothing but a fallen woman'. Although Perrault (2008) describes her as 'amazed to see how her grandmother looked in her nightclothes', this does not seem to make her suspicious or afraid. Furthermore, she has been given no warning whatsoever by her mother about wolves, who simply says 'Go, my dear, and see how your grandmother is doing, for I hear she has been very ill. Take her a cake, and this little pot of butter.' When met by the wolf in the woods, Perrault reports that she 'did not know that it was dangerous to stay and talk to a wolf', and therefore thinks nothing of directing him to grandmother's house when he asks. The wolf has plenty of time to dispose of the old woman, because the girl 'took a roundabout way, entertaining herself by gathering nuts, running after butterflies, and gathering bouquets of little flowers'.

The lack of warning given to the girl by her mother prompts Bettelheim (1976, 168) to dismiss Perrault's version as making no sense in moral terms.

All of this speaks clearly of an ignorant girl whose obliviousness to the possibility of harm is central to her fate. In terms of moral responsibility for her own and her grandmother's demise, Perrault's Red Riding Hood is an innocent since she knows nothing of the dangers that lie outside the home. In Perrault's narrative, innocence is the lens through which we are invited to view the lot of little girls whose naivety, ignorance of the evils of the world and trusting nature are attractive qualities for certain men who would take advantage of them. Therefore innocence carries a certain erotic quality but, as in pornography, it is a quality that has no transformative or developmental potential for the girl herself, remaining as she does ignorant of her allure in the eyes of others. It is therefore difficult to avoid the feminist criticism of Perrault's version that it is informed by an erotic binary relationship between men and women in which the latter are infantilized, sexualized and ultimately consumed by the former (Aristodemou 1999, 208–9). Perrault's young heroine as an innocent victim of sexual violence might in this way be compared to Sade's unfortunate young heroine Justine, who, throughout her ordeals at the hands of various powerful male libertines that she mistakes for protectors and upright pillars of society, remains, as Susan Sontag (1982, 100) puts it, 'in a perpetual state of astonishment, never learning anything from the strikingly repetitious violations of her innocence'. Like Sade's Justine, Perrault's Little Red Riding Hood is not a character so much as a thing: inert and unresponsive in any active way, unable to be anything other than an innocent vulnerable to betrayal, which of course is what lends her erotic appeal.

ii. Red Riding Hood as a Subject in Her Own Right   In some versions of the *Little Red Riding Hood* story we discover that the girl eats parts of grandmother's body at the wolf's invitation. This cannibalistic plot device is found both in an Austrian or Italian folktale collected by Christian Schneller (2007) in 1867 called *Little Red Hat*, and also in a French tale collected by Achille Millien (2007) in France in about 1870 called *The Grandmother*. Schneller's tale has the beast (here an ogre instead of a wolf) being so candid about what the girl is eating that we might reasonably presume that the girl really does understand that she is feasting on her Grandmother's body:

> Little Red Hat opened the door, went inside, and said, "Grandmother, I am hungry."
>
> The ogre replied, "Go to the kitchen cupboard. There is still a little rice there."
>
> Little Red Hat went to the cupboard and took the teeth out. "Grandmother, these things are very hard!"
>
> "Eat and keep quiet. They are your grandmother's teeth!"

"What did you say?"

"Eat and keep quiet!"

A little while later Little Red Hat said, "Grandmother, I'm still hungry."

"Go back to the cupboard" said the ogre. "You will find two pieces of chopped meat there."

Little Red Hat went to the cupboard and took out the jaws. "Grandmother, this is very red!"

"Eat and keep quiet. They are your grandmother's jaws!"

"What did you say?"

"Eat and keep quiet!"

A little while later Little Red Hat said, "Grandmother, I'm thirsty."

"Just look in the cupboard" said the ogre. "There must be a little wine there."

Little Red Hat went to the cupboard and took out the blood. "Grandmother, this wine is very red!"

"Drink and keep quiet. It is your grandmother's blood!"

"What did you say?"

"Just drink and keep quiet!"

The girl seems to be deaf to these gruesome facts, countering each clear and unequivocal revelation with the same faux-dumb response. Millien's version of the tale emphasizes even further the significance of the girl's own moral offence and also the possibility that she knows what is happening. While she tucks into her grandmother's freshly slaughtered meat, a nearby cat remarks: 'For shame! The slut is eating her grandmother's flesh and drinking her grandmother's blood.' Scenes of cannibalism sometimes appear in fairytales in order to denote extreme cruelty in a character, such as the witch in *Hansel and Gretel* who captures the two children in order to eat them. In other tales it is used as a device to trick unwitting characters into becoming morally involved in the wicked acts of others and to punish them for their own faults. In Grimm's *The Almond Tree* and also in Basile's *Sun, Moon and Talia* a wicked stepmother desires to murder her husband's children and then seeks to involve their father in the crime by tricking him into eating their flesh, served to him as animal meat. Those are stories in which a family patriarch fails to check the stepmother's murderous intent in his own home and being duped into eating his own children is his punishment for this weakness. In *Sun, Moon and Talia*, the woman is motivated to trick her husband into unwitting cannibalism as punishment for his adultery: the children (called Sun and Moon) are his by another woman (Talia) whom he found sleeping and impregnated her while she lay unconscious. In the case of the girl of the *Little Red Riding Hood* stories, she has allowed the wolf to eat her grandmother by directing him to the older woman's cottage and it is possible therefore that she is being led into cannibalism as punishment for this. However, it is significant that the ogre in the French folk variant of the *Little Red Riding Hood* story is candid about the true nature of the meat as grandmother's flesh and blood. This puts a slightly different light on things: at the very least it suggests a degree of knowing moral culpability on the girl's part and may also be an opportunity for us to challenge the 'innocence' reading of the tale. In Millien's *The Grandmother*, from the cat's disparaging remark that the cannibalistic girl is a 'slut', the narrative moves directly on to the stripping off of her clothes. We saw above how, in Perrault's version, the girl shows no awareness of the erotic implications of the stripping scene. However, in Millien's tale, she appears to welcome the simultaneously erotic and violent promise in the villain's explanations:

> "Get undressed, my child" said the bzou, "and come to bed with me."
>
> "Where should I put my apron?"
>
> "Throw it into the fire. You won't need it anymore."
>
> And for all her clothes – her bodice, her dress, her petticoat, and her shoes and stockings – she asked where she should put them, and the wolf replied, "Throw them into the fire, my child. You won't need them anymore."

This is significantly different to Perrault's own depiction the scene: Perrault was careful to keep the sexuality of the scene to the barest of innuendo for the amusement of his adult readers. His version informs us that the girl removes her clothes thus fixing our attention on her body, but without seeming to dwell on it unnecessarily. He avoids gratuitous carnality and thus nice bourgeois parents can read his version as a cautionary tale for their well-mannered children. On the other hand, Millien's *The Grandmother*, quoted just above positively revels in the carnality of the scene. It lavishes attention on the girl's stripping off of her clothes and since she is being explicitly told that getting into bed with this person may be the last thing she will ever do, it becomes more difficult still to maintain that she is ignorant of what is going on. If she does understand anything by the repeated assertion that she 'won't need [her clothes] anymore', then she must be beginning to appreciate that the person speaking is not her grandmother and that she is in mortal danger. This raises some potentially very uncomfortable questions. Could it be that she finds this situation, this new acquaintance with death and danger exciting, and furthermore, exciting in a sexual way? Reading these variants on the *Little Red Riding Hood* theme, we get the distinct impression that the young girl is becoming aware of, and is beginning to explore, her own sexual desire, and that this is made possible by her dawning awareness of the excitement of moral danger. We are beginning to depart from 'innocence' as an overriding theme and starting to move towards something more creative. The possibility for interpreting the *Little Red Riding Hood* story as one of sexual development is a familiar theme since the psychoanalytic readings of Bruno Bettelheim and various others. Bettelheim (1976, 176) was more interested in Grimm's tale than Perrault's; he too suggested that, in versions of the tale that give the heroine a little more chance to express herself, her evident interest in and temptation by the wolf's charm is evidence of the girl's own 'pre-conscious' Oedipal sexual desire for the phallic father. She is 'attracted and repelled at the same time' by the wolf as symbolic of dangerous, consuming masculinity.

It is true that in the tales death and new life reflect natural cycles and so, like the changing of the seasons, the passing away of the older generation makes it possible for the younger ones to flourish.[4] But here we seem to be confronted with the idea that a confrontation with violent death is itself linked to erotic desire, and that this confrontation is itself central to a person's developing subjectivity. For Bataille (1989, 33), eroticism is linked to death because both events are a violent interruption of ordinary life that is special to human experience. The violence of emotion that can accompany erotic delight – that 'always disturbs us, sometimes shatters us' – is, like the special significance that humans attach to death, something that sets human life apart from other species as far as we understand them. Bataille is surely correct that there are certain physical and emotional connections in effects that death and erotic pleasure produce in a subject, and it is precisely because these are experienced by a subject of desire (rather than merely an object of another's desire) that Bataille's observations are relevant for our reading of this tale and our effort to challenge the 'innocence' reading of it.

In Angela Carter's twentieth century re-telling of the tale in two short stories of her own (*The Company of Wolves* and *The Werewolf* 1996, 210–20), the young girl of the folktales is not consumed by the awareness of death; neither is she destroyed as a result of innocence to the wolf's desire to consume her as she is in Perrault's version. Instead she rises to the dangerous challenge and the danger posed. Carter tries to retell fairytales in such a way that reclaims the 'pornographic imagination' that informs the innocence reading of gender relations in Perrault's narrative – women as passive and men as predatory – may be revealed, challenged and reworked (Aristodemou 1999, 208–10). Carter's versions of the tales, which self-

---

4   For example, in the *Snow White* stories, the Mother who wishes for a child 'as white as snow' and then gives birth passes away shortly after.

consciously try to revive the adventurous spirit of the young heroine of the older folk versions of the tale that is muted by Perrault, emphasize the emergence of a young girl's own personality and developing sexual autonomy. They remind the reader that the age-old story of the young girl and the wolf may always be as much a story about self-discovery as it is about male aggression. In *The Company of Wolves* Carter begins by introducing the protagonist in terms of her virginity, thus drawing attention to the patriarchal gender politics of Perrault's narrative: 'She was an unbroken egg; she was a sealed vessel; she has inside her a magic space the entrance to which is shut tight with a plug of membrane ...' (Carter 1996, 215). When she first meets the wolf, he appears, as in Perrault's version, more of a man than an animal, and he comes to her disguised as a handsome huntsman. 'She'd never seen such a fine fellow before' and falls into his confidence, as in Perrault (Carter 1996, 216). But when the girl meets the wolf again in the grandmother's house, she is quite unlike Perrault's helpless victim. She notices that there was 'no trace at all of the old woman except for a tuft of white hair that had caught in the bark of an unburned log. When the girl saw that, she knew she was in danger of death' (Carter 1996, 218). The great coup of Carter's story however is her reworking the stripping scene. As in Perrault's story, the girl strips on the wolf's request, but here the girl's own sexual desire is not in doubt. Roles are partly reversed and the wolf's aggression neutralized by the girl's own sexual forwardness:

"What shall I do with my blouse?"

"Into the fire with it, too, my pet."

The thin muslin went flaring up the chimney like a magic bird and now off came her skirt, her woollen stockings, her shoes, and on to the fire they went, too, and were gone for good. The firelights shone through the edges of her skin; now she was clothed only in her untouched integument of flesh. This dazzling, naked she combed out her hair with her fingers; her hair looked white as the snow outside. Then went directly to the man with red eyes in whose unkempt mane the lice moved; she stood up on tiptoe and unbuttoned the collar of his shirt. (219)

Carter's handling of the scene, like previous versions, dwells upon the nubile virgin body of the girl, reminding us that for the wolf she is a sexual as well as a culinary prize. However, Carter makes it very clear that she is very much more than that – 'She knows she is nobody's meat' (219) – and in this way radically departs from Perrault's depiction of her as *mere* object. Therefore, the girl avoids death by countering the wolf's violence and sexual aggression with her own. Even when the wolf actually states that his big teeth are 'All the better to eat you with', the girl simply laughs at him and throws the rest of his clothes into the fire. She and the wolf end up in a tender embrace in the very bed where the old lady was so recently killed, he resting his head in her lap, she picking the lice from his fur (219–20).

This reading of the relationship between sex and death can be pushed further. Carter claimed that she wanted to appropriate the erotic dynamics at the heart of the fairytales – that is, the objectification of women and girls for the male gaze – for the empowerment of women as subjects of desire (Aristodemou 1999, 208–10). Carter's re-working of the character of the young girl draws attention to the patriarchal association between the passivity and innocence of children and that of women in the tale as Perrault presented it. It is clear therefore that the story of the young girl in the pretty riding hood offers a continuing opportunity for re-readings that challenge this patriarchal notion of innocence both in terms of gender politics and the representation of children.

For Carter, the stripping scene leads to equality in the physical encounter between the girl and the wolf and thus she undermines the reading of the story as a narrative of 'the misfortunes of innocence'. For Bataille (1962, 100), discovery of the erotic cannot be separated from the awareness of death, since both in sex and in death our individuality is ruptured leading to a feeling of 'crisis' and also a more profound sense of identity that exceeds the limitations of the individual alone. Bataille (1962, 19) writes of death and the erotic as a two-way revelation, contending that awareness of sexual desire is 'simply a sign to remind us constantly that death, the rupture of the discontinuous individualities to which we cleave in terror, stands there before us more real than life itself.' Indeed, the 'farthest bounds of possibility' can only be reached through the 'elemental violence which kindles every manifestation of eroticism' and with it the dissolution of the limited and self-contained self (Bataille 1962, 16). He equates the experience of the erotic with religious sacrifice of ancient times in which a community of spectators drew inspiration by witnessing the transgression of the taboo against killing. Recall that Freud (1950, 18) describes taboo as something both 'sacred' and also 'forbidden' or 'dangerous' since at its deepest level it exists to inhibit primal urges towards death and incest. It conveys 'a sense of something unapproachable'; commanding reverence but which is nonetheless unintelligible, very much the sense conveyed by the sacrifice. For Bataille (1962, 18), the erotic stripping off of clothes represents the violent stripping off of skin during the sacrifice of a sacred animal in primitive societies:

> Stripping naked is seen in civilizations where the act has full significance if not as a simulacrum of the act of killing, at least as an equivalent shorn of gravity. In antiquity the destitution (or destruction) fundamental to eroticism was felt strongly and justified linking the act of love with sacrifice.

If it is a story about the transgression of taboo and the erotic allure of sacrifice, then the girl's virginity may be significant. Perrault's version invites us to presume she is a virgin, and as I have said, Angela Carter explicitly draws attention to her virginity. Freud (1991, 265–267) referred to the curious fact that seemingly unrelated cultures and societies have traditionally placed significance, sometimes amounting to a taboo, on female virginity, albeit in vastly different ways. Freud

(1991, 269) tentatively suggests that what links the apparently opposing attitudes of traditional Western cultures, where loss of virginity is regarded as properly being conducted by a woman's husband, and some primitive societies in which defloration must be conducted ritually by a priest, is an ancient 'horror of blood' which in some cultures also makes menstruation taboo in the sense of being unclean. Blood, after all, is the 'seat of life'. However, in Carter's story it is the Grandmother and not the girl protagonist who is the sacrifice, since while the grandmother herself is killed and consumed, the girl escapes the role of the victim and instead enters into a relationship of equal sexual desire with the wolf. Of course, we are supposed to assume that the taboo on killing applied as much in this girl's world as it does for us. But in recognizing that her Grandmother has just been killed (for example, noticing her hair on the fire in Carter's tale), the girl understands that this taboo has been transgressed. Furthermore, she seems to have become somehow emboldened by this discovery, even excited by it, and if Freud's description of a taboo is correct then this should come as no surprise. Freud, after all, locates the very power of taboo in its contaminative capacity, ensuring that each transgression makes further transgression likely. The transgressor (in our case the wolf), 'possess the dangerous quality of tempting others to follow his example: why should *he* be allowed to do what is forbidden to others' (Freud 1950, 32). Bataille builds on Freud's comparison between the taboo regarding the shedding of blood in 'primitive' societies with modern notions of transgression. He notes that the allure of the live sacrifice in ancient religious practices lay in the transgression of the law of everyday life that was communicated to the spectators through death and the escape from taboo that it heralded. For spectators of the sacrifice, the death throes of the animal killed revealed the escape from taboo surrounding death and of killing in particular. In 'the fullness of the blood-swollen organs', the gathered people saw 'the impersonal fullness of life itself' (Bataille 1962, 91).

Bataille explores this idea that the awareness of the proximity of death can be a signal for an erotic experience in his novella *The Story of the Eye* (1982). It involves an adolescent couple (the unnamed male narrator who disdainfully shuns the 'insipid' pleasures of flesh that satisfy most people, and his partner Simone) who, through their shared obsession with sex and morbidity, seem to reach peculiar heights of mutual self-exploration. Like the young girl of the oral folk tales, their explorative journey towards self-definition is marked by trauma, tragedy and shocking violence, but rather than chastening them, these events excite them to ever more outrageous and obscene erotic acts. Like the girl of Schneller's *Little Red Hat* enthusiastically stripping in front of the licentious, murderous wolf, Bataille's characters are confronted with horror and desire simultaneously. Indeed, the first time they have sexual intercourse it is upon discovering the hanged body of their friend Marcelle. She has committed suicide and the couple, finding themselves sexually stimulated by the sight of the corpse, lie down next to it in order to make love (Bataille 1982, 43–4). If this seems like a bizarre reaction on the part of the couple, it is because they felt a connection with their dead friend outside the socially recognizable grieving process. The narrator reports that he 'loved Marcelle without mourning her' (43) and that Simone 'was frightened and furious, but in no way awe-struck' (44). The sense conveyed by the scene is that the lovers are moved by the tragedy in such a way that deepens their relationship with each other but also their isolation from the world. The narrator reports feeling 'very remote from anything we touched, in a world where gestures have no carrying power, like voices in a space that is absolutely soundless' (44). Could the young girl of the alternative versions of *Little Red Riding Hood*, with her bizarre response to discovering her Grandmother's death, have felt something like this? Angela Carter's depiction in *The Company of Wolves* of what happens after the girl discovers that the older woman is dead may have been an attempt to make sense of her behaviour in terms of this link that Bataille regards as connecting death and the erotic. In the retellings by Carter (1996), the young girl has seen the remains of Grandmother's hair on the fire and knows from this that she is herself 'in danger of death' (218). When she throws her clothes and those of the wolf onto that same fire, 'the old bones under the bed set up a terrible clattering, but she did not pay them any heed' (219). Like Bataille's adolescents' feelings for the dead Marcelle, this girl might be said to have loved her Grandmother without mourning her. She does not mourn her Grandmother because she understands that in order to transcend the limitations of her own everyday life, the experience of death is necessarily part of her discovery and exploration of desire. Carter's version of the tale is of course her own personal response to the meaning of the exchange between the girl and the wolf in the Grandmother's house as presented in the folk and fairytale version of the story. But incorporating as it does the striptease, the burning of the discarded clothes and the suggestive conversation about the wolf's body, Carter's emphasis of the erotic quality of the exchange liberates the story from Perrault's objectifying and victimizing theme. As Bataille (1962) argues:

> [T]he thing we desire most ardently is the most likely to drag us into wild extravagance and ruin us (86). ... Mortal anguish does not necessarily make for sensual pleasure, but that pleasure is more deeply felt during mortal anguish. ... Fear of dying makes us catch our breath and in the same way we suffocate at the moment of crisis. (105)

In other words the allure of the danger of death is a very strong and a very important part of life. Like the adolescent couple's bizarre response to discovering Marcelle's hanged body in the *Story of the Eye* – having sexual intercourse for the very first time – the girl's own response to her discovery of death is in Carter's story is also a discovery about herself.

A theory of pleasure in confronting death makes Bataille's argument unsettling, and in the *Story of the Eye* as in Angela Carter's retellings of *Little Red Riding Hood* this is not least because it involves adolescent sexuality. In this, Bataille's and Carter's erotic imaginings about sex and death arguably represent something darker than anything depicted in the fairytales in Perrault's bourgeois mould since the latter denies that the heroine herself has anything to do with the sexual undertones of the story. Even although Bataille seems to present a negative form of sexuality that threatens to obliterate its subjects (in *Eroticism* (1962, 17) he argues that eroticism leads to a dissolution of individuality, particularly for women), it is one that challenges and inspires rather than merely objectifies. I am aware that many people will object that to read an explicitly pornographic narrative style into a fairytale is a perversion, but I maintain that this is only so if we assume that the tale is primarily about innocence. However, if Carter was right to highlight the potential in the tales for reading them against these stereotypes then the trials of Bataille's adolescents is not so very far removed from the folk story of a girl who discovers her own desire and selfhood through cannibalism and a near death experience. In its brutal conjoining of death and the erotic, the writings of Bataille and Carter both suggest a way in which the often equally brutal misfortunes of the folk/fairytale heroines such as *Little Red Riding Hood* might be read in the absence of the debilitating innocence motif. As I remarked at the beginning of this chapter, the tales have always been the subject of political re-interpretation. As Aristodemou (1999, 193) says, 'The same motifs have been the subject of interested appropriations, imitations and reworkings for hundreds of years from peasants' hearths to the salons of eighteenth century Paris, to Victorian nursery rooms, to the twentieth century studios of Walt Disney.' The purpose of this chapter is to re-appropriate and rework the tale of *Little Red Riding Hood* and its oral ancestors in such a way as to challenge traditional readings about the inherent innocence of childhood or that disobedience must be punished. Taking the tale of the young girl in the red cap seriously as a story about developing autonomy compels us to focus on the apparent confluence of desire and death in the narrative – and in particular the young girl's dawning awareness of these two totems of self-knowledge.

The difference between the heroine of folk tales and the innocent victim that appears in Perrault's version is made starker still when one considers how much more she actually *does* in some other versions of the tale. The omission of any particular evidence of the girl's own competence as well as lack of awareness from Perrault is what chiefly marks her as innocent. In some versions of the folk tale however, the famous exchange between girl and wolf on Grandmother's strange physical appearance leads, not to the girl being eaten, but to her concluding that, being so physically strange ('why is your chest so hairy, Grandmother?'), the person in the bed with her *cannot* be her Grandmother. There are versions in which the girl fools the wolf with a clever and not at all ladylike trick. The following extract is taken from *The Grandmother*: the folktale collected in the nineteenth century in France by Millien (2007). The girl has just remarked on Grandmother's big teeth:

"The better to eat you with, my child!"

"Oh, grandmother, I have to do it outside!"

"Do it in the bed, my child!"

"Oh no, grandmother, I really have to do it outside."

"All right, but don't take too long."

The bzou tied a woollen thread to her foot and let her go. As soon as the little girl was outside she tied the end of the thread to a plum tree in the yard.

The bzou grew impatient and said, "Are you doing a load? Are you doing a load?"

Not hearing anyone reply, he jumped out of bed and hurried after the little girl, who had escaped. He followed her, but he arrived at her home just as she went inside.

The girl's request to go outside to defecate is well-timed: not only is it only just quick enough to avoid death, it also undercuts the violent horror of the bzou's sudden exclamation – 'The better to eat you with, my child!' – usually the dramatic climax of the preceding conversation which in all its versions simmers with mounting tension. It also underscores my view that the girl need not be assumed to be an innocent victim and neither does she regard herself as such. If we were to try to re-imagine how a girl in Red Riding Hood's place might actually behave, we might imagine a character more like this one in terms of competence. After all, the story is supposed to be set in a remote village community, and Grandmother's cottage can only be reached by making a risky journey through woodland inhabited by dangerous predatory animals. A child who is sent into that wood all alone would be expected to be resourceful, and to grow up fast. Angela Carter's modern retellings of the story in *The Werewolf* and also in *The Company of Wolves* seem to capture the spirit of survival that emerges from those older peasant tales. In Carter's stories, her mother equips her, not with a pretty little red riding cap, but with proper advice and equipment. In *The Werewolf*, her mother sternly and pragmatically warns her: 'do not leave the path because of the bears, the wild boar, the starving wolves. Here, take your father's hunting knife; you know how to use it' (Carter 1996, 210). Similarly, in *The Company of Wolves*, the girl wears 'her stout shoes' and like all children, carries a large carving knife: 'She does not know how to shiver. She has her knife and she is afraid of nothing' (ibid., 215). In *The Werewolf*, she does not stray from the path on her journey through the woods nor fail to recognize the dangers therein. When the wolf makes his first appearance she immediately understands that she must defend herself with force: she bravely and competently fights off the wolf who tries to bite her neck, cutting off its front paw with her hunting knife, sending the beast limping back into the woods. She wipes her blade and keeps the severed wolf's paw as her prize (ibid., 211). Although Carter does not explore the themes of sexuality that she does in her other story, events depicted in *The Werewolf* make it clear that she is no mere object of desire as Perrault imagines, but a desiring subject in her own right (ibid., 211).

iii. Grimm's 'Little Red Cap': Signs of Autonomy   Grimm's *Little Red Cap* has traditionally been read as depicting the girl heroine as just as naïve and silly a character as the girl depicted by Perrault. Aristodemou (1999, 206), for example, acknowledges no difference in character, noting that Grimm's provision of a 'strong man' to rescue her does nothing to rehabilitate the gender stereotyping. She says: 'in both cases the young girl is discouraged from being independent and exploring, let alone realizing, her capacities including her awakening sexuality.' Likewise Jack Zipes (1991, 29) asserts that Grimm's heroine is 'a delicate, bourgeois type, who is helpless, naïve and culpable, if not stupid.' Indeed, commentators who have written about the brothers Grimm and their project to collect and repackage the ancient folktales for the German bourgeoisie have tended to agree that the Grimms, like Perrault, were keen to present the young girl as an innocent. Having themselves been born into a frugal Protestant family, the Grimms worked with the belief that the old folk tales represented an ideal German culture – a vital form which they could use to educate the children of the middle classes in the Calvinist virtues of diligence, industry, honesty, order and cleanliness (Zipes 1988, 34). Of course, there was nothing distinctly German about the stories. As discussed above, various versions existed all over Europe, but the Grimms believed that the spirit of German people was captured in 'natural and pure forms of culture' (Zipes 1988, 34). They feared that this spirit was in danger of being lost underneath the development of the 'high' cultural forms and their project of collecting and reinvigorating old folk tales would preserve the purity of traditional German culture (Zipes 1988, 33). According to Zipes (1988, 34), Grimm's resurrection of old folk tales was based on their desire to 'resurrect the authority of their father and his heritage to regain a lost, untarnished home or realm'. Their own father had died and they had also been affected by the humiliating occupation of their homeland by Napoleon and dissolution of the Holy Roman Empire in 1806. The innocence of Grimm's young protagonists (Little Red Riding Hood included) thus represents the innocence and purity of the vital form of German culture that they feared was in danger both from within and without the borders of the now dissolved Empire. For Grimm, innocence was not merely a matter of titillation but a serious political idea, forming an important part of a larger patriotic agenda. They were 'bourgeois missionaries', whose 'bourgeoisification' of the oral folktales in forms such as *Little Red Cap* valorizes innocence and obedience in children (Zipes 1991, 47).

However, I believe that to read Grimm's version of the Red Riding Hood tale merely as narrating the dangers to innocence as we did Perrault's is to give insufficient credit to signs of emerging subjectivity in Grimm's heroine. Although the version as presented by Grimm does, like Perrault, depict the girl as innocent in the sense that she is clearly unaware of the dangers of the forest, there are some important characteristics of Grimm's *Little Red Cap* that distinguishes it from Perrault's *Little Red Riding Hood*. I believe that these may help form the basis for a move away from talking about innocence and towards a discourse of developing autonomy, although in a way far removed from Angela Carter's erotic retelling. Perhaps most obvious is that Grimm removes most of the evidence of paedophilia: unlike Perrault's protagonist, the girl does not remove her clothes or get into bed with the wolf. Instead, the famous conversation between the two at the grandmother's house takes place with Little Red Cap standing beside the bed. It is likely that this is simply to exorcize the more bawdy aspects of the oral tales familiar to peasant classes in order to suit the genteel tastes of Grimm's target market. Some critics have claimed that Grimm's wolf, unlike Perrault's, is *not* intended to remind adult readers of a seducer or a rapist: McGlathery (1991, 57) for example regards Grimm's wolf simply as a wolf, motivated by 'gluttony, pure and simple.' On the other hand, Grimm's version does retain a trace of a sexual motive for those willing to look close enough. In the forest, the wolf inquires lecherously, 'And what are you carrying under your apron?' Secondly, the 1857 edition of Grimm's tale refers to the wolf having 'satisfied his desires' having eaten the girl, before falling asleep (Grimm 2002). In any case, removing the girl's unwitting sexual display for the voracious wolf makes room for a shift of focus from the body of the girl as sexual object to her actions and character development as a subject in her own right. In Perrault's narrative, the reader is implicated in the wolf's desire by fixating on the flesh of the innocent girl. Her stripping off and jumping into bed with the wolf is a nod and a wink to Perrault's adult readers who, unlike his child audiences, would be expected to appreciate the innuendo.

Grimm then departs from Perrault in ascribing a stronger and more vibrant personality to the central character. While Perrault (2008) describes our heroine in objectifying terms as 'the prettiest creature who was ever seen', Grimm (2007) ascribes both personality and subjective will to her, describing her (albeit in language we might find rather sugary) as 'a sweet little girl', who 'wanted to wear [her red riding cap] all the time'. It is significant that in Grimm she herself *wants* to wear her red cap: her own desire – conformist and unremarkable though it may be – is nevertheless her own (McGlathery 1991).[5] Also, whereas Perrault has the girl rushing off into the woods without hearing any warnings, Grimm has her mother add: 'Mind your manners and give her my greeting. Behave yourself on the way, and do not leave the path.' We should presume that this warning is heard (if not fully observed) as the girl 'promised to obey her mother'. A hostile interpretation of this difference would be that Grimm is merely reiterating the bourgeois insistence on obedience. A kinder interpretation would be to point out that, unlike Perrault, Grimm did not want to send his heroine out into the woods completely unprepared. While Perrault's Red Riding Hood is sent out wholly blind to the dangers that lurk therein, Grimm's heroine simply fails to connect her mother's warning to the meeting with the cunning wolf. She is clearly not supposed to be entirely ignorant or stupid since in the initial encounter with the

---

5   McGlathery (1991, 57) suggests that Little Red Cap's desire to wear the pretty cap is like that of a woman who delights in wearing a lover's gift.

wolf her promise to obey her mother's command means that she is presented with a conflict between obeying her mother and being tempted to delay her journey, as the wolf suggests (Bettelheim 1976, 170–1). In terms of what causes her to divert from the path of duty, Perrault's Red Riding Hood is so naïve that the wolf can quite openly tell her that he is going to pay grandmother a visit. She needs no prompting to delay her journey and appears to temporarily forget her mission altogether while she is 'running after butterflies' and so forth. Grimm's wolf by contrast is required to go to significantly greater lengths to trick the girl, devoting a fairly substantial speech to the joys and beauty of the woods in order to delay her. Even then, Little Red Cap's motivation is to gather flowers to give to grandmother because she knows 'she will be very pleased' (Grimm 2007).

The crucial point here is that, whilst Grimm's heroine is still admittedly naïve, the story is much more clearly a learning experience and thus not merely a warning about the dangers that 'certain men' pose to the innocence of children. It is a representation of the path towards knowledge and independence, the negotiation of which involves a tension between conformity and desire: a tension also relevant and compelling for modern readers (Sellers 2001). This is demonstrated most clearly by the fact that Little Red Cap and her grandmother survive (albeit only with the help of the woodcutter who saves them) and later manage to despatch another wicked wolf by themselves (Bettelheim 1976, 183). There are also two moments during the narrative where Little Red Cap is visibly learning about the world, which do not appear in Perrault. First, when she enters grandmother's house, 'everything looked so strange that she thought, "Oh God, why am I so afraid? I usually like it at grandmother's"'. What is it that she is afraid of, and if she is *merely* afraid, why then does she not run away? She is aware that grandmother looks different, and that there is a strange and anxious atmosphere in the little cottage. But does she know that she is about to be eaten alive by a huge wolf? Grimm's story is fascinating because it subtly alludes to the fact that the world she thought she knew and in particular her life as a child shielded from the dangers of the forest is changing before her eyes as she gains knowledge of it (Bettelheim 1976, 172). The nature of the creature that presents itself in Grandmother's place in the bed is as yet unknown. And while she does experience fear, she is also aware that she wants to find out more about it – hence she stays to interrogate it regarding its strange appearance. Everything in the cottage 'looks strange' because for the very first time in her life she is conscious of both mortal danger and of her own desire for autonomy. In other words, she is beginning to lose her innocence in the profound sense of knowledge acquisition. Although as we have seen Grimm's narrative does remove the explicitly sexual content of earlier versions in order to be suitable for the 'respectable' bourgeoisie, the violence of emotion associated with the discovery of danger and self that Grimm narrates here must be indicative of the development of self-knowledge as the 'shattering' of one's composure in the face of death or the awareness of consuming desire. Georges Bataille (1989, 32) could be referring directly to this passage in Grimm's tale when he writes: '"Violence" overwhelms us *strangely* in each case: each time, what happens is *foreign* to the received order of things, to which this violence each time stands in opposition.' We do not need to follow Bataille all the way down the road that, as we saw above, he points towards in describing the utter dissolution of the individual self that experiences erotic desire as anguish. But a 'strange' and 'foreign' overwhelming of the young girl's senses and perceptions – that indeed renders her paralysed to defend herself at the last moment – is precisely the experience of dawning awareness of death and desire.

So far we have interpreted Grimm's version of the tale as quite different from Perrault's regarding the girl's own response to her situation inside Grandmother's house. Whereas Grimm's tale, thus interpreted, allows her to experience foreboding and disorientation that comes with discovering something both horrifying and exciting, Perrault's gives her no such opportunity since she is gobbled up without noticing anything particularly amiss. The second moment at which Grimm's narrative shows this learning process is the moment before the wolf attacks. The girl of Perrault's story delivers her last line as she did all the others: 'Grandmother, what big teeth you have got!' – is not in any way different in tone or perception to her earlier observations such as 'Grandmother, what big ears you have!' However, in Grimm, the girl's final observation clearly carries a degree of horror that is missing from her previous ones: 'Oh Grandmother, what a *horribly* big mouth you have!' (emphasis added). Perrault's undifferentiated line implies that she still mistakenly thinks she is merely addressing an oddly proportioned grandmother. Grimm's line, on the other hand, makes it clear that the girl had realized *something else* about the person in the bed. It is a lesson being learned in the moment before the terrible violent act. I believe that the exchange between Little Red Cap and the wolf at the grandmother's house is one of the great dramatic moments of European literature. Its finely balanced tension between ignorance and knowledge is far more subtle and than it is usually given credit for, covered over as it is by the crass innuendo and bland violence preferred by Perrault.

Conclusion

In our interpretation of this scene (and of the story as a whole) we have moved a long way from the static image of 'innocence betrayed'. The stillness and rootedness implied by the word derived from Latin expression 'to do no harm' gives way to an impression of movement and emotional development. A negative, passive state of being is replaced with dynamism and purpose. This image of the young female protagonist that resists the objectifying characterization of innocence is also to be found in the tales found in the collections both of Grimm and Perrault in which a woman narrowly escapes death when she discovers that her husband or husband-to-be is a misogynistic serial killer and intends to kill her. In some forms (including Perrault's *Bluebeard* and Grimm's *Fetcher's Fowl*) the woman discovers this through succumbing to the temptation of entering a room from which her husband has forbidden her, and therein discovering the bloody corpses of his previous wives. The other form (including the English tale *Mr Fox*, the American *Pretty Polly* and Grimm's *The Robber Bridegroom*) involves a woman making a journey to the house of a man she does not know well (sometimes her suitor or fiancé) where she witnesses him killing a woman in a sexual and/or cannibalistic ritual. Although in his *Bluebeard* Perrault tries to emphasize the fault of the young woman in her failure to resist temptation, these stories all present a narrative in which the rich man's new wife dares to defy the tyrannical man in order to acquire knowledge, and her triumph over death secured through her own presence of mind in mobilizing family alliances (Bacchilega 1997, 107–9; Bettelheim 1976, 299–303; McGlathery 1991, 66–71; Warner 1994, 255–7). Grimm's Little Red Cap's own ordeal brings opportunities for knowledge-acquisition of which the girl takes advantage, though rather too late to save herself without the help of the passing woodcutter. The girl was sent out into the woods before she was ready to adequately face the wolf. In *Bluebeard* and its variants, the power that accompanies such knowledge acquisition leads to freedom. As in the *Little Red Riding Hood* variants, the heroine of Perrault's version is markedly different to those of Grimm's tales.

Chapter 5

Innocence, the Image and the Unseen Paedophile: Spotting Indecency in Images of Children

What is it that causes certain images of children that are not obviously erotic to be condemned as 'indecent' (as English lawyers would say) or 'lewd' (for US lawyers)? Surely it cannot be the presence or absence of nudity, since this would condemn the majority of parents who keep 'baby in the bathtub' style photographs in their family albums. In 2001, the Saatchi Gallery in London exhibited photographs taken by Californian ex-fashion model and photographer Tierney Gearon in an exhibition called *I Am a Camera*. The photographs depict her family; some are posed, and others are natural. The photographs feature her two children – a son aged four and a daughter aged seven, as well as some other children. In some of the photographs the children wear masks. In six of the 15 exhibited, they are nude or partly nude. Gearon's photographs are not obviously sexual since they do not involve any sexual activity or posing, but depicting children either naked, partially clothed or in some way showing their genitals or genital regions could potentially excite the desire of a paedophile. The exhibition was visited by the police vice squad, which threatened to prosecute the gallery under indecency laws. The Saatchi Gallery defied the threats and the prosecution never took place, although the exhibition was condemned by sections of the tabloid press as child pornography.[1] The *Daily Mirror* and *The News of the World* reproduced some of the images with genitals blacked out, either to avoid causing offence or else to ensure that readers would interpret the photographs as sexual. The Protection of Children Act 1978 s.1 (1) (a) created the offence of 'taking, making, or distributing an indecent image of a child'. According to the English case of *R v Graham-Kerr*, whether or not an image is 'indecent' is an objective question to be determined by a jury in the absence of consideration of the original maker's motives. Indeed, there is evidence that a jury might have found Tierney Gearon's pictures indecent. *The News of the World*, as ever ready to seize an opportunity to cry paedophile, described the images as 'degrading snaps of naked children' and the reception of

---

1   We shall only consider the legal implications of images under 'indecency' laws relating to children. But see also the Obscene Publications Act 1959 s.1 (1), which allows prosecution for any publication that is deemed to be 'obscene' due to its tendency to 'deprave and corrupt'. Secondly, it is a common law offence of conspiracy to display a work deemed to be an outrage to public decency (*R v Gibson and another*).

the exhibition by the general public in the UK as a 'national outrage' ('Child Porn They Call Art' 2001). For some, the tabloids' apparent obsession with sex tends to undermine their simultaneous moral indignation on child sex issues. Dismissing the *New of the World*'s assessment, Polly Toynbee (2001) responded in the press by asserting that 'hypocrisy is far too weak a word for the News of the World'.

Tierney Gearon (2001) herself has been predictably defensive of her decision to exhibit her photographs, and has argued that her pictures are 'incredibly innocent and totally unsexual'. But despite Gearon's protestations, her images when looked at in the context of the furore that surrounded the *I Am a Camera* exhibition, undeniably do say something, not about child sexuality itself, but about the cultural *discourse* of child sexuality today. Indeed, child sexuality is such a thorny subject that it is difficult to conceive it as anything other than a textual phenomenon, that is, one of those issues that, due to cultural anxieties about the ubiquity of child abuse and paedophilia, cannot be addressed directly, but only by moralizing against perceived transgressions of the inviolable idea of childhood innocence (Stainton Rogers 1998, 195). Images such as Gearon's seem to expose a deep anxiety about the proper boundary between adult and child: sexuality is a feature of 'adult' life and must not be associated with 'innocent' children. That the word 'adult' has come to *mean* 'erotic' when referring to entertainment indicates that we think of erotica as necessarily being 'not for the consumption of innocents' (Stainton Rogers 1998, 196). I use Gearon's images to discuss this anxiety, arguing in this chapter that, given the nature of cultural discourse about innocence and childhood innocence especially, the relationship between innocence and sex is a close one. I believe that Gearon's exhibition and responses to it, like Grimm's *Little Red Cap*, invite us to reflect on the notion of innocence and its uses and abuses in cultural debates. The nature of 'innocence' when applied to images, in particular to images of children, is such as to cause great anxiety. In my view, innocence and indecency seem to be inseparable bedfellows and I suggest that there are two ways to read these images as indecent. The first approach is to argue that the photographs turn the children displayed into sexual objects for the gratification of paedophiles. This might be described as a 'viewer-centred' approach, and is arguably the most compelling for the tabloid moralists who protested about the exhibition. The argument is ethically problematic because it requires us to regard children's bodies as inherently erotic, the display of which turns them into passive victims of sexual violence and reveals something dark and uncomfortable about our society. The second way in which the images might be regarded as indecent is one that focuses on the image itself and looks to whether it seems to undermine accepted (patriarchal) sexual dynamics of mainstream depictions of children as innocent, inert, passive creatures.

1. Gearon's Photographs as Sexualizing Innocent Children

In her *Guardian* defence article, Gearon (2001) herself admits that photographs do not give very much scope for the children's own personalities to emerge:

> My pictures are about a captured moment, rather than about the person. They are about a feeling, and to that extent they preserve my children's anonymity. They are disguised somehow. I'm showing a moment of life, not part of their personality, and to that extent they could be anyone. ... After seeing my shots, you have no idea of what my kids are about.

Why should Gearon be so keen that her photographs do not reveal anything important about her children's personalities? One obvious answer is that Gearon simply wanted to emphasize that these are merely family snaps. Indeed Gearon seems to have even denied that she is an artist at all, since she has claimed to be utterly clueless as to the possibility of her photographs having any larger significance than mere family photos that just happened somehow to find their way into an art gallery (Edge and Baylis 2004, 80).[2] Gearon claimed that the viewer would have no idea 'what my kids are about' because, as private family photos, there is no clear narrative that speaks about the lives of the children, their thoughts or personalities, their likes and dislikes. However it is precisely the freedom accorded to the viewer to construct the children as they wish that causes the anxiety in responding to the photographs: if they are merely innocent family snaps, why is it necessary to display the children's genitals in such a public venue as an art gallery for strangers to look at? If the answer is that the photographs constitute 'art', then why would the 'artist' trivialize them by so fervently deny that there is an aesthetic, social or political narrative above and beyond merely family members having fun? (Edge and Baylis 2004, 77). We must conclude either that Gearon must have been so rattled by the accusations of having exploited her own children's bodies and privacy for her own fame that she decided simply to deny having any artistic intentions, or else that she really was ignorant about the existing artistic tradition of provoking viewers into unexpected reactions by blurring the boundary between the private (for example, lowly 'family album snap-shots' and other aspects of personal life) and the public (the ideals of the high art of the galleries of beauty, form and composition). A familiar example of such an artist in the UK is Tracy Emin, whose works, also bought and exhibited by Charles Saatchi, such as *My Bed* (1998) and *Everyone I Have Ever Slept With 1963–1995* (1995) provoke viewers' reactions both positively and negatively by

---

2   Edge and Baylis (2004) quote Tierney Gearon as claiming artistic naivety in interview (with the *Mail on Sunday*, 7 October 2001): 'How could anyone possibly be upset by those pictures? To me they were innocent, beautiful images. They were natural moments, funny moments, and real moments.'

presenting candid evidence of the artist's private life in the art gallery and thereby seemingly seeking to obliterate the public/private distinction.[3]

A possible interpretation of the disguise demonstrates the potentially stultifying and objectifying power of the innocence discourse. Recall that Charles Perrault's version of the *Little Red Riding Hood* tale clearly invites the reader to regard the little girl as the passive, innocent victim of an abduction committed with a sexual motive, her body the object of lust though lacking of any sign of awareness of the wolf's real intentions. The violence in the story comes from the wolf of course, but the violence of the story's bourgeois ideology is the disabling and disarming discourse of innocence. Reading Tierney Gearon's photographs as Perrault might have read those ancient folk tales from which he produced his own tale with its simplistic binary dichotomy between innocence and corruption, we would point out that the children are often depicted in such a way that seems to hide or disguise their own subjectivity. They are shown masked, wearing dark lenses, sometimes in a configuration of pose and lighting that obscures their faces. As such they are presented not as people with individual personalities so much as blank objects whose personalities may be constituted by the viewer. Three particular photographs might be singled out for more detailed analysis. In one image a boy urinates in the snow on the street. His exposed penis is viewed fully frontal in the sunshine, and his face is obscured by large black skiing goggles. In a second image, three children are seen playing in the yard of a house. Two are clothed and we see their faces clearly and the third child in the frame is naked and masked. In a third image two children are shown completely naked apart from their identical 'bimbo' masks. They pose in an apparently idyllic scene of spotless white beach, inviting sea and rich blue sky. The combination of the natural elements in the frame speaks of pure and untouched beauty. Perhaps this untouched quality reflects the virginity – and innocence – of children who, with their faces obscured by bizarre 'bimbo' masks, cannot return the gaze of the viewer. The configuration of masks and exposed genitals seems to guide the eye away from the face (thus muting signs of the children's own personalities) and towards the genitals. This is most obvious in the two pictures of the boy urinating since his bodily function captures the attention, while the masks hide the expressiveness of his face. Gearon has implicitly underscored her reluctance to allow the viewer to know very much about her subjects more recently. In 2007 Gearon published a book of 73 photographs provocatively called *Daddy where are you*, featuring landscapes of upstate New York in which her mother appears as central protagonist. Gearon's mother appears in these landscapes sometimes clothed, sometimes naked. We are told that she suffers from 'a mental illness' but are given no further information. All of which is presented without explanation or annotations. The critic Miranda Gavin (2007)

---

3   See also Edge and Baylis (2004, 80–2) who compare Gearon's apparent failure to acknowledge any aesthetic or political influence, with the photography of Sally Mann, whose collection of back and white images exhibited in *Immediate Family* (1992) show awareness of herself as part of an artistic tradition.

notes the way in which such a presentation seems to censor or limit the mother's personality:

> With no time line, no captions and no author's commentary, Gieron [sic] takes the reader into a strange domain, a place where the private is made public and time seems to stand still. Furthermore, with so much left unsaid ambiguity takes hold. What exactly is the nature of her mother's illness? ... How complicit is her mother in acting out these scenarios? How typical are these tableaux? ... In *Daddy, where are you*, we learn more about Gieron than her mother. The camera is a cathartic device for the author and the work possibly represents the visual equivalent of a year on a psychiatrist's couch.

For the purposes of our discussion we will focus upon the images of Gearon's children from the 2001 Saatchi exhibition *I Am a Camera* in the light of our discussion so far of innocence as a set of values that implies 'being' rather than 'doing'. The innocent is a prized jewel in the sense that, while it may be admired by others (subjects) it cannot return the gaze. Being innocent it is incapable of judgment of any kind. What worried the moralistic tabloid journalists was that, by publicly exhibiting these photographs, Gearon was in effect turning her own children into objects of lust for paedophiles. Although statistically unlikely, in a cultural climate in which the fear of abduction by paedophiles is periodically encouraged and commercially exploited by the tabloid press, this charge was a potentially serious one in terms of the meaning of the images. As Lynda Nead (1999, 205) argues, judgment as to what is indecent (although Nead uses the more common legal term 'obscene') is based *not* on the 'presence or absence of sexual content' but rather on the 'imagined presence or absence of sexual arousal in any given viewing public'. Gearon's photographs are a paradigmatic illustration of this point: the nudity of the children depicted is not in itself erotic and can only be regarded as such if they are viewed through the eyes of a paedophile. If we image paedophiles everywhere, then we see the image of the exposed child as indecent. Although to a liberal critic such a viewpoint is or should be irrelevant to making aesthetic, moral or legal judgments about the images, it has become significant in moral and legal discourse particularly with respect to children.

The argument about the powerlessness of the children in these photographs is augmented by a legal one about the impossibility of gaining meaningful consent from them to be depicted in a way that might excite paedophiles. Being innocent, the argument goes, children are by definition unable to understand why the depiction on their bodies may cause controversy and so consent must be withheld on their behalf.[4] By contrast, even if the young models that pose topless for the same tabloid newspapers that condemned Gearon's images are being commercially exploited,

---

4   The photographs of Alice taken by Lewis Carroll were of course 'innocent' as images in their own right, but are viewed differently now given modern attitudes towards Carroll's apparent sexual interest.

at least the editors can justify their apparent double standards by pointing to the fact of their models being 18 and therefore assumed competent to consent.[5] For images *intended* to be erotic there does need to be a black and white cut off point at which competence to consent to being photographed and displayed erotically can be assumed. But it raises another question: why should we assume that a nude image of a child is erotic at all? Is nudity *in itself* erotic, justifying a ban on all nude images of children, no matter what the intention of the photographer or the manner in which the photograph was taken? Of course, paedophiles might find Gearon's photographs erotic, and what upset the moralizing tabloid press about the Saatchi photographic exhibition in 2001 was that the innocence of Gearon's children had been violated by depicting them nude and thus exposed to the perverted gaze of any passing paedophile. But so what? What relevance does the paedophile's view of things have in interpreting the images unless the pictures are *already* sexualized? Gearon's defenders object that her pictures are not sexual and only perverts believe them to be. As Polly Toynbee (2001) puts it in her *Guardian* article, to treat the kind of candid nudity of Gearon's photographs as sexual and the viewing of them as perverted 'lets paedophiles set the standard of what is normal': that is, children's bodies are treated as if they are sexual by nature. The *News of the World* view implies that since a few people might be sexually aroused, then the images are sexual. In their reporting of the Gearon story, the *News of the World*'s decision to black out the children's genitals ensured that their readers could not fail to view tham as sexual objects.

The supposed 'innocence' of childhood and the corresponding anxiety that this innocence is in danger of being lost, means (to a tabloid mentality at least) that if there is any doubt as to whether an image is sexual, then it must be viewed as such. Calvin Klein's advertising campaigns of 1995 and 1999 and the furore these created in the US is an interesting example. The 1995 campaign featured teenagers modelling jeans, which Calvin Klein defended as conveying a positive message, that 'regular people in the most ordinary setting' can be glamorous. In 1999, a campaign involved young children jumping on a sofa in their underwear, displayed in Times Square, New York, which intended, Calvin Klein said, 'to show children smiling, laughing and just being themselves. We wanted to capture the same warmth and spontaneity that you find in a family snapshot' (Fenner and Standora 1999). In both cases then, Calvin Klein protested that the images were ordinary, innocent snapshots and misunderstood by critics. The critics condemned them as exploitative child pornography on the basis that they could be read in a sexual way:

---

5   The Protection of Children Act 1978 prohibits the taking, making and distributing of indecent images of 'children' only, which according to s.7 means young people who either *are* (7(6)) or *appear to be* (7(8)) under 18.

People were right to take offense at Klein's commercials and posters featuring half-dressed teens who look like they're auditioning for a do-it-yourself porn flick in somebody's basement rec room. ... These models weren't selling jeans. They were selling sex. Adolescent sex. The ads were sleaze, appealing to the prurient interests of pedophiles and other gutter dwellers. ('Calvin Klein's Dirty Obsession' 1995)

Unlike Tierney Gearon, Calvin Klein very quickly removed the images from view. Was a wrong committed in using images of children in their underwear? Were those children the victims of an immoral act or a sexual offence? Again, it depends on whether those images are indeed sexual and thus sexually exploitative of people who (unlike 18-year-old models) cannot give legally valid consent to being exploited. Amy Adler (2001a, 257) takes what Calvin Klein's critics would regard as a liberal view of the 1999 campaign:

I went back and looked at the picture ... One of the little boy's underpants seems baggy as he jumps in midair. Is that the outline of his genitals I wonder? It was then ... that I realized I was participating in a new order, a world created and compelled by child pornography.

Adler is arguing here that it is a new public hysteria over child pornography and childhood innocence itself that sexualizes images that would previously have been viewed more positively. I think that what Adler seems to be claiming is that some images *really are* innocent when it comes to images of children. These are photographs such as those of children in the bathtub or on the beach that fall foul of a culture that fetishizes innocence and thereby unnecessarily sexualizes otherwise innocuous scenes. The cases of family members threatened with prosecution over private photographs of their children in the bathtub and so on are infamous both in the UK and the US. The British newsreader Julia Somerville was arrested and questioned in 1995 over photographs of her seven year old daughter in the bath (Fowler 1995). And on the other hand, there are those images that cynically exploit the idea of innocence in order to titillate and elicit desire for commercial reasons. The trouble with this view is that the innocence discourse itself creates such anxiety that it becomes difficult to distinguish between the two kinds. What adds to the controversy of Gearon's photographs is that on the one hand they seem to be the sort of family snaps that every parent has in their family album, but, on the other hand, in being displayed in the art gallery they also contradict the normally 'private' context of such images. This is not determinative of indecency law, since although the Protection of Children Act 1978 originally required either actual distribution or intent to distribute, the mere private possession of an indecent image is now also a criminal offence under the Criminal Justice Act 1988 s.160. However it means that an otherwise innocent picture is corrupted by the possibility that it may be seen by a corrupt viewer who takes sexual pleasure from it.

The courts in both the US and the UK have grappled with this distinction. In both jurisdictions attempts have been made to determine which kinds of images should be prohibited and which should not. The trouble is that there is no clear way to determine whether an image is *in itself* innocent, since children depicted as innocent are often a target of paedophilic desire, as well as children depicted as sexually precocious or inviting. Given that paedophiles find clothed and un-posed pictures stimulating as well as more obviously 'erotic' ones, then to judge from the perspective of the paedophile would mean that no picture of a child is safe from prohibition. In the US, the debate about what constitutes a 'lascivious exhibition of the genitals' (the definitional test for illegal child pornography), has become incredibly nuanced, not least because, unlike material that is merely 'obscene',[6] child pornography is defined as 'action' rather than 'speech' and as such cannot claim protection under the First Amendment on the grounds of artistic or other merit (*New York v Ferber*). In the influential judgment of *United States v Dost*, the Californian district court laid out a six part test, including 'whether the setting of the visual depiction is sexually suggestive, ... or ... whether the visual depiction is designed to elicit a sexual response in the viewer' (at 832). Images in which children's genitals are visible – whether covered or uncovered – must be scrutinized and interpreted in terms of their capacity to excite desire in people who are sexually attracted to children. As Adler (2001b, 955–6) argues,

> [a]pplication of the *Dost* test thus requires an inquiry into the intended effect of the material on an audience of paedophiles. ... But how are we to get inside the head of the paedophile and to see the world from his eyes? ... Child pornography law's focus on the perspective of the paedophile creates a further problem: as explained above, paedophiles like so many pictures of children. ... [W]hen viewed from the perspective of paedophiles, all children could be erotic.

Because innocence is such a highly prized quality for some, the very innocence – in the sense of being non-sexual – of an image may very well be what appeals to the paedophile. What might look to most people a perfectly innocuous picture of a child, say, in a paddling pool or in a beginners' ballet class, is both innocent and erotic at the very same time and for the same reasons. Such is the double-edged nature of 'innocence'. This is precisely what is disempowering about the characterizations of *Little Red Riding Hood* and other fairytale children as innocents: it removes their own opportunity for defining themselves. According to the *Dost* test then, all pictures of children might be pornographic in the sense of the child being treated as an object – rooted to someone else's desire and someone else's gaze. This way of interpreting images universalizes indecency/lewdness and the US courts thus 'constitute children as a category that is inextricable from sex'

---

6   Defined by the US Supreme Court in *Miller v California* as material that is 'patently offensive', that 'appeals to a prurient interest in sex' and lacks any 'artistic, political or scientific merit'.

(Adler 2001a, 263). Using the law to protect children from becoming the subjects of pornography therefore in fact *creates* child pornography by constructing images of them as sexual. According to the current CPS charging standards in the UK, what constitutes 'child pornography' is judged objectively, based on a checklist. Even so, a picture can be regarded as 'indecent' for the purposes of Protection of Children Act 1978 even if there is no erotic posing, which means that, as in the US, English prosecutors must scrutinize such images to determine whether 'indecency' can be discovered therein. As in the US, English law does not accord the same protection for 'indecent' images of children as it does for merely 'obscene' material, which has the defence of 'being for the public good on the ground that it is in the interests of science, literature, art or learning, or of other objects of general concern' (Obscene Publications Act 1959, s.4 (1)). In the English case of *Graham-Kerr*, the defendant took photographs of a boy at a swimming pool. Even though the defendant himself admitted to being sexually aroused by the boy, the photographs themselves were only indecent in the sense that the boy was naked. There was no erotic posing. As we have seen, on appeal it was held that the motivation or attitude of the person who takes or makes the images is irrelevant in determining whether or not an offence has been committed: intentionally taking or making an indecent image is sufficient and so it is no defence for a defendant to say that they themselves did not regard the images as indecent. Graham-Kerr's conviction of taking an indecent photograph was overturned by the Court of Appeal, since, even although the he did in fact admit to paedophiliac tendencies, this should have been irrelevant to the jury's assessment of the images. If an image does not involve erotic posing, then whether or not it might be described as indecent very much depends upon the message that we feel is being communicated by the photograph. As I have said, Gearon denied that there was any message at all to be taken from her 'incredibly innocent' photographs, which only makes the task of interpreting them more difficult.

If it really is possible to read Gearon's photographs as a kind of sexual violence against her children then this indignant response is quite understandable. How could she so brazenly display her own children as sexual objects for the perverted gaze of the paedophile? For some, for instance those who campaigned in England for the so-called 'Sarah's Laws' allowing members of the public to see whether someone with regular, unsupervised access to children is listed on the sex-offenders register (which recently underwent trials in Warwickshire, Peterborough, Cambridgeshire, Southampton and Stockton) predatory sexual violence lurks around every corner (Arrest After 'Sarah's Law' Call 2008). For such people the public display of child nudity may in itself be enough to constitute an unnecessary risk to children. James Kincaid (2000, 108–9) challenges this view of the prevalence of paedophilia as a cultural phenomenon when he asserts that our preoccupation with sexual violence against children is often a 'virtuous glibness' that diverts attention away from the many thousands of cases of non-sexual violence, neglect, poor healthcare and so on that are more pressing issues. Kincaid's dismissal of the significance of sexual abuse as a form of child maltreatment is somewhat at odds at least in statistical terms with research recently published in *The Lancet* (Child Maltreatment 2008) that 15 per cent of girls and 5 per cent of boys in the developed world have been subject to some form of sexual abuse, while 10 per cent of all children suffer emotional abuse every year. However, the relevance of sexual abuse to the interpretation of images such as Gearon's is far from apparent for liberals such as Adler and Toynbee. There is an imaginative leap to be made in connecting these two things (abuse and images) because the liberal view dismisses the idea that there is an intrinsic link between naked images of children and actual sexual abuse. It is indeed very tempting to simply dismiss as hysterical nonsense the tabloid reports of outrage over the display of the naked child. However, there is a more complex and interesting question regarding a possible link between images of the body and the erotic. Lynda Nead (1999, 222) argues that any attempt to engage critically with an aesthetics of the body is to risk surrendering the objective, detached position which claims critical distance from the image and thus a purely intellectual aesthetic and interest in form rather than content – and falling instead into a physical, affected, passionate one. This physical reaction may be one of arousal (as in the paedophile) or disgust (as in the outraged tabloid journalist) or simply intrigue, but all are implicated in what Nead (1999, 206) calls a 'cycle of desire and gratification'. Both the moralist who condemns the images as disgusting and the liberal who praises them as touching portraits of family life are claiming a certain distance from the photograph: both are claiming to be separate from and thus competent to judge and classify what it is they see there. But Nead (1999, 206) argues that in both cases this claim to critical autonomy is often illusory and the effect of images that present the naked body is that the viewer 'all too often finds unity [with] and becomes a part of the corporealized, sensual discourse it seeks to contain and regulate'. Nead's comments are specifically directed at the reception of erotic art and sculpture that has traditionally been regarded as the preserve of the 'gentleman connoisseur' (as the only kind of person sufficiently educated and enlightened to view erotic material purely as 'art' without being corrupted by it). However, her argument is helpful for us here because it points towards the reason why it was specifically the *public display* of Gearon's photographs that caused such a moral storm: the indecency of the images might be said to lie not so much in the images themselves but the fear that in some people they will excite an unhealthy sexual desire. This is to treat the image of the child's body as a taboo, that is, something that should simply not be seen because of its potentially erotic effect in some viewers. I would agree with Polly Toynbee and Amy Adler and other liberal critics who say that to treat the image of the naked child as taboo in this way only exacerbates the problem of the sexualization of the child and childhood innocence, but it is its very status as a taboo that means that prohibition and violation together exacerbate desire and anxiety.

George Bataille's argument about erotic desire being driven by the violation of taboo takes this point about the unavoidably physical reaction to particularly unsettling depths. Bataille's cultural analysis of sexuality leads him to identify an association between the allure of proscribed sexuality and the spectacle of blood sacrifice in 'archaic societies'. As we have seen, the definition of what constitutes child pornography and what does not has caused intense debate due not only to the combination of widespread disgust at the sexualization of the child, but also because of the undoubted allure of innocence, the combination of which makes any concession to possibly exploitative images seem so dangerous. The problem, argues Bataille (1962, 178), is that anxiety and desire are inextricable: 'Where would pleasure be if the anguish bound up with it did not lay bare its paradoxical aspect, if it were not felt as unbearable by the very person experiencing it?' The prohibition of sexual desire with respect to children itself incites it because it makes a sacred object (and therefore a sacrificial object) out of innocence. The result is a confusing paradox of dread and desire, a taboo and its transgression (see also Freud 1950, 29–30).[7] The implication of Bataille's argument, shocking enough in itself, is that in order to feel that an image such as Gearon's could be sexually degrading pornography and exploitative of the children depicted, is to understand the erotic power of the transgression of taboo. Freudian psychoanalysis locates erotic desire as originating from within taboo itself: the oedipal frustration of being prohibited from having the object of our desire and the consequent desire to violate it (Adler 2001a, 249). Bataille reports that in certain 'archaic societies', human flesh is ritually consumed, not because it is regarded as food, but because its consumption is normally prohibited by taboo. It is normally 'forbidden, sacred, and the very prohibition attached to it is what arouses the desire'. Bataille (1962, 71–2) argues that in such societies, we can recognize the Freudian idea of the taboo as a 'protective barrier against excessive desires', where the taboo on eating human flesh being 'the reason why the pious cannibal consumes it'. This is the really shocking thing about the tortuous wrangling in the courts as to what constitutes 'lewd display of the genitals' or 'indecency' in photographs that might in previous years have not excited any interest at all: it is only because we have constructed the displayed image of the innocent child as sacred – as the 'forbidden fruit' – that it has become to be seen as objectified and victimized by display. For Bataille (1962, 178) the ability for the suggestion of paedophilia in an image to rouse such strong passion in the form of condemnation is simply proof of the 'immutable necessity' of the 'dread' that pleasure demands. Bataille's own fiction takes up the Sadean mantle of exposing this nightmarish picture of sexuality. The adolescent couple in his *Story of the Eye* (1982) discussed in the previous chapter are morbidly fascinated witnesses of a gruesome road crash. They find themselves 'fully absorbed' by the sight of a 'very pretty' female cyclist who has had her head 'almost totally ripped off' by the wheels of a car: 'The horror and despair at so much bloody flesh, nauseating in part, and in part very beautiful, was fairly

---

7   Freud (1950, 29) describes how, in obsessional neurotics, the instinctual desire for a prohibited object is repressed, resulting in a 'fixation' on it, a 'continuing conflict between the prohibition and the instinct', and an 'ambivalence' of the person for it, encompassing unconscious desire and conscious detestation.

equivalent to our usual impression upon seeing each other' (Bataille 1982, 11). This is a morbid depiction of sexuality in which the trigger of desire is utterly objectified in death for the sexual pleasure of the living. In the eighteenth century, Sade's writing shocked those of his own society because his stories sexualized the virtuous life: it was her unswerving adherence to virtue and chastity that made his unfortunate Justine – who seeks protection from one apparently upstanding representative of public life after another, only to be beaten and abused each and every time – a sexual object. Thus what should not have been connected in any way to sexuality became, for Sade, in fact an incitement of desire. In our own society it is the sexualization of the innocent child that incites the greatest fear and dread. It is this dread that means that the very implication that a child might be viewed as an object of sexual pleasure causes such huge anxiety and must be met with fierce condemnation, but also that which continues to ensure that innocence, formerly preserved for the society maiden bride, is placed on such a high pedestal.

Although the liberals are certainly right that to regard the child's body as inherently erotic says something very depressing about our society, the conservatives who insist that the images must be viewed with a paedophile's eye are unwittingly confirming Bataille's Sadean nightmarish picture of human sexuality as bound up with violence. There is a violence committed on the sexualized body of the child who, like the pretty French cyclist whose horrible road accident provides a mesmerizing sexual object for the adolescent couple of the *Story of the Eye*, becomes a pure object of desire. In a slightly different context, Alison Young describes a phenomenon that she calls the 'aesthetics of disgust': an effect of the conjoining of elements in an image that challenge and undermine the distinction between innocence and corruption. In her analysis of three controversial art exhibitions, Young argues that what accounts for the vitriolic and often physically violent reactions to certain artworks that seem deliberately to provoke religious indignation is that they conjoin themes that ought never to meet. I have argued above that the controversy surrounding Gearon's work relates to the anxiety caused by presenting the image of a child in such a way that might imply that they could be the object of sexual desire – the association of childhood innocence with sexual desire is what makes people uncomfortable. For Young, this tendency for artists to provoke uproar through making uneasy associations is a repeated characteristic in the reception of contemporary art. One example that Young cites, which is also relevant to our own discussion of Tierney Gearon is Marcus Harvey's *Myra*, in which the infamous 1965 police photograph of the child murderer Myra Hindley was reproduced as a huge painting and displayed in the Royal Academy in London in 1997 as part of the Saatchi 'Sensation' exhibition. Since they took sexual pleasure in torturing and murdering their child victims, one might wonder if Hindley and her boyfriend Ian Brady might in fact represent the modern sadist that Bataille identifies as at the heart of (rather than alien to) humanity. The painting caused huge furore in the British media, involving a boycott led by the tabloid press, the mother of one of Myra Hindley's victims and even Hindley herself (Young

2005, 34). What made the painting so controversial was firstly that its immense size meant that it could be a monument to Myra Hindley (Young 2005, 36); and secondly that the original photographic pixels were represented in the painting by the shapes of children's hands, suggesting that the bodies of children had been used to recreate the child killer. This also seemed to imply that the image of the child killer 'swallows up' those children just as the larger image 'swallows up' the pixel dots that make up the photograph (Young 2005, 37). To the extent that the reproduced images of children's hands were, so to speak, the building blocks of the painting, children are thus depicted as objects within the larger picture, in which Myra Hindley herself is subject: her defiant face appears in stark contrast to their passive and probably unknowing handprints. The close association between the innocent children and the image of the face of a person that tortured and murdered children caused not merely anxiety but disgust. Young argues that the significant thing about *Myra* is that in seeming to collapse the distance between apparently distant concepts (the 'illegitimate touchings' of innocence and corruption) it seems to signify also a collapse of critical distance between the viewer and image: instead of inviting viewers to stand back and assess the work as an object, it provokes a physical response – one of anger, dismay, disgust (Young 2005, 41–4).[8] The anger here is directed at the objectification of children by using their handprints to represent the pixel-dots of the police photograph, which is a second violation of children in the adult viewers' minds. Like Sade's eighteenth century readers anxious for the safety of their daughters, the work causes a dread about what Bataille claims to be the dark heart of humanity. The collapse of critical distance that Young refers to in connection with *Myra* finds a resonance with this reading of Gearon's work. As in Gearon's case, the artist responsible for *Myra* probably only exacerbated public anxiety about the children in the image, to the extent that they are noticeable at all, as mere passive victims to a crime that they are incapable by their innocence of understanding. Harvey explained that he chose to depict Myra Hindley constituted by children's hands because that was 'the most simple image of innocence in all that pain' (Lack 2008; Young 2005, 36). Even if Gearon's protestations of artistic innocence are to be believed, Harvey must have known that to hang a picture of Myra Hindley in a public art gallery would cause a stir. He may have felt it safer simply to 'play dumb' about the painting's provocative power rather than embrace further controversy by admitting that the stirring up of public anger and disgust was his primary purpose in choosing to represent a child-murderer. After all, moral indignation is surely better for any artist's profile than tepid approval or worse, indifference. In Gearon's pictures violence is arguably implied by the possibility of the presence of an actual paedophile viewer in the gallery or else by the imagined presence of the spectral or theoretical paedophile which the *Dost* test invites us to assume always to be present when we interpret

---

8   Others have argued that any phenomenon that seems to efface the boundary between supposedly separate notions such as innocence and sexuality that explains cultural obsessions with, say, 'child brides' (Stainton Rogers 1998, 196).

an image of a child. In Harvey's painting however, the violence takes the form of a real historical event committed by a perpetrator still living at the time of the exhibition, which he implicitly recreates using the children's handprints.

2. Gearon's Children as Sexually Precocious

The interplay between representation, desire and disgust that informs the arguments of Nead, Bataille and Young taken together do go some way towards explaining why Gearon's 'incredibly innocent' photographs caused so much controversy. However, the weakness of the discussion thus constructed is that in focusing on the significance and the use of the 'innocence' discourse, it emphasizes the position and gaze of the viewer to the cost of the people depicted in the images. Having explained the power of innocence – whether its allure in the form of sexual desire or disgust and dread at its perceived violation/corruption – we stand in need of an explanation of why this reading does not inevitably and finally *fix* their meaning. If we are to regard Gearon's photographs as art, and in being hung in the Saatchi gallery we are clearly being invited to do so, then they deserve to be dislodged from tabloid sensationalism. It is worth bearing in mind that the images themselves do not speak as such and, as Roland Barthes (1977, 39) argued, there is a certain terror associated with images whose connotative meaning remains unfixed. As Barthes himself puts it, 'traumatic images are bound up with an uncertainty (an anxiety) concerning the meaning of objects or attitudes.' Gearon's scenes of children playing games, laughing, urinating, interacting with other children and adults and so on cannot of themselves reveal their meaning. In any case, the images do not only depict children; the children, and adults also, appear always in a specific context and against a specific landscape. We are shown urban landscapes, snowy scenes, beaches, parks and rural settings, trailer parks, interiors and exteriors of houses and so on. All of these scenes could tell many different kinds of stories and may be open to all sorts of interpretations about the view of American life represented. Why should we be so interested primarily in the bodies that also appear? My own interest in these photographs and my interpretation of them as images of children and in particular children's naked bodies implicates me as much as the paedophile in imposing my own subjective reading on them. But even if we set aside the question of why we should focus on them as images of children and children's bodies primarily rather than, say, images of American suburban settings, we might still try to question the assumption underlying the tabloid reaction that the children in these photographs are inevitably powerless objects fixed by the paedophile's gaze. As we saw above, those critical of the exhibition read them as images of violence and victimization in which children were unknowingly made to display themselves in postures that in their innocence they could not have known would attract the lust of the paedophile. But that meaning is not in any way inevitable. Like any text, it is in the stories we tell about Gearon's photographs, or to put it another way only the sense that we as viewers bring to them that tells a story about what they are about. This is why it is not necessary to accept the view that they are in themselves violations of innocence or instances of sexual violence. In the previous chapter, the story of *Little Red Riding Hood* was re-interpreted as narrating a young girl's emergence as a subject of desire through gaining awareness of death and danger. There are obvious difficulties of a legal, ethical and political nature in attempting to interpret an account of a sexual encounter between an adult and a child as anything other than a serious crime and a violation. However, I believe that it is an association between awareness of death and the erotic identified by Freud and later by Bataille that helps us further to understand the controversy of Gearon's images as challenging patriarchal notions of the child as passive to and innocent of adult sexuality.

In re-reading Gearon's images I want to highlight the importance in the debate of the role of the subjective personalities of the children depicted, disconnecting them from the objectifying gaze of a supposed paedophile viewer. Masks such as those that appear in Gearon's photographs are used in storytelling, not merely to hide and disguise, but also to bring to light new characters and personalities. It is possible that Gearon's use of masks and light and dark can be read in this creative way, which does not hide the children's subjectivity so as much as play on it. In one photograph, the four year old boy stands in a confident pose, inquisitively regarding an old man whose face is obscured by a bird mask. In another, a baby watches a nearby adult with keen, focused eyes. In another, two children are shown hiding in the corner of a room. They are illuminated by a desk lamp and on the other side of the picture we see the dark shape of an adult – presumably searching for them – lurking in the shadows. The children are smiling and clearly enjoying a game of hide and seek. The overarching impression of the photographs is that the children are actively engaged in social intercourse both with each other and with the adults. Even in the image of the two children on the beach completely naked apart from their identical bimbo masks, we must acknowledge that the children are both looking directly at the camera. Although we cannot see their eyes, we know that they are in fact returning the viewer's gaze and thus resist being fully constituted by it. In this light, the children themselves take control of the elements of the image – including the bimbo masks which can be read as representing simply the play of identities that children adopt in games of role-play and make-believe on their journey of discovery and maturation.

However, the fact that the children are shown displaying their genitals seems to invite the viewer to interpret the playfulness as sexual precociousness, and where we might have seen only fun games of hide and seek and role-playing with masks, we might now see invitation for sexual activity. Such an implied invitation causes offence because a) it anticipates paedophilic desire in the viewer; and b) affirms this desire positively by returning the gaze. In other words, the indecency of the photographs lies in the challenge they throw out to the viewer's own self-identity:

rather than merely carrying the risk of being arousing to the sexually deviant paedophile, they appear in fact to invite the *normal* viewer to adopt the role of the paedophile. This is, I think, even more of an upsetting interpretation than the one discussed in the previous section (that of the images as violence against innocent children) because it undermines the ordinary viewer's very reason for looking. We have already seen how a child's very 'innocence' as depicted in 'ordinary settings' could lead courts in the US to judge that a photograph is not at all innocent if a paedophile might look at it with lust. According to the court in *Dost*, the same absurd assessments may also be made with regard to whether 'the visual depiction suggests sexual coyness or a willingness to engage in sexual activity' (at 832). Sexual coyness or a willingness to engage in sexual intercourse could be determined in obvious erotic posing, such as a 'come hither' look or whatever. But Gearon's photographs do not contain any erotic posing at all. Instead, the possibility of an erotic element to her images (other than the mundane fact of nudity which as I have said cannot in itself be erotic except for a paedophile) is provided by the danger that some of them arguably communicate, the possibility that the children, like Lolita herself, might themselves be complicit in a dangerous and erotic game. In the photograph showing the children hiding in a corner of a room the apparently innocuous game of hide and seek might be read as implying danger, possibly of a sexual nature, in the form of the dark and ominous shape of the adult. In the image of the two children on the beach wearing 'bimbo' masks, one of the children points a toy gun at the photographer/viewer, as if in playful self-defence – against whom?

Interpreted thus, Gearon's photographs are to be distinguished from the vast array of mainstream representations that Kincaid argues really do exploit 'childhood innocence' for the unacknowledged erotic pleasure of adults. James Kincaid (2000, 25) has argued provocatively that, since 'most adults in our culture feel some measure of erotic attraction to children and the childlike', there is a huge public demand for material that dwells on the child's body as an object of adult desire. However, mainstream audiences certainly do not want to identify with a child-molester, which means that depictions of the child as an object of lust must never threaten us with overt sexuality on the part of the child. Kincaid (2000, 94) argues that the demonization and scapegoating of the paedophile is convenient cover for mainstream society to unreflectively indulge in its own eroticization of children through the innocence fetish. For Kincaid, it is mainstream films such as *Home Alone, Sleepers, My Girl, Stand By Me*, and so on, and even classic novels such as *David Copperfield, The Catcher in the Rye* and *Tess of the D'Urbervilles* that really appeal to a paedophilic interest in children. These apparently non-erotic depictions of childhood and innocence are for Kincaid evidence of a deep and widespread exploitation of the erotic appeal of childhood innocence. Focusing upon the bodies and minds of children allows adults to look with a paedophiliac gaze on those bodies, safe in the knowledge that the real paedophiles are monstrous perverts who have nothing to do with us. 'Our culture has enthusiastically sexualized the child while denying just as enthusiastically that it was doing any such thing' he argues (Kincaid 2000, 13). Kincaid's commentary on popular culture is important in forming a critique of the innocence discourse.

> [D]esirable faces must be blank, drained of colour; big eyes round and expressionless; hair blond or colourless; waists, hips, feet, and minds small. The physical make up of the child has been translated into mainstream images of the sexually and materially alluring. (Kincaid 2000, 17–18)

Kincaid does not restrict himself to popular contemporary culture however. He sees children and young people everywhere depicted as blank, empty vessels, ready to be filled out with and violated by the mainstream viewer's erotic desire. Dickens's David Copperfield for example is 'so pure, so insistently empty, that we might have trouble not occupying him, taking him over' (Kincaid 1992, 306). Depictions of childhood that avoid controversy tend to be those that clearly separate the child's body from the viewer's desire by means of intervening adult characters. There needs to be a villainous adult for viewers to vilify and preferably also a rescuer figure who, being beyond reproach, viewers can comfortably identify with. Viewers certainly do not want to be asked to identify directly with a prurient interest in children's bodies. However, unlike Gearon's photography, Dickens was not initially condemned for producing pornography. This may be because, unlike Gearon's children, David Copperfield's helplessness in the rough hands of Mr Creakle and Mr Murdstone invites the reader to identifying with an imagined rescuer and thus can enjoy the torture without becoming complicit in it: 'We mistreat the child with one hand in order to perform a rescue with the other, but we may never get around to rescuing, so enticing is the torture' (Kincaid 1992, 308). In Gearon's photographs, the viewer is being asked to identify positively with these scenes of potential violence, and if, as some critics did, the scenes are interpreted as scenes of danger acted out – possibly even sexual danger – then this invitation to associate is uncomfortable. The image thus becomes indecent in the eyes of some people because there is no mediation between the viewer of the image and the apparent act of child molestation being depicted as normal and enjoyable for all.

What arguably makes Gearon's images controversial in the eyes of some people then, is the coincidence of playful danger and nudity, which the children seem to find enjoyable, even exciting. The photographs themselves do not need to have been intended to be erotic in order to convey this effect to some viewers. It is enough that in the combination of these elements, certain viewers feel an uncomfortable jarring against the more familiar presentation of children as innocent. It is an explanation for the furore regarding Gearon's work that other critics have identified in the reception of other works. For example, Martha C. Nussbaum considers why works by James Joyce and D.H. Lawrence were initially condemned by critics as obscene or disgusting: although sexually explicit in parts (and on this point distinguishable from Gearon's photographs anyway), works such as *Ulysses* and *Lady Chatterley's Lover* caused initial controversy because, as Nussbaum (1999, 41) writes, they 'asked their readers to look at the body; the reader's antecedent disgust with the body (especially the female body) gets projected back onto the work, as a way of warding off the challenge it poses'. For Nussbaum (1999, 42–4) it is ironically the *lack* of disgust for the female body in these works that posed such a challenge for and hence indignation from their contemporary critics (and arguably that later guaranteed their acceptance into the canon of serious literature) and distinguished them from the truly degrading treatment of women in pornography. A similar explanation applies to Nabokov's *Lolita* and the two film adaptations of that novel. *Lolita* was first published in Paris in 1955, Nabokov having first been refused by four American publishers, and was initially banned in the UK and France. Stanley Kubrick spoke in interview of his frustration at having to dilute the eroticism between the adult male professor Humbert Humbert and Lolita in his 1962 adaptation in order that the film could be given a certificate at all. Major film distributors who were worried about the risk of bad publicity initially refused the 1997 film starring Jeremy Irons. The reason why *Lolita* caused such offence was not that it depicted a child in a sexual setting. Rather, it was because it suggested that the child involved was not ignorant of Humbert's paedophilic intentions, but in fact desired to explore her own sexuality through her association with him. *Lolita* was difficult for mainstream audiences and critics to digest because like Carter's *The Company of Wolves* or for that matter Larry Clark's film *Kids* (1995), it presented the girl not merely as a passive object but a *subject* of desire as well, and furthermore prepared to take serious risks in the pursuit of fulfilment. Because Lolita is depicted as returning the adult male's proscribed desire for her, the story seems positively to affirm paedophilia and thus implies that the reader/viewer might also feel the same way. If the story could have depicted Lolita as a mere victim of Humbert's manipulation, then it would not cause offence, but would conform to the bourgeois notion of sexuality that makes Perrault's *Little Red Riding Hood*, for all its innuendo, acceptable as reading for a mainstream audience. Gearon's children's bodies are presented without disgust; they challenge the viewer to look upon the naked body of the child. It is therefore precisely *because* these photographs may be interpreted in the absence of the innocence motif that they have suffered a hostile reception in some quarters. Innocence certainly has erotic appeal as I have discussed but it would be wrong to think of Gearon's photographs as exploiting this.

It is a bizarre consequence of this argument that the more 'innocent' the depiction of the child, the more suspicious it becomes. In applying Kincaid's argument, it is important that we find ways of escaping his rather nauseating reading of texts that in casting the generalized reader as paedophile-voyeur cannot help but dumb it down to the level of tacky smut. Like Humbert himself, Kincaid invites readers everywhere to confess their own grief at the loss of the child when, for example, David Copperfield or Holden Caulfield grow up. Referring to the former, Kincaid (1992, 309) writes: 'the child vanishes from us, probably accounting for the fact that we find the rest of the book a sad falling-off'. It is easy to balk, as I did, at Kincaid's seemingly crass and sweeping dismissal of a vast swathe of classical literature and popular culture as voyeuristic or as pandering to latent mainstream mass-paedophilia. However, in the light of Kincaid's identification of the voyeuristic gaze of the reader/viewer, we can see the sexual duplicity of, say, Perrault's version of the *Little Red Riding Hood* story, offering readers titillation by focusing their attention on the young girl's body whilst at the same time denying any such motive by casting her as lacking any desire of her own. In Perrault's *Little Red Riding Hood* just as in the mainstream novels and films discussed by Kincaid, erotic undertones can be brushed over because the object of desire herself shows no precociousness and therefore no affirmation of paedophilic desire in the reader. While we can view the child as a victim in need of rescue we can enjoy the tale and the body of the violated girl voyeuristically without being implicated in the violence of the crime described. What the mainstream films cited by Kincaid have in common is that they allow the adult audience to identify with the responsible adult associated with the child, possibly rescuing the child from the clutches of a paedophile. *Lolita* cannot fit into this bracket of films because the audience's interest in the child is not mediated by this acceptable adult character. Instead it asks the viewer to identify directly (or at least to sympathise with) the child molester whose defence is that the child in question was an active participant in her own seduction, and hence the offence it caused. If the children of Gearon's pictures are comparable to *Lolita*, then it is not at all difficult to see why they caused the controversy that they did.

Conclusion

In this chapter I have argued that the way in which we deploy the idea of innocence, and in particular how we identify innocence in the characters of stories and images, provides a useful way of reflecting critically on our own current troubled preoccupation with the image of the child and how to interpret it. I have argued that the language of innocence and corruption has much to answer for in warping cultural and social attitudes towards images of children. As long as children are constructed as 'innocents', we will continue to worry that images like Gearon's are in fact images of sexual exploitation – which either expose children to a malignant paedophilic gaze or else offensively accuse the ordinary viewer of latent paedophilic desire. Whether a child is depicted as lively or blank does not really matter regarding the cultural anxiety about child pornography; in a society that identifies the child's body with sexuality, the image of such a body is caught up in a discourse of sexual perversion either way through the prizing of innocence. If it is the discourse of innocence that I have described that informs our perspective, then what we see in any image of a child is the capacity to be corrupted, and their innocence to be lost forever. It is a discourse which, as we saw in the context of both US law (*US v Dost*) and English law (*R v Graham-Kerr*) ensures that the fear that the innocence of the child might incite sexual desire and thus sexualize the image in fact *causes* sexualization by imposing the paedophile's desire onto the image. Just as Grimm's tales can be re-read in order to spot not merely the unpreparedness and ignorance of the child protagonists but also their ingenuity, bravery and developing autonomy, so photographs of and other images of children that would seem suspicious from an 'innocence' perspective can be re-read or re-viewed in such a way that does not violently replace the child's own subjectivity with that of an adult viewer.

Chapter 6

'I must not let anyone in; the seven dwarves have forbidden me to do so': The Violence of Innocence

Fairytales undoubtedly derive much of their dramatic tension, as well as their moral character, from the theme of the honest, hard-working family that comes to be threatened by dangers lurking outside. As a place of safety, comprising its own patriarchal moral and legal order, the home is a neat and easy metaphor for the moral certainties that fairytales appear to herald. That which lies outside the home, in the dark forest away from the reassuring glow of the oil lamp certainly cannot be innocent or it could not survive. It is therefore likely to be malevolent and must not be trusted too easily. It must not be allowed in to harm those inside the home with the tricks or disguises it uses to gain entry. In medieval times, in which one generation of peasants in remote European rural communities used folk tales to warn the next of the very real dangers of the forest, the advice was often intended to be as much pragmatic as entertaining. Looked at this way, the tales of wicked stepmothers who seek to murder or expel the children out of spite or jealousy narrate the same theme as those in which beasts of the forest – the wolves and bears of which those remote medieval peasant communities lived in fear – all are threats to the fragile sense of safety fostered by the family and its home. However, at the same time this neat sense of moral coherence between the familiar and the sinister is not quite so straightforward. Fairytales are very often marked by an anxiety that threats to the moral integrity of family life come from within the family itself: Red Riding Hood finds a wolf where her grandmother ought to be; the wicked queen that becomes murderous with jealousy for her stepdaughter Snow White is the same woman that brought the little girl up almost from birth; when Sleeping Beauty pricks her finger, her father leaves her to the mercy of fate. There are also tales, less familiar now due to their more difficult plotlines, of incestuous desire in which kings bankrupt their kingdoms in order to win the heart of their own daughter. In our own society this anxiety is reflected all too clearly. We worry that our children will be snatched away by a paedophile lurking outside on the streets, and react indignantly when a responsible parent is separated from their children unnecessarily (Pope 2008). But on the other hand we fear that the mistreatment of children by irresponsible or cruel families may go unnoticed because of the incompetence of local child services and react with fury when Social Services fail to avert a child's death. This chapter examines the moral link between the ways in which we read this home/forest or inside/outside distinction in both fairytales and in public discourse about child safety. I argue here that the binary distinction between that which originates from the home itself on the one hand and that which comes from outside the home provides a way of understanding our own attitudes towards distinguishing different kinds of violence against children. In an age in which children may be lawfully assaulted for the sake of discipline so long as the violence is deemed 'reasonable', and yet the physical abuse against children is also considered one of the worst possible offences, there is certainly a need to reflect critically upon the moral categorization of violence in society and how it comes about. The discussion of fairytales here is directed towards defining what is meant by 'reasonable' violence on the one hand therefore in the interests of families and children more broadly, and excessive or cruel violence on the other.

1. Reasonable Violence: Protecting the Home and Family Life

a) Learning the Hard Way: Physical Suffering as Moral Education in Fairytale

One way in which Grimm's tales in particular promote their particularly favoured idea of the family as a productive bourgeois unit is by depicting the various trials and tribulations of their protagonists that eventually lead to their gaining maturity and wisdom. Although we might expect our Snow Whites and Little Red Caps ultimately to survive the finale of a Grimm tale, they are nevertheless made to suffer along the way. Written down in an age in which parents were permitted to use a far greater degree of force to chastise their children than is the case today, it is not surprising that Grimm's moral tales for instilling the right values in bourgeois children are characterized by often severe and sometimes life-threatening violence. The fairytales suggest that the stability of the family may be strengthened by the reasonable chastisement of immature characters if it brings them into line with expectations. Bettelheim (1976, 173), whose critical response to the tales is characterized by his belief in their educative function, argues that the girl's punishment in Grimm's *Little Red Cap* by being eaten is right because by her own weakness and lack of wit she directed the wolf to her grandmother's house. The experience of being eaten (or whatever else we are supposed to imagine) teaches girls that to practise self-restraint and obey instructions is to protect oneself from the dangers of the world (Bettelheim 1976, 182). Bettelheim (1976, 183) writes that characters such as Little Red Riding Hood and Snow White are 'twice-born' in order to gain the independence and wisdom to deal with 'future wolves'. As a story, *Snow White* is like *Little Red Cap* inasmuch as it is about the development of values proper to family life (a little girl learns to be less narcissistic and more caring). It goes beyond *Little Red Cap* however in that through the contrasting fates of the stepmother queen and the girl she tries to kill, it provides a lesson on just deserts. Whilst the stepmother queen ends her life in agony and despair dancing on red hot shoes, Snow White is eventually married to the handsome prince. The lesson that one should care for others applies both to the queen and Snow White, although it is only actually learned by the latter. Snow White, although showing weakness in allowing herself to be tricked into disobeying the dwarves' injunction not to open the door to strangers, must endure three apparent deaths and a lengthy spell in a comatose state before she can awaken as a new woman. Three times she is tricked by the stepmother queen (disguised as an old woman) into accepting various items that turn out to poison and choke her. Bettelheim (1976, 203) argues that in being made to suffer in this way, Snow White is being punished for being dangerously self-absorbed. The reason why the jealous queen so easily overcomes her three times is because Snow White is herself obsessed by her own beauty and therefore cannot resist the old woman's gifts. The comb and the brooch promise to make her look even more beautiful, and the shiny apple with its bright red half that the girl bites, may represent sexuality (Bettelheim 1976, 209). Snow White's apparent death by poisoning is a plot device that Bettelheim identifies as being shared also by *Sleeping Beauty* and *Little Red Riding Hood*: the protagonist is punished for her immaturity by being forced to spend a period of time out of the world (the hundred year sleep in *Sleeping Beauty*, the time spent in the wolf's belly in *Little Red Riding Hood*, the period of unconsciousness in *Snow White*) in order to be reborn chastened and ready to obey and serve a husband (the prince who finally rescues her) (Bettelheim 1976, 213).

Such an interpretation of the tales as being about the imaginative education of children makes a certain moral sense. However, Bettelheim seems to assume that fairytales are simply this and are thus primarily stories for children. This is probably why Bettelheim does not address the broader questions regarding fairytales as myths: their implications for gender or the patriarchal overtones of such plots, although feminist critiques have been offered more recently by other commentators.[1] The theme of physical suffering as education is taken to extreme lengths in certain modern versions of the fairytales. In Anne Rice's erotic retelling of Sleeping Beauty as a story about S&M, *Claiming Sleeping Beauty*, 'Beauty' learns the virtues of unquestioning obedience to her prince through being thoroughly and absolutely dominated in a series of publicly humiliating sexual and violent rituals. Not only does he determine the when and where of their own sexual activity, he also forces her to eat her meals from the floor like a dog, naked except for a chain that he holds, and invites strangers to beat her on the buttocks and molest her while he watches. The brutal prince prohibits Beauty from ever complaining about his methods: '"You must never protest", he repeated. "Not with sound, not with gesture. Only your tears may show your prince what you feel"' (Rice 1999, 18). Whenever Beauty displeases her prince he punishes her with a savage beating. Despite its explicitly erotic content, this modern story of cruel domination can be categorized as conforming to traditional fairytale morality in some crucial ways. It presents the violence suffered by its innocent young protagonist as necessary for her passage from childhood to adulthood and the autonomy that comes with this passage which is got through suffering on

---

1   See discussion in Chapter 4 of Angela Carter (1996), Christina Bacchilega (1997), Susan Sellers (2001) and Maria Aristodemou (1999).

account of the actions of more powerful characters. If Bettelheim is correct to say that Red Riding Hood's being eaten and Snow White's three temporary 'deaths' are warranted punishment for their failure to obey instructions, then the ultimate survival and flourishing of the Beauty of Anne Rice's story is properly regarded as consequent upon, not despite of, her physical trials.

b) Reasonable Violence in the Life of a Child

The idea of reasonable violence that comes to us from Grimm's fairytales, first published as they were at a time when to give boy a good thrashing for a minor offence was not unusual, strikes many modern readers as absurdly cruel. In English common law, the remarkably durable nineteenth century case of *R v Hopley* set out the correctional defence to assault by Cockburn CJ as 'moderate and reasonable chastisement may be used to correct what is evil in a child but such punishment should be neither excessive nor protracted'. Cockburn CJ held that *un*reasonable (and therefore unlawful) chastisement was force applied 'for the gratification of passion or rage' (206). The defence is now unavailable for the use of force on children by third parties outside the home.[2] However, in *R v H (Assault of Child: Reasonable Chastisement)* the Court of Appeal affirmed that in the home, the old common law formulation continued to apply since Cockburn CJ's dictum was flexible enough to be applied in a modern context, such as the exclusion of force that leaves bruises or other signs of harm from the definition of 'reasonable'.[3] Reasonable chastisement claims it own justification through the same moral distinction that we see drawn in the tales. That is to say, if violence can be interpreted as necessary to bring about conformity with a desired standard that is itself authoritative then it is itself productive rather than destructive. As a moral perspective this view seems to justify not only the smacking of one's children in order to enforce discipline, but also a more relaxed attitude to violence that strays into the realms of the *un*reasonable, legally speaking. Researchers Keenan and Maitland (1999) report that police and the Crown Prosecution Service (CPS) often take the view that, since a degree of physical violence is lawful for parents and a degree of physical violence is a normal part of family life, authorities ought not be overly concerned to police the 'boundaries' of what is reasonable. One officer said in interview that, whilst an offence would probably be committed if there was constant hitting, 'if you've got a one-off, it's not their fault and provided the child's not severely injured, then I don't think that there is role for us because realistically you would have to say that most children, if not all, get smacked by their parents at

---

2   See the Education Act (No. 2) 1986 (state schools), the Schools Standards and Framework Act 1998 (private schools) and the Day Care and Child Minding (National standards) (England) Regulations 2003 (child minders and day care nursery carers).

3   It looks like it will continue to do so in England and Wales after MPs in Westminster voted against a proposal to ban smacking, as reported by *Epolitix* ('MPs Fail to Impose Smacking Ban' 2008).

some time in their lives' (Keenan and Maitland 1999, [3])⁴ Cases involving older children and signs of remorse on the part of the parent at losing control in cases of physical violence would be treated sympathetically, as suggested by these two officers when interviewed:

> when you are looking at a 15-year-old girl ... it gets back to, if a parent is at the end of his tether, which all parents must get to, then it would be silly to think that the police would intervene every time a parent hit a child.

> He was saying that he wanted her to have good moral values and discipline ... and I suppose I admired him for trying to do his best for his child really ... I certainly disagree with the way he went about it, his behaviour was inappropriate and wrong, but I also felt he was trying to do a good job. (Keenan and Maitland 1999, [6])

Whether or not it is right to hit one's children to discipline them is something of a polarizing debate. A perceived increase in violent crime and antisocial behaviour committed by young people in recent years does seem to have hardened attitudes, at least for certain journalists (Womack 2006; Robertson 2008). For their own part, Keenan and Maitland (1999, [9]) accept with disapproval that while sexual abuse is rightly considered to be always unacceptable (both in law and measured public opinion), physical violence in the form of hitting and chastisement is still widely considered to be acceptable within certain boundaries.⁵ Keenan and Maitland (1999, [9]) are of the view that 'we should be concerned about any development which could make a child complainant who has been physically assaulted feel that what has happened to him is considered to be less bad than if he has been sexually assaulted by an adult'. There are two issues here – whether the existing reasonable chastisement defence is right in itself, and secondly how investigating officers ought to determine when excessive force amounts to prosecutable abuse. Although we should be careful not to confuse these two as legal questions, in moral terms they are linked by the notion of the family as a place where a certain level of violence is tolerated. Keenan and Maitland's research focused on investigations into allegations of physical assaults that would, if taken to trial, probably exceed the level of force justified as 'reasonable chastisement'. What is significant about the research is that the officers who advocated declining to prosecute isolated incidents of excessive force justified their opinion through their view of family life as inherently violent from time to time, and that the common acceptance of 'reasonable' chastisement means that there will inevitably be times when this crosses into more severe force. But surely the ubiquity of a harmful act should

---

4   Page references to Keenan and Maitland article in square brackets refer to downloaded source.

5   For example, they report that Creighton and Russell found that 72 per cent of surveyed adults responded that 'a slap was a justifiable way of punishing a child for misbehaviour'.

not necessarily mean it is of no public concern, any more than the frequency of any offence excuses it. After all, child sexual abuse is apparently also very widespread – and according to some may even be the majority experience (as reported sceptically by Kincaid 2000, 252) – but in this case few would claim that it is therefore trivial. As I have been arguing in this chapter, determining which kinds of violence are to be tolerated and which are to be regarded as abuse has nothing to do with how widespread they are, but rather depends upon a moral notion about secure and productive family life that we derive in part from from fairytales.

The general landscape of debate regarding the 'reasonable chastisement' – whether it is right in principle or is discriminatory against children and a violation of their human dignity and bodily integrity, whether in practice it serves an educational purpose or in fact merely reinforces beliefs about the positive use of violence and negative beliefs about children – are thoroughly discussed elsewhere and I shall not go into detail about them here. Neither will I consider the extent to which reasonable chastisement is consistent with international conventions on human rights.[6] There remains a widespread view that there are good reasons to preserve the defence, which relate to the bourgeois moral idea promoting the productive family life. This idea has been debated in the legal sphere, in some countries at the highest level of judicial authority. Take, for example the constitutional appeal of *Canadian Foundation for Children, Youth and Law v Canada (Attorney General)* in which the Canadian Supreme Court ruled by a majority that 'reasonable chastisement' by way of smacking of children aged between 2 and 12 years by parents and teachers, legalized by s.43 of the Criminal Code did not violate the Canadian Charter of Rights and Freedoms or any international obligation relating to child welfare. The majority judgment delivered by McLachlin CJ is largely informed by what he felt to be a reasonable interpretation of what society at large would regard as acceptable in the interests of preserving the privacy of the family and the child's need for a family free from heavy-handed interference from the criminal law. He states that his reluctance to allow 'minor disciplinary contacts' on children to be subject to the general prohibition of non-consensual assaults is justified by the 'impact this would have on the interests of the child and on family and school relationships. Parliament's choice not to criminalize this conduct does not devalue or discriminate against children, but responds to the reality of their lives by addressing their need for safety and security in an age-appropriate manner' [51]. In McLachlin CJ's view, the harm that might be suffered by a child through being subject to lawful physical chastisement must be balanced against the harm suffered both by the child and the *family as a whole* if that chastisement were treated like ordinary criminal assaults: 'Children also depend on parents and

---

6   The European Convention of Human Rights 1950, art. 3 prohibits 'torture and degrading treatment', as does the International Covenant on Civil and Political Rights 1966, art. 7. The United Nations Convention on the Rights of the Child 1989, art. 19(1) requires all states to 'protect the child from all forms of physical or mental violence, injury or abuse, neglect or negligent treatment, maltreatment or exploitation …'

teachers for guidance and discipline, to protect them from harm and to promote their healthy development within society. A stable and secure family and school setting is essential to this growth process' [58]. The dual emphasis on health and a secure environment to encourage its growth speaks very much to the idea of the family a unit of production and the court's duty being to sanction whatever best removes the weeds of violence without damaging the precious flower of family life. In this regard the criminal law is a 'blunt instrument' which is appropriately engaged to 'punish force that harms children, is part of a pattern of abuse, or is simply the angry or frustrated imposition of violence against children', but if used in response to 'transient or trifling impact ... that is part of a genuine effort to educate the child' [59], then it 'risks ruining lives and breaking up families – a burden that in large part would be borne by children and outweigh any benefit derived from applying the criminal process' [62].

Although denying that upholding the legality of reasonable chastisement amounts to moral approval of the smacking of children – McLachin CJ prefers to justify his decision by referring to the 'lived experience' of the child [60], the 'critical need of all children for a safe environment' [58] and the 'reality of their lives' [51] – the Chief Justice's speech surely appeals to a moral theory of the home as I have described it here. As both critics and dissenting judges in the same appeal have pointed out, from a liberal individualistic perspective there are compelling moral reasons for regarding a law that removes legal protection from one particular group of people to be a violation of their rights and dignity.[7] The view expressed by the majority of the Canadian Supreme Court in this case depends on accepting an interpretation of the rights of the child that places the family unit as a whole on the same level as the individual child. This logic is accepted even by the part-dissenting Binnie J. On the one hand, Binnie J expresses his grave 'difficulty with the proposition that a child 'needs' correction through conduct that, but for s.43, amounts to a criminal assault' [102], and insists further that in his view 'to deny protection [against physical force] at the hands of their parents, parent-substitutes and teachers is not only disrespectful of a child's dignity but turns the child, for the purposes of the *Criminal Code*, into a 'second-class citizen' [109]. But on the other hand, he nevertheless concedes just a few paragraphs later that 'the intervention of the police or criminal courts in a child's home in respect of 'reasonable' correction would inhibit rather than encourage the resolution of problems within families' [113]. This is certainly a dramatic softening of his initially fierce defence of the child's right to be defended against the use of any force by adults. The distance between his initial furious rejection of McLachlin CJ's interpretation of the child's 'needs' and his eventual support of the reasonable chastisement exception must

---

7   See the judgment of Binnie J (dissenting in part), para. [72]; also para. [106] – 'Few things are more demeaning and disrespectful of fundamental values than to withdraw the full protection of the *Criminal Code* against deliberate, forcible, unwanted violation of an individual's physical integrity.'

indicate just how powerfully the moral idea of family integrity continues to influence views about the place of violence within family life.

2. Excessive, Dangerous and Unjust Violence Against Children

a) Innocence and Experience in Morally Distinguishing the Characters of a Story: The Victoria Climbié Report and its Legacy

I remarked in Chapter 4 that in the fairytales, villains and heroes share a common trait – they are proactive and passionate in pursuit of their goals and knowledgeable about the dangers and opportunities of the world. Grimm's disguised wolves, jealous stepmothers, evil sorcerers and so on that people the tales are all driven by feverish activity in bringing about the object of their desire – namely the destruction of an innocent heroine. The character that we would recognize as *heroic* in these tales is not the innocent child who unwittingly and passively allows herself to stray into danger, but the manly figure of the rescuer who acts to defend the home and prevent its destruction. Typical of the heroic type is the woodcutter who cuts Little Red Cap and her Grandmother from the wolf's belly; the handsome prince who discovers the body of Snow White and brings her back to life; the travelling prince who cuts through the magical forest of thorns to wake Sleeping Beauty with a kiss. How would we feel about the woodcutter if, upon suspecting something amiss in the forest, he had decided to give the wolf the benefit of the doubt, not wishing to interfere? Or about the adventuring prince who decided that the thorns surrounding Sleeping Beauty's castle were just too sharp and tangled to be bothered to hack through? Naturally we would feel thoroughly dissatisfied. As readers, we distinguish not so much between heroes and villains, but between the innocent and the knowing – the passive and the active. This distinction between the innocent (passive) protagonist and the knowing (active) villain/hero can help us understand our attitudes towards issues relating to child welfare today, and this is where we consider the case of Victoria Climbié (2000, Haringey, North London, in which the abuse and neglect of a little girl led to a Parliamentary report on the failings of the Social Services and caused widespread public dismay) and the depressingly similar case eight years later of 'Baby P' (2008, Haringey, North London, on which a serious case review was scheduled to report at the end of March 2009). In January 2000, 8-year-old Victoria Climbié died of cardiac arrest and multiple organ failure, reported to be caused by 'hypothermia, which had arisen in the context of malnourishment, a damp environment and restricted movement' (Laming 2003, 36). In his report, Lord Laming identified that the central reason for Victoria's death (apart from the dire cruelty of her great-aunt Marie-Therese Kouao and Kouao's partner Carl John Manning who were convicted of her murder) was the inadequacy of Social Services in failing to identify that she was in grave danger and in taking no effective action to remove her to safety. Every mention that Lord Laming makes of Social Services alludes to the fact that, although they had plenty of contact with Victoria and Kouao and opportunities to take action, they failed to do so. Below are some quotations from the report that illustrate the crucial importance of knowledge and activity in Laming's narrative:

> The bathroom in Manning's flat was small and the door opened out onto the living room. There was no window and, although there was a heater, it was either broken or unused. When Victoria was inside, the door was kept closed and the light was switched off. She began to spend her nights alone, cold and in pitch darkness.

> However, Ms Arthurworrey [a social worker] noticed nothing untoward when she made the second of her two pre-announced home visits to Somerset Gardens on 28 October 1999. ... Victoria seems to have been all but ignored during this visit as she sat on the floor playing with a doll. The fact that she was still not attending school was raised during the conversation, but no questions seem to have been asked about how Victoria was spending her days. (Laming 2003, 33)

> The dreadful reality was that these services knew little or nothing more about Victoria at the end of the process than they did when she was first referred to Ealing Social Services. ... The extent of the failure to protect Victoria was lamentable. Tragically, it required nothing more than basic good practice being put into operation. This never happened. (3)

The failure of the council services to obtain the knowledge that would have been necessary to save Victoria's life was a failure, as Lord Laming (2003, 6) said, of leadership, staff skills and structures. In November 2008 a baby named as 'Baby P' died of a skull fracture and his various other injuries, including a broken back, fractured ribs, missing nails and bruises, were widely reported (*Economist* 2008, 40). The media almost unanimously condemned the inadequacy of the same local area child services which, having largely implemented Lord Laming's recommendations of 2000, should have been able to prevent the tragedy. In contrast to the sheer lack of activity blamed for the local council's inadequacy in 2000, the media reported that Baby P was seen several times and observations were recorded and communicated. What seems to have gone wrong this time was that the information gathered was naively interpreted giving the benefit of the doubt to the apparently 'chaotic but loving' family. The baby's broken back went undiagnosed despite an examination by a paediatrician because Baby P was 'too cranky' to be properly examined. Chocolate smeared on the baby's body successfully hid from social workers most of the bruising (*Economist* 2008, 40). A doctor who examined Baby P in hospital noted that he should not be allowed to return home, but failed to ensure that his advice was taken. Baby P was reported in *The Guardian* as 'being seen 60 times by social and health workers. Each one meticulously recorded their concern' (Jenkins 2008). For the tabloids the inaction of Haringey Social Services in failing to prevent the death of Baby P shows that they now have 'blood on their hands' ('Baby P Petition reaches 850,000' 2008); the liberal broadsheet press spoke of 'reticence on the part of professionals' and a tendency to be 'insufficiently assertive with parents' when investigating suspicions of abuse (Brindle 2008).

In both of these upsetting child abuse cases then, the observations of Lord Laming and the media indicate that the local services' moral fault was in failing to show the characteristics of a competent rescuer in the mould of the wood-cutter in *Little Red Cap*. What would have been expected of Social Services was not necessarily that they acted heroically (since heroism is, with good reason, never expected as a standard of care) but that they had shown some of the characteristics of the knowledgeable saviour. If the woodcutter that had been keeping an eye on the wolf's movements had entered the Grandmother's house and upon seeing the newly fattened beast decided to assume that no action was necessary (leaving Grandmother and Little Red Cap to dissolve and digest in the wolf's belly), we would be justified in thinking that there was something wrong with the moral coherence of the story. It is for this reason that the story of Victoria Climbié as it is narrated in the report – whose cuts, bruises, bites and burns were not hidden to Social Services but explained away as 'self-inflicted' – sits so uneasily with anyone who reads it. This is also why reports of the failure to diagnose Baby P's broken back or to notice that chocolate smeared on his body hid bruises generated such outraged comment in 2008. No-one on the front line or leadership of social services in either case was accused of doing anything wilfully wrong. Their crime was to do nothing; they *did no harm* and yet terrible harm resulted from their failure to respond adequately to the available signs of harm. To put it another way, they showed too much innocence when knowledge and activity were required. In contrast to the inaction of social services, the behaviour of Marie-Therese Kouao – Victoria Climbié's great aunt who later became her guardian – and that of the family in the later case of Baby P conform to the villain of fairytale narrative. Kouao was reported to be not merely neglectful as a guardian, but also devious, cruel, jealous, and most importantly of all *active* in all of these things. We learn of her frequent changes of address – taking Victoria from Ivory Coast to France, then to England, and then moving in with her new partner Manning. We learn how Kouao actively deceived a social worker from Tottenham child services – first by preparing her house especially for the visit concealing the fact that Victoria was made to sleep in a plastic bag in the bath and later her efforts to qualify for re-housing by the north Tottenham local council by falsely alleging that Manning had sexually abused Victoria (Laming 2003, 33). However, the Laming Report's focus upon her canny manipulation of the council's child welfare and housing services are important, not just in charting a series of events leading up to Victoria's eventual death, but also in characterizing Kouao as a true villain. The reader is left in no doubt that, like the sly wolf and the murderously jealous stepmother, Marie-Therese Kouao's very soul is consumed with malignant desire. Likewise in 2008, Baby P's mother, boyfriend and lodger, all convicted of 'causing or allowing the death of a child', were archetypes of villainous cunning, described as 'very clever', and as having pulled off a 'skilful deceit' in outwitting the authorities for so long (Brindle 2008).

b) The 'False' Family Relation and their Dangers

Marina Warner (1994) has remarked on the way in which the fairytales may have served to narrate the difficulties that accompany the cohabitation of different generations and also the joining of families through remarriage. Amongst the peasant families from which the Grimms claimed to have collected their tales, the frequency of deaths of young women in childbirth led to a higher number of men seeking second wives to take care of their children. It was also traditional for surviving elderly relations to be looked after by younger family members (and their spouses). Both situations could be fraught with familial conflict: resentment on the part of the younger woman for her husband's mother and the older woman's anxiety about being abandoned by the young (Warner 1994, 228). Warner argues that the two situations might both be narrated together in the tales, since until the nineteenth century the expressions 'stepmother' and 'mother-in-law' were often used interchangeably to distinguish the birth mother from other women who otherwise took on the role of mother (Warner 1994, 219). This is an explanation for the great frequency of a wicked 'step' relation (usually mother) to provide the villain of many fairytale plotlines. Warner's historical analysis has shown that in the years preceding Grimm's first collection of 1812, the tales involving stepmothers and mothers in law served as a warning to younger generations that the older family members should not be ignored or abandoned (Warner 1994, 236–8).

Other commentators have suggested that the 'step' relation is simply a literary device – perhaps added by Grimm himself – for narrating violence without compromising his idealization of the bourgeois family (Zipes 1988, 121). Whatever the correct explanation, the fact that it is a 'step' relation that is to blame for family strife is essential to the identification of cruel, excessive, dangerous violence, coming as it does from outside the family and not from within it, which would undermine the moral integrity of the very idea of family and thus of Grimm's project as a whole. Grimm must have realized this shortly after publishing the first edition of his collection, since only in the first edition of 1812 is the character of the jealous queen Snow White's actual birth mother (McGlathery 1991, 122; Zipes 1988, 120–7). The moral culpability of the stepmother character is that she has usurped both the mother's role by attempting to harm the children she is meant to protect and the father's role as master of the house. The threat she poses to the patriarchal order of the home and her wilfulness marks her out as an archetypal villain who must be destroyed at the end of the story. Her repeated destruction in the range of tales narrates the constant vigilance necessary to prevent the intrusion of danger into the home as the environment in which children learn that society is naturally patriarchal. This is why the threat to the home so often takes the form of a woman: in seeking to harm rather than nurture, and to effect events rather than passively wait to be helped, wicked stepmothers are the very antithesis of bourgeois femininity. A good woman in Grimm's view is one who accepts her place in Freud's gendered scheme of sexual development, accepting her lack of a physical means (i.e. a penis) of fully associating with patriarchal authority and internalizing her role as wife and mother (Freud 1991, 321). The rejection of the wilful or strong-minded matriarch – the 'phallic mother' – is central to the triumph of patriarchy as understood by feminists who use psychoanalytic theory (Barnett 1998, 152). If fairytales are readable as myths in the same way as the Greek drama discussed in Chapter 2, then the defeat of the wicked stepmother that makes possible Snow White's successful passage from childhood into adult married life represents women's association with the castrated woman (that is, with the patriarchal ideal of feminine as passively accepting of male authority) and acceptance of her secondary place in society. From a patriarchal perspective, the wicked stepmother represents the dangerous and lamentable failure of natural family affection and thus moral culpability. Unable to accept her place as second wife to a widower and carer of his children, the stepmother is commonly a catalyst for violence in the home that the fairytale logic tends to see punished in the final moments. In *Snow White*, the voice of the mirror drives the stepmother queen wild with jealousy, and we can read that voice as reflecting the queen's own failure to overcome her vanity and narcissism (McGlathery 1991, 122). In this story it illustrates the queen's moral failings as one who has never been able to embrace the joys of family life, which would have brought her to see her own image in the context of her care for others. As such a character, she is incapable of regarding Snow White as her daughter in need of love, but only as a reminder of her own fading beauty.

Violence that undermines family life is not monopolized by the stepmother/step-daughter relation. Other well-known tales create other kinds of false family relations. As discussed in Chapter 4, when the protagonist of the various versions of the *Little Red Riding Hood* story arrives at her Grandmother's house she finds not the safety of a home from home but rather the wolf waiting to pounce on her. In Perrault's version particularly, it is clear that Red Riding Hood has unwittingly directed the wolf there and the Grandmother invited him in. However, is it possible that the wolf was *already* living the cottage – before the story began, perhaps even before Little Red Riding Hood was born? Recall that in Angela Carter's modern retelling of the story in *The Werewolf*, the girl manages to fend off the wolf that attacks her in the forest by chopping off its front right paw. When she reaches the isolated cottage a little later, she finds her grandmother in a near-delirious fit of fever. The girl unwraps the piece of cloth in which she had stored the wolf's severed paw to make a cold press and the 'paw' drops out:

> But it was no longer a wolf's paw. It was a hand, chopped off at the wrist, a hand toughened with work and freckled with old age. There was a wedding ring on the third finger and a wart in the index finger. By the wart, she knew it for her grandmother's hand.

She pulled back the sheet but the old woman woke up, at that, and began to struggle, squawking and shrieking like a thing possessed. But the child was strong, and armed with her father's hunting knife; she managed to hold her grandmother down long enough to see the cause of her fever. There was a bloody stump where her right hand should have been, festering already. (Carter 1996, 19–20)

This is a disturbing course of events. Whereas in Grimm and Perrault the wolf and Grandmother are clearly different characters, Angela Carter's *The Werewolf* suggests that the wolf's disguise is not merely grandmother's nightcap, nightdress and glasses, but grandmother herself. Angela Carter's story alludes to the historical fact that remote medieval and early modern peasant communities of Europe did live in fear of wild animals such as wolves and that a popular association between wolves and the devil sustained a belief in werewolves. Records indicate that it was not uncommon in the sixteenth and seventeenth centuries for an accusation of being a werewolf to be used as a form of scapegoating, and fears of possession by the devil are narrated in other folk tales that have survived (Zipes 1991, 28–9). It is possible that, in its various forms as an oral tale circulating amongst the medieval peasantry, the story emerged from the same class of stories as those other tales, representing an imaginative take on such superstitions. The grandmother as a kind of disguised monster places the tale more squarely within that class of stories in which children are the victims of violence within the home itself. Like the tales of wicked stepmothers, Carter's version of the Red Riding Hood theme narrates the anxiety that the family as a place of safety and moral integrity is constantly under threat, and always in need of defending from malign influences.

When we turn our attention back to current debates regarding violence against children, two examples of the idea of the 'false relation' (or the false *familiar* or friend) come to mind. Lord Laming's report for the Victoria Climbié Inquiry makes a point of being clear that Marie-Therese Kouao was not Victoria's real mother, but her great-aunt who pretended to the authorities and Social Services that Victoria was her daughter. Kouao and Victoria first met when Kouao (who lived in France) 'turned up' at in the Climbié household in Ivory Coast and 'told Mr and Mrs Climbié that she wished to take a child back to France with her and arrange for his or her education' (Laming 2003, 25). We learn also that Kouao took Victoria first to France and then to the England on a passport that falsely named Victoria as 'Anna', Kouao's daughter (2003, 26). Of course, Kouao did not act like a mother towards Victoria. She never, for instance, sent Victoria to school or provided any sort of education. We learn from the report not just of the physical and emotional abuse inflicted but also that when Victoria was hospitalized in July 1999 with a scald to her face, 'Kouao [n]ever brought Victoria anything in the way of clothes, food, toys or treats throughout the fortnight she spent in hospital' (2003, 31). We are also told of 'a marked difference between Kouao's appearance (she was always well dressed) and that of Victoria (who was far scruffier)' (2003, 27). If Kouao's striking lack of familial care can in any way be explained by the fact that she was not Victoria's 'real' mother, the report certainly alludes to it. Although Kouao represented to Social Services that she was Victoria's mother, when complaining to a friend that Victoria was incontinent, she added that she was not her real daughter – a remark that made Victoria cry (2003, 32). In the fairytales, the 'false' mother character represents the dangers that children face when a person claiming the role of carer fails to live up to the required responsibilities. If Zipes and McGlathery are correct to suggest that the 'step' relation in fairytales is merely a dissociative artifice added by Grimm, this may explain why the report draws attention to the lack of a true mother-daughter relationship between Kouao and Victoria. In the case of Baby P in 2008, the woman involved was the baby's real mother; however the involvement of the other defendants – the mother's boyfriend and a lodger – introduces an element of uncertainty as to the relationship between the various parties. A Parliamentary report has been promised, and time will tell if the fact that the three convicted of the offence of 'causing or allowing the death of a child' were not a traditional married couple in the sense of a married couple will be treated as being significant as in Victoria Climbié's case. There is evidence from the media reports however that this may be so. For example *The Economist* (2008, 40) does draw attention to this in its description of the failings of the local social and health services when it remarks that 'no one realized the two guilty men had moved into the home', suggesting a significant moral difference between this 'family' and the ideal.

The second example of the idea of the false familiar as an indicator of dangerous violence against children is the current public consternation and legal discourse regarding child grooming and abduction for sexual abuse. It is common for liberal critics of the *News of the World*'s infamous campaign to 'name and shame' all convicted paedophiles in Britain to complain that such a public approach to identifying offenders will 'drive the wretched paedophile underground' (Linklater 2007). The metaphor of the burrowing animal chimes with the fairytale distinction between the homely innocent victim and the wandering, rootless villain. In its briefing paper for the Home Affairs Select Committee report for the Sexual Offence Bill,[8] Childnet International (2002) described the need for a new offence to criminalize the (at that point unregulated) grooming of a child for sexual purposes. The new offence was believed to be especially necessary because of the explosion of access to the Internet where paedophiles could get to know children under the pretence of being another child, who could win their trust and then convince them to meet. Childnet International (2002, 4) argued that the real danger of the Internet is that it 'allow[s] contact to be made even while the child is using the Internet in the secure surroundings of their own home, even their own bedroom'. The passage conjures the horrific notion that the home – which ought to be a sealed box of safety for vulnerable children – can now be penetrated from outside by the tentacles of paedophilia thanks to the Internet. This impression is strengthened by the way in which the Select Committee report describes the wrong committed by the men

---

8   The bill later became the Sexual Offences Act 2003.

in the cases used to support the creation of the new offence. In Milton Keynes, a thirteen-year-old girl arranged to meet a boy she had chatted to on the Internet, but 'instead of a fifteen-year-old boy, awaiting the girl was a forty-seven-year-old man who had travelled all the way from Newcastle to Milton Keynes to meet the girl' (Childnet International 2002, 4). The report also describes how another man had met a thirteen-year-old girl he had contacted on the Internet and 'drove her to his flat many miles away where he began a series of indecent assaults'. Having been released on bail for those assaults he made contact with another girl and 'drove hundreds of miles across the country to commit a similar assault' (2002, 4). The assaults themselves are of course the harm that the existing law aimed to punish (and the intention to commit them that the then new 'grooming' laws aimed to punish), but it is the cynical use of the chat-room to win the child's trust and the vast distances travelled in order to breach that trust that provides the moral fibre to the proposed offence. The integrity of the home as a place of safety must be protected from violation from outside. In the fairytales, villains who mean to do harm to children put on disguises and false voices in order to win their victims' trust: the use of the Internet chat-room is a twenty-first century legacy of these strategies.

c) Sexual Transgression as Violence

We have already seen that predatory sexual violence is an important part of some tales (for example, Perrault's *Little Red Riding Hood*). However, there are a few tales which also shed some light on attitudes towards incestuous sexual desire and its disruptive and destructive effect upon family life. Fairytales involving sexual relations between family members tell of a disruption of family life at least as damaging as the jealous spite of 'false' family relations such as wicked stepmothers and werewolf grandmothers. Three tales in particular seem to shed some light on our own views about transgressive or damaging sexual relations, including but not limited to incest biologically understood and sexual relations otherwise legally proscribed. First, there is Perrault's *The Sleeping Beauty in the Wood* and the related tale written by Giambattista Basile in 1634 as *Sun, Moon and Talia* and based on Italian oral tradition, which critics has subsequently suggested may relate to incestuous sexual desire. In *Sleeping Beauty* and *Sun, Moon and Talia*, a princess's father does all he can to prevent the fulfilment of a prophesy that he fears will take her away from him. When in *Sun, Moon and Talia* (Basile 2005) he fails to avert his daughter's 'death', his reaction is extreme:

> As soon as the wretched father heard of the disaster which had taken place, he had them, after having paid for this tub of sour wine with casks of tears, lay her out in one of his country mansions. There they seated her on a velvet throne under a canopy of brocade. Wanting to forget all and to drive from his memory his great misfortune, he closed the doors and abandoned forever the house where he had suffered this great loss.

McGlathery agrees with Bettelheim that the central theme is the father's desire not to lose his daughter to marriage, although McGlathery also reads incestuous sexual desire into his efforts to avoid losing her. Why, asks McGlathery (1991, 99), does the father–king of Basile's Italian version disappear from the narrative so suddenly when his daughter 'dies' as prophesized? In a reversal of the more common explanation of fairytale sexuality as the oedipal desire of a child for a parent, McGlathery suggests that the father's anxieties come from his fear of being tempted to violate her body. It is true that, immediately after the father–king's sudden departure, we are told that, 'after a time, it happened by chance that a king was out hunting and passed that way' (Basile 2005), which McGlathery reads as insinuating they are the same person. Finding the beautiful sleeping Talia, the visiting king wastes no time: 'he beheld her charms and felt his blood course hotly through his veins. He lifted her in his arms, and carried her to a bed, where he gathered the first fruits of love.' In case there remains any doubt in the reader's mind as to what this means, we learn next that Talia gives birth to two children nine months later (Basile 2005). Bettelheim is a more traditional Freudian reader of fairytales, and he focuses his attention on the sexual symbolism in the better-known versions of the tale: of the daughter's climb to the very top of the tower of her father's castle in Perrault's *The Sleeping Beauty in the Wood* and Grimm's *Sleeping Beauty*, where she accidentally pricks her finger, precipitating a one hundred year sleep (Perrault 2005; Grimm 2005). Bettelheim (1976, 228–9) suggests that the father–king who tries to prevent his daughter's fate in Basile, Perrault and Grimm and the prince who subsequently discovers her in Perrault's story could simply represent the shift of the daughter's desire from her father to a lover; the long sleep symbolizing her resolution of Oedipal immaturities by transferring her desire onto a more suitable object, and the long sleep imaginatively symbolic of the passage of time from girl to woman.[9] However, if we accept McGlathery's interpretations of the father's anxieties to prevent the loss of his daughter to womanhood then the distinction between father and lover is troublingly blurred. However there is no indication from these tales that the father's incestuous desire – if such it is – is fatal for the success of the family. In both cases the usual fairytale narrative of the natural reproduction of life plays out to its inevitable conclusion, arguably supporting Bettelheim's reading of the stories as successful resolutions of Oedipal anxieties.

While it requires some effort of imagination to interpret these tales as narrating incestuous desire, there are also tales in the collections both of Grimm and Perrault that *explicitly* involve a king who desires his own daughter because his wife implicitly condones or even requests it. Grimm's *Cat-Skin* and Perrault's equivalent *The Donkey's Skin* both involve a dying queen making her husband–

---

9   This interpretation is rejected by Marina Warner (1994, 220), who instead contends that the sleep represents the 'dark time' of inter-generational strife for a young woman that follows her first encounter with the mother-in-law.

king promise never to remarry unless he finds someone quite as beautiful as she.[10] In both the tales, the initially inconsolable king eventually realizes that the only woman who can match his dead wife's beauty is his own daughter, and ignoring dire warnings from courtiers, tries desperately to have her. An important common feature of the fairytales *Cat-Skin* and *The Donkey's Skin* is the price demanded by the daughter before she agrees to her father's amorous advances. In Grimm's *Cat-Skin* (The Brothers Grimm 2005), the daughter responds, not with 'No!', but with an elaborate request:

> Before I marry anyone I must have three dresses: one must be of gold, like the sun; another must be of shining silver, like the moon; and a third must be dazzling as the stars: besides this, I want a mantle of a thousand different kinds of fur put together, to which every beast in the kingdom must give a part of his skin.

Rather than being put off, the king invests huge resources and dispatches hunters to every part of his kingdom in order to have every single beast therein killed and skinned. In Perrault's *The Donkey's Skin* (Perrault 2008b), the price of the incestuous match is similarly incredible. The daughter's godmother advises her: 'You must demand the skin of the ass he sets such store by. It is from that donkey he obtains all his vast riches, and I am sure he will never give it to you.' The donkey is the king's prized possession since the 'bushels of gold pieces' that it magically produces every night ensures that the kingdom is never poor. However, here too the king's desire is so strong that he has the donkey slain without hesitation, to the dismay of his daughter. The meaning of this plot device is not difficult to decipher: it represents the counter-productive nature of incestuous desire and the danger that it represents for family relations and the home in which those relations operate. Both tales show the daughter driven into squalid hiding in order to escape her father's amorous advances. Disguised in rags, she becomes a servant at the palace where she coyly allows herself to be discovered by a Cinderella-type plot device involving a gold ring that she drops into the king's soup and readmitted into royal society. Perrault's tale makes more moral sense than Grimm's, ending with the girl's marriage to a prince and her forgiving her repentant father. Therefore for Perrault, in directing physical energies towards an unproductive end, sexual acts within the family are deemed to be disruptive of family life and thus as morally culpable. It is possible that for his own part, Grimm himself never quite understood the moral import of his own version of the story, because it ends 'happily' with the princess entering fully into the role of her father's wife. The delighted king, who seems to have forgotten the identity of this girl and she his, exclaims: 'You are my beloved bride, and we will never more be parted from each other' (The Brothers Grimm 2008). Ashliman (2008) also comments on the moral incoherence of the

---

10   The Brothers Grimm (2005): 'Promise me that you will never marry again, unless you meet with a wife who is as beautiful as I am, and who has golden hair like mine.'

ending of Grimm's story, commenting that 'the final sentence notwithstanding, this tale is a tragedy, a story that symbolically – but lucidly – portrays the unhappy life of a sexually abused child. ... This is not a story of happiness and fulfilment, but rather one of coping and surviving.'

If fairytales are, as I have suggested, expressive of moral and social anxieties, then it should not be very surprising to find some of the same anxieties in laws regulating sexual behaviour. I discussed in the last chapter how current anxieties about paedophilia have profoundly affected the way in which we interpret images of children which in former ages may have been regarded as innocuous. Here I want to consider anxieties over sexual behaviour that takes place between consenting persons competent to make choices for themselves, whose sexual lives the criminal law nevertheless seeks to protect and regulate. The Sexual Offences Act 2003 introduced a raft of new offences into the criminal law of England and Wales, committed with the consent of a 'victim' who, but for a particular set of circumstances, would be deemed competent to consent to sexual intercourse (the age of consent in the UK being 16). I want to highlight two aspects of these. First there are the 'abuse of trust' offences. According to sections 16 to 24 of the legislation, a criminal offence with a maximum sentence of 5 years imprisonment is committed where 'sexual activity' takes place between a person over 18 and a person under 18, where the older person is in a position of 'trust' or 'care' over the younger. For the purposes of the offence, a position of trust includes teachers of students who are 16 or 17, but it does not include employers who take on apprentices of that age.[11] Secondly, the Sexual Offences Act 2003 abolished the old incest offences and replaced them with a range of offences criminalizing sexual activity between adults of proscribed 'family relationship[s]'. According to section 25, where 'sexual activity' takes places between people of a 'family relationship' where the younger person is under 18 and the defendant over 18, the defendant may be liable to imprisonment for up to 5 years for non-penetrative sexual activity and up to 14 years for penetrative activity. What makes these laws more controversial than the old incest laws from a liberal perspective is the breadth of definition accorded to 'family relationship'. According to s.27, a family relationship exists in three circumstances (where 'A' is the defendant and 'B' is the victim):

> 27(2) – one of them is the other's parent, grandparent, brother, sister, half-brother, half-sister, and or uncle or A is or has been B's foster parent;

---

11   This offence (known as 'abuse of trust') was originally created in 2000 as a concession to opposition MPs who argued that lowering the age of homosexual consent from 18 to 16 would effectively legalize sexual activity between schoolteachers and 16- and 17-year-old male pupils.

27(3) – step-parent, cousins, stepbrother or stepsister, where A and B live or have lived in the same household, or A is or has been regularly involved in caring for, training, supervising or being in sole charge of B;

27(4) – anyone living in same household and is regularly involved in caring for, training, supervising or being in sole charge of B.

The offences are drafted to apply where both parties are over 16 and otherwise deemed to be fully competent to consent to sexual activity. Sections 64 and 65 criminalize both penetrating and being penetrated by a family member irrespective of consent and age. Should these reforms be regarded as anything other than sensible pragmatic formalizations of relationships we deem to be harmful anyway? There is an obvious tension in these sex laws between a liberal approach (that regulates by looking to the capacity of a person to consent but otherwise allows the individual to make their own moral decisions) and a moral one, which looks beyond the formal requirements of autonomy to the specific nature of the relationship involved. The question of what the age of consent should be differs from country to country. In Europe it ranges from 14 to 16, while in the US the range tends to be between 16 and 18, depending on state law. However, the age of consent tends to reflect prevailing notions about the age at which a person is regarded as being competent to comprehend the meaning of sexual intercourse, rather than social or moral views on the nature of relationship or other factors affecting the balance of power between the persons involved. There are two important exceptions to this general rule which indicate that moral attitudes about the nature of a relationship as well as the competence of a person to consent may continue to be relevant. First, varying moral attitudes towards homosexuality means that in many countries homosexual intercourse either remains illegal or else a higher age of consent applies, and in many countries where no distinction is drawn, this is as a result of fairly recent legal reform.[12] Secondly, in some countries sexual intercourse is only lawful within marriage.[13] It is precisely because the 'abuse of trust' and 'family relationship' provisions in the Sexual Offences Act look not to the young person's competence but to other factors about the nature of the relationship that has caused controversy since, like jurisdictions with special provisions on homosexuality or marriage, they seem to reintroduce an element of legal moralism (Spencer 2004, Hanson 2008). In fact, the relationship of 'family member' for the purposes of criminalization includes many relationships that may constitute a lawful marriage (for example, cousins, step-siblings, former step-parents, anyone involved in training/supervising the other). S.28 does provide an exemption from criminal liability for such family members that are lawfully

---

12   For example in England and Wales, homosexual and heterosexual intercourse were equalized at 16 by the Sexual Offences Act 2000.

13   Sexual intercourse outside marriage is illegal in Iran, Oman, Pakistan, Qatar, Saudi Arabia, Sudan and Yemen. See AVERT (2008).

married, but critics such as Spencer (2004, 357) have commented that it is hardly a comfort to a married person to know that had they not been married, one of them would be deemed to be a sex offender. Similarly, a mentally competent person of 16 or 17 who chooses to stay on at school is arguably discriminated against by these provisions, since their choice of sexual partner will continue to be the business of the law in such a way that the choice of young people who leave school at 16 will not be. The sexual activity prohibited by ss.16–24 is clearly a serious breach of professional codes of teaching, is unethical and involves a significant power imbalance. However, this fact could only be relevant if we regard it as necessary and desirable for the criminal law to look beyond the young person's own competence to consent. If young people are generally recognized as being competent to consent at 16 then to criminalize sexual activity of this kind as the offence of beach of trust undermines this recognition.[14]

In order to justify using the might of the criminal legal process to prevent such relationships we must indeed look beyond matters such as competence of young people to give consent to sex, and whether or not selecting certain relationships to criminalize without finding lack of consent in the ordinary sense is discriminatory. In other words, arguments about autonomy and discrimination are not quite sufficient to justify the prohibition involved here and so we must make use of more deeply ingrained moral ideas about the harm of sexual relations, not to young people themselves, but to the unproductiveness of sexual desire within a de-sexualized context. The justification for the law of abuse of trust must lie in the belief that the *idea* of family as an asexualized space is a moral notion that can be applied outside actual families. For the familial sex offences also, since the definition of a family relationship applies even to relationships that do not involve any blood relation at all (for example, step relations, former foster parents) and the offences deem consent to be irrelevant, it is necessary to look slightly deeper than the tried and tested eugenics and sexual brutality arguments for a convincing justification. The moral justification for both of these offences is related to incest: the moral status and responsibility of the teacher towards students and the proximity of a person living in a young person's household to provide training (s.27 (4)) invests the relationship with a moral dimension for which sexual desire is disruptive and abusive. The teacher or carer stands in for the parent and as such is conceived as occupying a moral space within the boundary of the home. To introduce sexual desire into that picture contradicts that moral association, just as the grandmother's betrayal of her granddaughter (at least in Angela Carter's *The Werewolf* in which the grandmother turns out to be a dangerous shape-changing beast) introduces an unwelcome element into what ought to be stable and secure. Those who have sought to critique this offence have tried to distance themselves from any association with moralism: the arguments from autonomy

---

14   One comment on the Michelle Hanson (2008) article: 'If there is a genuine feeling that 16-year-olds are not capable of making informed decisions about who they have sex with, then the age of consent needs to be changed.'

and discrimination are liberal values that purport to rely instead on a view that the autonomous individual must not be prevented from pursuing their own idea of the good life without paternalistic interference. However, unless one comes from an extreme libertarian position it is difficult to isolate the critique of 'abuse of trust' provisions without conceding the basic principle of a necessarily asexual zone notwithstanding capacity to consent. For those who are convinced by the moral analogy between parents and teachers, the paternalism of the new abuse of trust offences seems a sensible way to formalize the necessarily asexual relationship between teachers, trainers or carers and pupils. The teacher is *in loco parentis* and thus the obviousness of the incest taboo between parents and their own children is applied to teachers and pupils as well. Liberals, on the other hand, tend instead to draw analogies between teachers and professionals whose responsibilities towards young people who come within their sphere of influence are not generally regarded as amounting to parental.[15] Such critics have argued that although a relationship between teacher and a pupil is one that raises concerns about power imbalance, this is not properly a matter for the criminal law of sexual offences. The argument is in fact simply a denial that the relationship between a person in a position of trust and the person over whom they exercise care (as defined in ss.16–24) is one that invokes the moral idea of the family as a taboo on sexual relations.

The Sexual Offences Act 2003 is by no means innovative in being explicable not by its practical benefits in averting actual violations of autonomy, but rather by reinforcing existing moral structures of illicit sexuality. The ancient incest taboo, which is common to many different cultures irrespective of any awareness of genetic dangers of incestuous reproduction, exists to enforce sexual conformity (Freud 1991, 4–13). As discussed in the previous two chapters, the nature of taboo is such as to ensure the persistence of the danger of its transgression. In modern times, the incest taboo arguably both militates against and encourages the development of potentially problematic sexual desire between 'in-law' parents and children. For example, Freud is typically alert to the dangers posed by sexual desire within families, causing a perceived moral offence even where, as in the Sexual Offences Act there is no actual violation of the incest taboo in terms of blood. He argues that an older woman will sometimes compensate for a lack of emotional or sexual fulfilment in her own life by identifying with her daughter, which 'can easily go so far that she herself falls in love with the man her daughter loves ... [and] this may lead to severe forms of neurotic illness as a result of her violent mental struggle against this emotional situation' (Freud 1991, 15). A young man who in infancy managed only to repress

---

15   Another respondent to Michelle Hanson's (2008) article wrote: 'Why should the child at work have the freedom to have sex with exactly whoever they please whilst the child *of the same age* at the sixth-form college is limited? Is limited sexual freedom worthy of the name? Is this not the same situation that existed when homosexuality was criminalized, that you could only have consensual sex with a person of the State's choosing? It's all a little bit dodgy and to be honest, I think that the social stigma connected to the "offence" (along with the inevitable sacking) is punishment enough.'

rather than eliminate his Oedipal desires may be also tempted to recall his first natural sexual object as an infant (his mother) and desire his mother-in-law, although his internalization of the incest taboo will fight vigorously against it (ibid., 16–17). Freud's theory of Oedipal sexual development is of course a specific instance of the operation of the incest taboo outside strictly blood relations. However, it is not necessary to fully accept his argument in order to understand the moral dynamics of the legislation examined here. The familial and abuse of trust sexual offences under the Sexual Offences Act 2003 are not explicable so much by reference to a *practical* need for protecting vulnerable people from harmful sexual acts, but rather because of the horror associated with the perceived transgression of a taboo engendered by the sexual ambivalence pertaining between a desexualized zone such as the home and what lies outside it. In terms of providing practical protection to young or vulnerable people from physically or psychologically harmful sexual activity, surely no-one should be prosecuted unless their activity falls within one of the other offences, such as sexual activity with someone under the general age of consent (16 in the UK) or in the absence of consent. The offences are defendable instead because of a need – perceivable, as we have seen, in legal and literary texts – to protect the moral integrity of the idea of the 'home'; to signal that within the boundaries of the family (and its extended sense including teachers and others that stand in for various facets of the parenting role) sexual relations are disruptive and unproductive.

Conclusion

Reflecting on the violence and relationships of desire depicted in fairytales allows us to develop a critical perspective on current attitudes towards the different kinds of violence that children suffer today. I have tried to suggest that reading contemporary social attitudes critically means examining the ways in which certain acts of violence are regarded vis-à-vis the promotion of an idea of secure and productive family life. The metaphorical representations of the idea of 'home' and that which appears to threaten it from the outside are not restricted to a discourse of innocence, discussed in the previous two chapters. They also allow us to consider the moral character of certain acts – are they to be understood as justified physical labours necessary for a child's emotional maturity, needed for balancing the scales of justice, or on the other hand, are they to be denounced as unjust, excessive, vicious and unproductive? When we consider the kinds of violence or sexual relationship that ought to attract the attention of criminal lawyers and what our response to them ought to be, we are engaged in a process of negotiating the moral integrity of the idea of family. An act of violence or a relationship is assessed according to its anticipated effects, that is, whether it will support a productive family life or whether it will undermine or disrupt it. Whether we are concerned with violence or sex, behaviour that we condemn tends to be that which we regard as lacking the security, productivity or growth that we want from family life.

PART 3
Imagination, or Ghosts of Violence Yet to Come

Chapter 7

'What they are, yet I know not: But they shall be the terrors of the earth': Nightmares of Science/Fiction

The controversy surrounding the rapid advance of biotechnology and its promise to genetically enhance human beings is a recurring theme in political and academic debate. Aldous Huxley was not the first to express discomfort at the possible consequences for human society and Margaret Atwood will of course not be the last. There have always been conservative critics to warn against 'artificial' enhancements (corruptions) of nature, whose worries about the possible consequences for humankind are based not on measurable benefits and harms but rather on notions of the mystery, sacredness and uniqueness of human nature. It is well known that science-fiction literature has been used simply to affirm the conservative critique of genetic enhancement, including the literary texts I focus on in this chapter. 'Brave New World' for instance has become a stock slogan for anyone who objects to some new scientific development or other but is unable or unwilling to argue the case more fully. The purpose of this chapter is certainly not to use literature to show that the awful fate that critics such as Habermas warn may be in store for liberal democratic societies may in fact materialize. Nor am I at all interested in using literature to assess just how awful life might be if such fears are in fact realized. Rather, the literature is used to draw attention to the moral and dramatic dynamics of conservative cautionary critique of what Habermas pejoratively calls eugenic programming.

One theme common to science fiction literature is the radical separation of society into 'haves and have nots'. The three novels discussed in this chapter and the next all share this theme of such an apartheid and all strongly hint towards the dire implications that this has for the ideals of liberal democratic political society. In Aldous Huxley's *Brave New World*, the civilized world of perfect peace and harmony in which citizens' desires and needs are both controlled and satisfied through a combination of genetic programming and suggestion contrasts starkly with the primitive reservations – left uncivilized as a social experiment – in which the people are free from state and commercial control, practise strange rituals and have fierce and unpredictable passions. In Margaret Atwood's *Oryx and Crake*, society is dominated by biotechnology companies which seem to be responsible for the organization of political society. Attwood thus imagines society as divided into secure, clean and safe 'compounds' that house the well educated elite who work for the biotech companies in the production of drugs to be sold chiefly to the occupants of the 'pleeblands' – areas outside of the compounds where the air is polluted, security non-existent and consequently life is, to paraphrase Hobbes, nasty, brutish and short. Finally, Kazuo Ishiguro's *Never Let Me Go* imagines a parallel twentieth century in which children are cloned as a source of organs for transplant well before they reach middle age, and that due to the miraculous treatments made possible by this arrangement are necessarily regarded as less than human by 'normal' people. All three novels involve a young protagonist who emerges from the 'wrong' side of society's divide – John the Savage who travels from his New Mexico reservation to discover the horrors of civilized British society in *Brave New World* and Tommy and Kathy who are childhood friends in England and who are eventually forced to come to terms with their identity as clones that society accords mere instrumental rather than having intrinsic value in *Never Let Me Go* – or one who otherwise comes to reflect on the society in which he finds himself (Jimmy, the young wastrel of *Oryx and Crake*). Prima facie then, the three novels that are discussed in this chapter and the next rely on the same premise with regard to eugenic programming: that it has dangerous implications for liberal democratic society and that that the seductive material benefits that it promises will erode ethical commitment to social solidarity, equality and human rights.

1. The Rhetoric of 'Eugenic Programming':
Biotechnology, Liberalism and Morals

Before beginning, I must pause to explain that the label of 'conservative' has a particular meaning in this chapter and the next. To be 'conservative' for the purposes of this discussion is interpreted here as being opposed to the development of biotechnologies, in particular technologies for the genetic enhancement of future persons, on *moral* grounds. This conservative moral opposition to biotechnology is represented here chiefly by Jurgen Habermas and also by others such as Leon Kass. Their objections to biotechnologies such as genetic enhancement, cloning and PGD are definably 'moral' since the arguments they advance relate to their picture of what we might describe as an 'authentic human life'. As I shall describe, for both of these commentators such biotechnologies threaten to obscure or even obliterate precious or in some way unique aspects of human life that are not related to any particular empirically measurable disadvantage. Their arguments are moral in the sense that the disadvantages they identify in biotechnologies are losses of principle that are not (for them at least) dependant on empirical proof: autonomy, personal identity, dignity, uniqueness, equality with others. The definition of a conservative moral commentator therefore does not include those who for non-moral reasons (say, legal or economic) oppose the development of such technologies. Neither does it include those who, aligning themselves with leftist politics, reject the technologies on the grounds of the potential for social exclusion and environmental problems that may accompany their commercialism, or the global financial implications of making them available on the market. Theorists who proceed from a Marxist critique of capitalist commodity culture may have been influential on what I categorize here as current conservative ethical positions (in particular the communitarian positions such as that of Michael Sandel), but these are not directly relevant to the discussion here on the basis that they are primarily economic and social theories, rather than ethical. Neither does my definition of a conservative include any particular political position vis-à-vis the role of government or the state and its relationship with or exercise of power over the individual. In political discourse in the US, the progressive left may oppose development of biotechnologies, orientated as they are towards a critique of the use of technology for purposes of state control and surveillance, while at the same time encouraging the privatization (and thus profiteering from) resources that ought to be publicly available. Of course, biotechnology is an area in which debate often focuses upon the impact of powerful commercial interests (in the form of large biotech firms) and consequent implications for social justice. The opposition to biotechnologies on these pragmatic grounds does not form part of the moral arguments against biotechnologies that I define in this chapter as 'conservative'. The liberal ethical positions that are offered to refute the conservative arguments are discussed in detail in the next chapter.

a) Habermas's Undemocratic Argument from Democracy

Conservative arguments against allowing for the genetic enhancement of future persons and other such technologies tend to be couched in the form of warnings: *if* such and such were permitted, *then* even if this brings great benefits for those who are able to take advantage of them, human life would be degraded in a deeper sense. Consider, for example, this argument put forward by Jurgen Habermas (2003, 65):

> Eugenic programming establishes a permanent dependence between persons who know that one of them is principally barred from changing places with the other. [This is] foreign to the reciprocal and symmetrical relation of mutual recognition proper to moral and legal community of free and equal persons.

For Habermas, eugenic programming would erode commitment to the values that make human rights and democracy possible, namely the freedom and equality of all citizens, because the power of genetic pre-determination draws a formal distinction between the decision-making powers of one generation and the next. This is an imbalance which, for Habermas, is fundamentally incompatible with liberal democracy because it can never be rectified. Human dignity does not simply attach to human beings by virtue of their capacity for reason and observance of moral laws, but rather is dependent upon what Habermas (2003, 33) calls 'relational symmetry' between members of a moral and legal community. Personal identity is constituted by one's involvement in this community: each person's self-conception depends upon the mutual and symmetrical respect there accorded. Full subjectivity therefore depends upon the moral and legal community providing equality in this regard (Habermas 2003, 34). In order to appreciate one's own equality it is necessary for each person to accord others respect as persons in themselves and see this respect reflected back to them.

In his analysis, allowing parents to fulfil their desire to control the outcome of reproduction leads to loss of autonomy in future generations. Since that which is produced by eugenic programming is an altered humanity, humankind as a species ceases to be 'master' of that which they produce, but becomes part of the array of produced goods: abstracted in the exchange economy (Habermas 2003, 47). Desire on the part of the chooser against a background of competition and productivity becomes the only guiding ethic and this is offset against the dreaded 'vertiginous awareness' in the product of that desire that an essential part of themselves has been objectified (Habermas 2003, 53). Habermas claims that to allow genetic enhancement and other types of eugenic programming would erode not just discrete aspects of human life, but the moral character of human life as such. For Habermas, the gains promised by biotechnology – freedom of reproductive choice, prolongation of life, increased health – all contribute towards an erosion of fundamental principles essential to the possibility of universal participation in the public life of liberal democratic society. Therefore, legal resistance to, pre-implantation genetic diagnosis (PGD) and cloning in Germany provides a moral image, which is in danger of being reinterpreted as 'artificial barriers in terms of taboos' by the tangible benefits of biotechnology (Habermas 2003, 25). The freedom and health benefits are bought at a high cost, argues Habermas (2003, 24), namely the 'instrumentalization of humanity's inner nature', since the inability to choose the genetic make up of one's children is part of the essential moral and political life of our species. Eroding the distinction between 'chance and choice' may bring empirically measurable personal economic and social benefits, but simultaneously damages human beings' self perception as autonomous persons of equal worth and thus also undermines the possibility of the liberal legal, political and moral attitude of universal equality and participation (Habermas 2003, 29).

The trouble with this is that, despite being premised on the importance of open ethical and political debate, the argument is essentially a demand that certain procedures – which could bring great benefits to people – must be prohibited in law without their effects being known. In other words, Habermas is asking us simply to take his word for it that the effects of radical biotechnology will be disastrous for the democratic process and liberal commitment to equality and human rights. *How* is autonomy and equality violated? *How*, assuming that resulting children are not prevented from developing normal cognitive faculties, are PGD, sex selection, cloning, genetic enhancement and so on qualitatively more damaging for the lives, self-perception and opportunities than other forms of control and influence that parents seek to exert on their children? If we are to believe Habermas, these are all questions that the law must prevent from being fully tested in the interests of preserving liberal democracy itself. In seeking to exclude such testing in open debate, there is therefore an undemocratic aspect to Habermas's idea of using legal prohibitions to create a 'moral image', despite his taking every opportunity to couch his arguments in terms of democratic participation.

b) Taboo as a Conservative Argument

What is and what is not 'essential' to human nature and democratic society is very much a matter of opinion. There are many commentators who, without any sense of irony, agree with Habermas about the legal prohibition of 'eugenic programming' without providing any reasons further than the possible harm to liberal equality and democratic openness. Taking up the theme of the power imbalance between one generation and another, Leon Kass (2003, 16) for example, warns of the 'risks of despotic rule' that may accompany 'even partial control over genotype'. Adam Wolfson (2003, 61) has argued that liberal values of equality and autonomy must be understood not as scientific empirical facts but as political decisions. Not everything is appropriate for scientific analysis, Wolfson insists, otherwise we may be persuaded to throw away some of our most important values. Just as we should rely on our moral ideas about humanity and not enquire whether *in fact* all people are equal, we should be guided by 'our moral intuitions and religious judgments' and assume that, say, the life of the embryo is valuable and may therefore not be used at will. Like Habermas, Wolfson (2003, 63) believes that the proper role for the law is to set a firm example:

> ... there is also the need for some absolute limits or bans on certain biotechnologies. One needs to establish bright lines and firewalls, to say thus far but no farther. We might consider bans, just by way of example, on human cloning or sex selection of children for nonmedical purposes.

Wolfson does not go into detail as to how or why such a need arises, except insofar as it threatens the *a priori* equality and freedom of all people. Habermas is surely correct to worry that the 'moral image of society is indeed in danger of being, as noted above, reinterpreted as 'artificial barriers in terms of taboos', since by the very process of the open democratic debate that must be protected against the development of biotechnology, 'just so' arguments fail by Habermas's own standards of rational argument. For conservative commentators, 'taboo' is not merely the pejorative term that it is for liberal consequentialists.[1] Rather, taboo represents shared moral feelings and beliefs that gain authority simply from their continued existence. Yuval Levin presents a passionate defence of taboo as a morally significant entity which through its depth and mystery gives shape to the moral life of a society and, as such, should sometimes not be subjected to question. His argument is non-rational and seeks to produce a physical response, and this is indeed the very point of a taboo as understood by Freud: 'Taboos stand at the

---

1   For example John Harris (1998, 181) who likens those worried about the nature or 'humanity' of human clones to racists.

border crossing between the realm of the properly human and those of the beasts and the gods. When the boundaries are breached, when degradation or hubris is given expression, our stomachs recoil, even if our minds at first do not' (Levin 2003, 54–5). Similarly, Leon Kass (1992,105) regards taboos such as those against incest, adultery and cannibalism as necessary foundations of civilized society and its institutions, such as the family. In other words, taboo is simply that which gives us our moral framework, but its existence cannot be ultimately explained except with reference to customary moral feelings that have developed in a culturally and historically arbitrarily fashion. There is thus a pragmatic aspect to respecting taboos. Why, asks Cora Diamond, is it generally considered wrong to eat people? Diamond (1995, 322) explains that what makes it 'wrong' is simply that people are not generally regarded as things one eats. Anyone living in a modern Western society who thought and acted differently would be committing a violation of deeply ingrained norms, but this does not mean that it would be impossible in theory to conceive of a functional cannibalistic society. We might say that, while we live in a society that linguistically distinguishes between people and food as being, respectively, subjects and objects, cannibalism will remain a taboo. However, if we take Habermas at face value we would have to concede that the 'wrongness' of cannibalism is a social and cultural construct and that it is possible to imagine a society with different conditions that regarded such a belief a mere prejudice.

In an arguably more honest (though ultimately rather feeble) conservative response to the issue, Levin (2003, 58) presents the conservative critique and democracy as mutually incompatible: 'in appealing to clear and explicit rational argument, we begin to overcome our deep repugnance, and diminish it in others. We create an argument that rests, as arguments do, on premises and postulates, rather than a deep taboo …'. A good thing, surely, since, as Levin himself concedes, moral repugnance tends to fade with habit. In any case, has 'deep taboo' in the context of, say, mixed-race marriage and homosexual acts shown itself in the past to be 'unreliable' (Levin 2003, 56), 'wrong or unjust' (Levin 2003, 57) as a moral guide? Usually yes, but not in the case of biotechnology, replies Levin. Determined to stick to his conservative hymn-sheet, Levin defends taboo as an absolute defence against the disintegration of society's moral life, whilst at the same time conceding its incompatibility with democratic argument: '… we risk losing much if the process of transforming sentiments into arguments is not carried out properly, in a sober and responsible way, and with an eye to what is worth preserving and protecting' (Levin 2003, 63). Given his suspicion of 'rational argument', it is perhaps not too surprising that Levin offers no reason why some moral sentiments are more reliable than others. Presumably we must simply rely on his moral sense to lead him in the right direction.

I have discussed taboo as the basis for ethical principles elsewhere in this book. In Chapters 4 and 5 I discussed George Bataille's arguments on how the construction of a taboo invites its own transgression by stimulating desire. By drawing a line which simply must not be crossed only adds allure to the object of the prohibition and furthermore turns it into a scared thing, the sacrifice of which becomes an experience of great temptation. Recall that the taboo that Freud (1950, 32–4) imagined as being erected to curtail dangerous primal desires is inextricably bound up with the desire to transgress it. I would argue that in basing their arguments on aspects of human nature being 'taboo', Habermas, Levin, Wolfson and others risk simply (and unconsciously) rewriting the Oedipus complex, in which the sincere and serious attempts to reinforce the law (the taboo) perpetuate the desire to violate it. Indeed, the rhetoric of these commentators, full of unsubstantiated admonitions and imperatives – for example, Wolfson's 'thus far but no farther' – are indicative not of a democratic spirit but of an attempt to invoke an almost God-like 'just-so' authority on the debate. However, without being able to point to any specific dangers, but only abstract threats, these are arguments that exist in the realm of the imagination and are easily undercut as soon as one demands specifics. We are reminded of the impotent rage of King Lear, railing against his powerful daughters:

> I will have such revenges on you both,
> That all the world shall – I will do such things,
> What they are, yet I know not: but they shall be
> The terrors of the earth. (II, ii, 453–6)

Just as the terrible admonitions to the Israelites in Leviticus, Deuteronomy and Numbers are merely poetic bile (though no less arresting for that) unless one believes them to issue from a source of binding authority, so those of Habermas and others who issue 'don't do it … or else!' arguments against genetic enhancements and other biotechnologies are meaningless as arguments in the scientific sense of testable hypotheses. This is why science-fiction novels are an important aspect of the debate. Because the central purpose of science-fiction is to imaginatively conjure images of future societies and worlds which are the products of trends and attitudes contemporary to the authors' own societies as they saw them, they allow us to reflect on arguments, such as those considered here, that admit of imagination rather than reasoned argument.

c) Science-fiction and Taboo

Huxley provides an imaginative picture of what society might be like if twentieth-century taboos are broken down. In *Brave New World*, state encouragement for each person to believe that 'everyone belongs to everyone else' means that the passionate possessiveness that formerly marked romantic love has been eradicated in favour of a more sociable, stable and generous expectation of universal promiscuity. This idea was first tried by Huxley in his early novel *Crome Yellow* of 1922, which describes the future in the way in which his Brave New World would later be arranged: birth in the natural sense made obsolete and replaced by a modern system of incubation and consequently motherhood, family and monogamy would be made redundant. Being freed from such strictures, 'Eros ... will flit like a gay butterfly from flower to flower through a sunlit world' (Woodcock 1972, 85). The reversing of sexual morality is central to *Brave New World*; when John the Savage realizes that Lenina cannot comprehend the importance of monogamy and passionate love, he loses the will to live in the civilized world. Love, like any exclusive or solitary activity such as the enjoyment of literature, is considered too antisocial to be encouraged in Huxley's future.

Furthermore, as in *Crome Yellow*, the replacement of families with a state controlled mass incubation system means there is no significance to words like mother, father, brother, sister, and so on, and hence no incest taboo. At the beginning of the novel, the Director of the London Hatchery explains how people of the lowest castes (Gammas, Deltas and Epsilons) can be produced in this fashion from a single egg, thus creating hundreds of identical twins. There is a scene in which the Director of the London Hatchery demonstrates the infant children being encouraged to engage in erotic play. The Director recounts with disapproval to his students how, in the time of Our Ford, children were actively discouraged to explore their sexuality at such a young age and consequently suffered all sorts of antisocial mental problems in later life, such as attaching unseemly attachment to one particular person. Huxley's depiction of future society encouraging erotic play in children is very clearly a critique of some perceived implications of Freud's theory of infantile sexuality and the role of the Oedipus complex in the normal development of sexual morality in particular. Freud had argued that a child's awareness of sexual morality and particularly the incest taboo is formed in early childhood when a child first experiences the conflict between his own desire and society's prohibitions. In Huxley's world, the lack of prohibitions on children realizing their infantile sexual desires means that the unconscious Oedipal desire to kill one's father (which manifests in rebellion against the law) in order to have the object of desire has disappeared. In his 1932 review of *Brave New World*, Joseph Needham notes that Huxley's account of a society without sexual taboos was probably motivated by contemporary discussions on how the Oedipus complex might explain political activism and social unrest. In Freud's analysis, the incest taboo functions to deny children the initial object of their desire (their parents): a girl who wants to be the person most loved by her father and the boy who wants his mother as 'his own property' find that their desire unreturned and this leads to the child being 'cast out of [his] fool's paradise' (Freud 1991, 315). Being cut off from his mother, the boy turns his attention to his own penis but finds that his parents also disapprove of him masturbating and bed-wetting and threaten him (he thinks) with castration (Freud 1991, 317). Thereafter, entry into the phallocentric adult world of language, authority and rules – a redirecting of sexual desire to other women – is then the only way for boys to avoid castration and make up for the loss of his mother as sexual object (Freud 1991, 319). This separation from the mother through taboo – painful and frustrating as it may be for the child – is essential for normal development and the internalization of moral norms which are then perpetuated. A notion that Needham suggests might have influenced Huxley's idea of sexuality in a 'happy' future was the possibility of altering Freud's picture of child development for social engineering. For without the incest taboo imposed on the child through the threat of castration, the child would not be denied the object of his desire, would not experience the fear and frustration with respect to the father's authority and thus perhaps by the same token dissatisfaction with legal authority might similarly be eliminated. Therefore, if social sexual taboos could be removed then social unrest might be similarly eliminated (Watt 1975, 203). Huxley's response to this kind of social application of Freud seems to be that the removal of the taboo leads to the infantilizing of the people, incapable of deeper feelings of love or loyalty. The scenes from Huxley's novels that deal with his vision of a society that trains people to lack such feelings are a critique of where he felt twentieth century consumerism was headed. It is well known that Huxley's own moral sensibilities were drawn from Late Victorian and Edwardian English Protestantism. It is also known that his sister and mother died when he was young and coupled with his loss of sight at a young age also, some biographers have suggested that these experiences of tragic loss contributed towards his views and his writing in later life. His satire of the cheapening of attitudes towards sex, family, culture and history that may be a consequence of the drive towards generalized happiness leaves little doubt as to Huxley's values (Thody 1973, 57).

More recent science-fiction is, of course, lighter on the Victorian moralism, but here also, depictions of future societies tend to involve the general lowering of moral expectations. Atwood's *Oryx and Crake* is full of passages that imply that in a future society in which traditional bonds of social solidarity become broken down in a world dominated by divisive biotech giants, anything non-commercial such as morality and the arts may all become irrelevant, even meaningless. Like Huxley's Savage, Atwood's Jimmy is an outsider in his own society, although to a lesser extent. Jimmy is moved by Shakespeare in a society for which the arts have become irrelevant to personal and political life (Atwood 2004, 97). His marketability in Atwood's ruthlessly utilitarian world, in which the only hope of career success is to make oneself useful to a large biotech firm, is compromised by the fact that he is not a 'numbers person' (2004, 29). Instead of one of the highly competitive and opulent science driven universities, he attends a crumbling, funds-starved arts institution (Atwood 2004, 226–7). Although he does eventually find a job writing promotional slogans meaningful only in a commercial sense, he preserves his integrity to a certain extent by approaching the job creatively, if cynically – inventing his own words to fool his bosses. He is morally an outsider also. Jimmy listens with astonishment and rage as Oryx, his lover, coolly recounts how she was sold into child slavery by her mother and then on to hardcore child pornography at the age of eight (Atwood 2004, 104–5), which Jimmy himself regularly consumed as a teenager. Her story, which she narrates with no trace of self pity, anger or regret is punctuated by Jimmy's exclamations – 'pervert!', 'I'll kill him, the bastard!' In response to Jimmy's expressions of disgust at her story of sexual and commercial exploitation, she says (with no hint of sadness) that it is better to have monetary value than no value at all (Atwood 2004, 147). Indeed, Oryx denies Jimmy the smallest opportunity to try and treat her as the victim of any kind of wrong, since she even refuses to understand him when he tries to offer acceptance of her past: 'It's all right' he told her, stroking her hair. 'None of it was your fault.' 'None of what, Jimmy?' (2004, 132). Commodification has become so far reaching in Atwood's imagined future that Oryx's indifference to the abuse of her own body for commercial purposes seems orthodox and even rational. Jimmy's frustration at Oryx's inability or unwillingness to regard herself as the victim of abuse is unsettling for the reader (Atwood 2004, 162–3, 166–7). As we shall we below both in this chapter and the next, the association of biotechnological futures with a mutated form of consumerism is an important part of the conservative critique, whether by way of a simple cheapening of attitudes towards one's own body in the case of Leon Kass, or by effecting a collapse of the distinction between consumer and commodity through taking eugenic control of future generations, as in the case of Habermas.

The discomfort alluded to in those scenes from Huxley, Atwood and Ishiguro is at the heart of the conservative critique of biotechnology and its perceived claims to improve the material and physical well-being of human life. As literary devices, Atwood's vegetable chickens and Huxley's children at erotic play elicit strong feelings about a society that has transgressed certain invisible lines. In this chapter and the next, I discuss this device as tapping into a powerful moral narrative of the body and its relevance to the conservative critique. However, nothing dates like moral repugnance and such images are more difficult to utilize in political, legal and philosophical writings. As we see here, Habermas's objections to a range of biotechnologies – including Pre-implantation Genetic Diagnosis (PGD), cloning and genetic enhancement that he collectively labels pejoratively as 'eugenic programming' – are ostensibly focused upon liberal democratic concerns for equality and freedom. At the root of his arguments is an appeal to the physical body, squeamishness, feelings of violation, and so on, for which he has been criticized by liberal commentators, but which also raise interesting questions as to the relationship between literary and philosophical responses to biotechnology.

2. Justice and Bodily Integrity/Injustice and the Dismembered Body

Metaphors of corporeality and physicality and images of the human body have often been used by theorists seeking to mount a critique of law and justice. For example, Dworkin (1977, 105–130) gave us the vivid image of Hercules as the superhero lawyer of integrity who judges impartially, without susceptibility to bias or favour.[2] Representing an ideal of legal reasoning for actual judges, this Hercules must 'construct a scheme of abstract and concrete principles that provides a

---

2   Dworkin introduces his Herculean judge as 'a lawyer of superhuman skill, learning, patience and acumen' (1977, 105).

coherent justification for all common law precedents and ... constitutional and statutory provisions as well' (Dworkin 1977, 116–7). Although Dworkin speaks of a heroic man, this superhuman picture of judicial perfection can only be an abstraction of judgment. In response, feminist critics have corporealized this image, complaining that in conceptualizing justice as a male superhero affirms gendered stereotypes of law and justice as discriminating against 'flesh and blood' judges who do not look like the ideal of masculine detachment and independence. Erika Rackley (2006, 219) understands Dworkin's Hercules sartorially, as 'stripped of self [and] reclothed with the magical attributes of fairness, impartiality and independence' and the woman judge, who threatens to undermine the strictures of impartiality with her womanly empathy and ethic of care, 'cannot easily wear Hercules's bespoke suit' (Rackley 2006, 221). What Rackley (2006, 223) wants is a judge who not only loses his clothes, but also 'sheds his skin' and 'steps into the skin of those before [him], weeping silently as he begins to judge' (Rackley 2006, 231). Although the Hercules of Greek myth stands aloof on Mount Olympus (and in Dworkin's imagination over and above the whole vista of legal knowledge) this critique of him as an image of justice brings him back to earth with violence. He is first revealed as a body (stripped and re-clothed) and then skinned in the name of a more caring and empathetic, embodied justice. Hercules as the supreme hero of myth and upholder of Dworkian integrity is certainly a worthy sacrifice. As I discuss in this section, conservative responses to the perceived radical threat to justice posed by biotechnology also draw upon metaphors of the body. In the rhetoric of Habermas and others, we discern a critique that appeals not to reasoned argument as such, but rather to the physical experience of dread and disgust and the susceptibility of the body to hurt and harm.

a) The Savage Vomits and Crake's Children Eat their Own Shit: Ethics of Disgust

In the section above I noted that Habermas (2003, 53) refers to the experience of inequality between present and future generations as a dread 'vertiginous awareness' that an essential element of one's identity has been objectified. Habermas (2003, 39) argues, for example, that our perceptions of the use of embryos may be guided by 'disgust at something obscene rather than moral indignation proper'. The appeal to physical reactions and unreasoned moral sentiments has come closest to a moral argument in itself in the writings Leon Kass (2003, 17): 'We are probably repelled by the idea of drugs that erase memories or that change personalities; or of interventions that enable 70-year-olds to bear children or play professional sports ... we sense that it may have something to do with ... the attitude that is properly respectful of what is naturally and dignifiedly human.' As a moral argument, Kass's reliance on what he calls the 'wisdom of repugnance' has been met with derision by liberal consequentialists who argue that such 'wisdom' fails to offer an argument beyond his own prejudices (Harris 2007).

Fictional works that imagine societies in which biotechnology delivers on its perceived promises are full of references to bodily functions that stand as a substitute for reasoned arguments which also trouble the liberal and democratic critiques such as that of Habermas. Huxley has John the Savage vomiting when he visits the London Hatchery. He is disgusted at the sight of identical faces of the children that crowd around him and his dying mother's bed at the hospital. In the final scene of Huxley's novel we find John providing a spectacle for his neighbours by whipping his body and vomiting some more. This exchange between John and Bernard and Helmholtz who come looking for him nicely illustrates the critique of biotechnology that fails to find rational expression:

> "I say", Helmholtz exclaimed solicitously, "you *do* look ill, John!"

> "Did you eat something that didn't agree with you?" asked Bernard.

> The Savage nodded. "I ate civilization."

> "What?"

> "It poisoned me; I was defiled. And then", he added, in a lower tone, "I ate my own wickedness."

> "Yes, but what exactly? ... I mean, just now you were ..."

> "Now I am purified", said the Savage. "I drank some mustard and warm water."

> The others stared at him in astonishment. (Huxley 1974, 188)

Mustard and warm water, John explains, is a remedy familiar to the Indians on the New Mexico reservation and, like self-flagellation, is a ritualistic method of purification that is utterly incomprehensible to citizens of civilized society. The feeling of defilement is associated in Marxist and other leftist critique with consumer society in which desire becomes synonymous with mass-produced goods. Baudrillard shares the revulsion reported by Huxley's Savage at the levelling of cultural differences. In a passage about his disgust for modern consumerism and in particular the development of vast climate-controlled indoor shopping centres offering 'eternal springtime' and 'abstract happiness', he expresses his perspective by employing a metaphor of excretion: 'Everything is finally *digested* and reduced to the same homogenous fecal matter ... All that is past (passed): a *controlled*, lubricated, and *consumed* excretion (*fecalité*) is henceforth transferred into things, everywhere diffused in the indistinguishability of things and of social relations' (Baudrillard 1988, 34–5). Baudrillard finds it horrifying that the convenience and pleasant atmosphere of the shopping mall may become the blueprint for modern life as a whole and generalized abstract contentment be transferred into all parts of private, public and social life. We may very well imagine that the vitriolic manner in which Baudrillard writes about contemporary consumer society stems as much from a feeling of physical sickness as much as his intellectual reflections on Marx. Baudrillard's references to digestion and excretion are interesting here because they relate very directly to the imaginative responses of science-fiction writings. In Atwood's *Oryx and Crake*, the two young men at the centre of the story are school friends who grow up in very different ways. One (Crake) becomes a highly gifted scientist and as such rises to the very top of society. The other (Jimmy) is less gifted and struggles to get by, drifting from one meaningless job to the next. Jimmy sees ethical objections (which, like John's, are expressed as physical revulsion) where Crake sees only commercial value. Jimmy feels nauseous upon witnessing a new kind of GM chicken grown like a vegetable with just a huge breast and a tiny mouth to 'dump the nutrients' (Atwood 2004, 238–9). In his capacity as 'mad scientist', Crake develops a new race of people that he believes will replace humankind. His creation is designed to be superior to human beings in various ways. For example, they have no conception of hierarchy or competition, they have no notion of the divine and they have no aggressive instincts. Furthermore they eat grass which they must eat twice to digest properly. Jimmy objects that this effectively means that the new species must 'eat their own shit', and Crake dismisses Jimmy's objection as 'merely aesthetic' (Atwood 2004, 188). Crake's dismissal of Jimmy's objection is of course correct from a consequentialist point of view: *so what* if the mixing of eating and excreting seems disgusting to some people, if it means that, as a society, they live peacefully? *So what* if chickens are reduced to a breast and a tiny mouth and grown like vegetables if the bird is not conscious anyway and the meat tastes just as good? The difference of perspective between Crake and Jimmy on this point neatly captures an important aspect of the debate. Baudrillard's objections to consumer culture, like Jimmy's, may be disregarded as merely aesthetic.

Perhaps the same may be said of Habermas's argument that the distinction between subjects (that is, persons) and objects (things, consumer products) must not be allowed to be effaced by permitting one generation to effectively *produce* the next according to their desired mould through eugenic programming. Throughout his writings on liberal democracy, Habermas has been keen to assert that his conception of the individual is not the disembodied self of Rawls's theory of justice in which the moral powers of rationality and reasonableness arise and assert themselves prior to any political or social context. He has always been careful to insist that in his view of liberal democracy the conditions for equality and democracy arise *within* the context of public life. Thus the voice of the individual person has always been crucially important to Habermas's conception of the state. On the other hand, until now his writings have tended to neglect the physical body itself as a site of moral reflection. However, his moral critique of biotechnology contains various references to the physicality of his reaction. Habermas (2003, 39) writes, for instance, that an ethical self-perception of our own species can only emerge from feelings of 'disgust' at practices which appear to be obscene because they undermine and erode previously unalterable species-boundaries.

b) Habermas's Vertigo and the Rape of Lavinia: Justice and the Abused Body

The 'dread' and 'vertigo' that we saw above that Habermas (2003, 39) reports feeling in response to the increasing opportunities to control the individual steps of the reproductive process is very much the physical disorientation that the word implies. In this choice of description, the metaphorical impetus of 'moral foundation' is given new life: the ground (of social morality) beneath Habermas's feet is removed and he finds himself falling through the thin-air of unfettered personal freedom. Habermas's confession of physical revulsion is quite revealing and illustrates the difficulties involved in engaging in reasoned debate on bioethics. The importance of the physical in Habermas's critique is shown most vividly in one passage of *The Future of Human Nature* in which he is discussing the necessity that individuals are fully the authors of their own 'intentions, initiatives and aspirations' for free democratic debate. He states that each person must 'be at home, so to speak, in their body' (2003, 57). There is violence in this language, all the more violent for its implication that responding to biotechnology involves an irresistible self-harm if one does not feel, 'so to speak', at home in one's body. After all, what makes vertigo so disorientating is not merely the fear that one *will* fall, but the sensation that one is *already* falling through a world that to everyone else is firmly fixed and still.

Other conservative commentators make use of a violent rhetoric of physical discomfort in their responses to biotechnology and not only in their often fanciful predictions of actual violence which may be committed on or by, say, clones or post-humans. In these passages quoted below, Yuval Levin (2003) could be writing about body-snatchers illegally exhuming and cutting up a corpse by lantern-light in the small hours:

> … the taking apart of taboos, and the dragging of the hidden into the open, is not only a challenge as we argue, but also what has drawn us into the argument to begin with. … Embryologists in the laboratory are, quite literally, dissecting taboos. … the extra-corporeal embryo has been ripped from its human context. (61–2)

There is much violence in Levin's forthright statements about dragging, dissecting, and ripping. In fact, Levin is here lamenting the unravelling of long established taboos as reasons in themselves for not, say, experimenting on embryos or cloning in the face of open, democratic debate. As we saw above, Levin seems to be sadly resigned to such a fate due to the violence that democratic debate necessarily does in 'dragging' taboo into the open for scrutiny.

Thus the human body and its demand to be treated properly, is powerfully symbolic in conservative critiques of biotechnology. Levin's deliberately unpleasant allusions to cutting up and dragging away, Kass's revulsion at 70-year-old birth-mothers and Habermas's vertigo at the thought of inhabiting a 'eugenically programmed' body; the arguments all appeal to the symbolic power of the body. It is important to Habermas that a person 'feels at home' inside their own body because if they do not, then they may not be able to become fully integrated into the public life of society or its democratic processes. Thus a concern for the *bodily* integrity of individuals translates to a theory about the integrity of democratic society as a whole. The physical body that enjoys 'integrity' is one that is complete in itself; all of its limbs are present and correct and thus support a full and complete working physical life. Likewise, Dworkin (1977, 117) describes Hercules, his imagined judge of 'integrity', as one who wields the full array of legal sources: 'Hercules must arrange justification of principle at each of these levels [the constitution, the US Supreme Court, various legislature, lower courts] so that the justification is consistent with principles taken to provide the justification of higher levels'. In coming to the right decisions in the cases he judges, it is vital that Hercules is not disconnected from any relevant legal source, so that the 'seamless web' of law does not become disjointed. The loss of integrity for both the human body and for the body of law as a set of enmeshed principles of justice is about the loss of independence through the loss or destruction of necessary constituent parts. It is all too easy to imagine the dire consequences of Hercules falling short of his arduous task: both the ordinary body and the state become bruised, broken and dismembered and justice goes missing. In Shakespeare's *Titus Andronicus*, discussed below, Titus comments on the state of chaos and violence in Rome by remarking that justice has left the earth ('Terras Astraea reliquit', IV, iii, 4), and he has good reason to think so. In a scene in *Hamlet* in which Rosencrantz and Guildenstern try to ascertain from Hamlet the whereabouts of the freshly slain body of Polonius in order that they take the body to the King, Hamlet replies: 'The body is with the King, but the king is not with the body' (IV, iii, 26). Hamlet speaks this line having just killed the 'rash intruding fool' Polonius, whom he mistook for the King. We may interpret this phrase in various ways. Literal interpretations of the remark are provided by the notes to the Arden Hamlet. Since the King may have been Hamlet's intended target it makes literal sense to say, as Jenkins (1982, 338–9) does, that although the body in question is in the palace (and thus 'with the King'), it is not itself the body of the King ('... the King is not with the body'). It also makes literal sense to say that Hamlet is stating that kingship itself is not contained within anyone's body.[3] However, given Hamlet's belief that the usurpation of Old Hamlet's throne by Claudius was unjust and harmful to the state to the extent that he showed himself willing to kill the rightful King, it is equally possible to read 'the body' as referring both to the physical human body and also the body of the state. If a person's head – the rational part – is to rule the body, we might read the sentence as alluding to Hamlet's belief that Claudius is not the rightful ruler, Denmark effectively has no head at all. 'The body is with the King' in the factual sense in which the ruler of Denmark is a man with an ordinary human body, but 'the King is not with the body' in the sense that having gained the throne unjustly, the King does not have a legitimate place at the head of the state,

---

3   For other interpretations see also Johnson (1967).

leaving the body of law headless. Being thus separated from its head, Claudius's own laws have no moral or legal validity.

Habermas's remark that one must feel at home in one's own body should be read as similarly metaphorical. He seems to regard a person's body, not merely as a vehicle for a personality, but as a symbol of political and moral autonomy. A body whose fundamental characteristics have been pre-determined does not represent a truly independent and autonomous self. The self and the body it inhabits must be right for each other and this will not be possible if there is some fundamental disjuncture between the two parts. Decapitation and mutilation of the physical human body as a metaphor for injustice and disintegration of public order under a tyrannical leader is an evident theme in Shakespeare's early tragedy *Titus Andronicus*. The speeches of Titus's brother Marcus allude to this theme on at least two occasions. At the beginning of the play Marcus Andronicus offers the crown to Titus and conjures an impression of Rome as a decapitated body in order to convince him to accept:

> Be candidatus then, and put it on,
> And help to set a head on headless Rome. (I, i, 205–210)

But Titus refuses the crown and the new leadership of 'headless Rome' becomes engulfed in a bitter feud. At the very end of the play, the cycle of revenge and counter-revenge having come to its bitter and bloody conclusion with the deaths of Tamora, Lavinia, Titus and Emperor Saturninus all in quick succession, Marcus again employs a metaphor of the wounded body – as well as metaphors of ornithology and agriculture – in an appeal for calm:

> You sad-fac'd men, people and sons of Rome,
> By uproar sever'd, as a flight of fowl
> Scatter'd by winds and high tempestuous gusts,
> O, let me teach you how to knit again
> This scattered corn into one mutual sheaf,
> These broken limbs again into one body. (V, iii, 66–71)

When Marcus discovers Titus' daughter Lavinia brutally raped and her hands and tongue cut off by Tamora's sons Demetrius and Chiron in revenge against Titus (II, iv), his speech draws attention to the larger symbolic importance of Lavinia – an innocent – within a play so full of betrayal, revenge and bloodlust, and particularly the association of justice with the body.

> O, had the monster seen those lily hands
> Tremble, like aspen leaves, upon a lute,
> And make the silken strings delight to kiss them,
> He would not then have touch'd them for his life!
> Or had he heard the heavenly harmony

Which that sweet tongue hath made,
He would have dropp'd his knife, and fell asleep,
As Cerberus at the Thracian poet's feet. (II, iv, 44–50)

The allusions to music in Marcus's speech are significant for a wider concern for justice; harmony was central to Plato's conception of the ideal state and the association between the harmony of music and harmony of the state was a familiar political symbol in the early modern period (Raffield 2008, 214–215). The Thracian poet referred to by Marcus Andronicus is Orpheus – the God of music – the mythology surrounding whom in Greco-Roman mythology presents an early example of an association between music and the harmonious state (Raffield 2008, 215). Of course, after her mutilation, Lavinia appears in the play only in the speeches and conversations of the other characters and in the stage directions. Having lost her tongue she cannot report what has happened to her, preventing justice from being done on her behalf. However she remains onstage almost until the very end of the play; her hideous mute appearance a constant reminder of violence done to her and to Rome itself (Foakes 2003, 55; Raffield 2008, 219). Shakespeare's use of the image of a dismembered and silenced body to represent disorder and injustice also finds resonances in the Bible. The Old Testament story of a travelling Levite and his concubine who spend a night in an old man's house in the Israelite town of Gibeah is another in which the abused and dismembered body of a woman comes to symbolize the injustice of a society. In this story, the men of Gibeah demand that the travelling Levite is brought out to them to be sodomized. The old man refuses to give him up and instead puts out the concubine, who is taken away and gang-raped throughout the night until dawn, when she is left for dead:

> In the morning her master got up, opened the doors of the house, and when he went out to go on his way, there was his concubine lying at the door of the house, with her hands on the threshold. "Get up", he said to her, "we are going". But there was no answer. Then he put her on the donkey; and the man set out for his home. When he had entered his house, he took a knife, and grasping his concubine he cut her into twelve pieces, limb by limb, and sent her throughout all the territory of Israel. Then he commanded the men whom he sent, saying, "Thus shall you say to all the Israelites, 'Has such a thing ever happened since the day that the Israelites came up from the land of Egypt until this day?' Consider it, take counsel, and speak out." (*Judges* 19, 27–30)

The distribution of the woman's limbs across the nation was intended to provoke universal disgust and anger amongst the Israelites towards the guilty men, and concerted action to restore justice. Indeed, it succeeds in producing a display of unity between all of the tribes of Israel, 'and the congregation assembled *in one body* before the Lord at Mizpah' (*Judges* 20, 1).[4] As Lavinia signifies beyond simply a dismembered body, the human body in this Old Testament story represents justice itself: its division and dissemination across Israel speaking of disharmony and injustice and the eventual unity of the Israelites into one body, the concerted restoration of justice. We can read this association between the abused body and the fear of disorder and injustice in Habermas's references to the 'vertigo' and 'dread' with respect to changes to human nature. Both Jurgen Habermas and Marcus Andronicus refer to qualities of the body that are vulnerable to hurt and degradation in their reflections on justice and the body politic. While Marcus invokes the God of music in his reflections on the rape of Lavinia and of the body politic itself, Habermas appeals to a metaphor of balance. As a philosopher of universal concepts, Habermas would certainly accept that one person's experience of vertigo is an inadequate basis from which to build a theory of harm. On this level, the consequentialists are correct to reject Habermas's conservative arguments about biotechnology. However, we should read Habermas as saying something much more profound about the nature of justice itself as it relates to the human body. The science-fiction novels discussed in this chapter do not compare with *Titus Andronicus* in terms of horrific violence. However, they each share something with Shakespeare's play through the strong emphasis that they place on the associations between the rupturing of the body and the rupturing of justice. Let us consider a particular relationship between the rape of Lavinia and the central theme of Kazuo Ishiguro's *Never Let Me Go* – the harvesting of the students' organs for donation. In that novel, the characters, all apparently orphans, are raised at an odd sort of boarding school in England, seemingly cut off from the rest of society. They are clones of people in the outside world, raised to accept their role as organ-donors and to give up their organs by the time they reach their mid-thirties. In effect they are all eventually cut open and plundered when their time for 'donating' comes. The word *rape* derives from the Latin *rapere*, which before its association with sexual violence meant to seize, carry off by force, abduct and plunder. The Latin word is also related to *rapidus* – which in the seventeenth century gave rise to the English *rapid*, meaning 'hasty, snatching, tearing away'. In this sense of plunder, the bodies of the students are raped and things taken from them that should not be taken. There is a parallel here between the symbolic significance of the bodies of Kathy and Tommy in Ishiguro and Lavinia in Shakespeare – in both cases the violated body serves as a sign of a ruptured body politic. In the case of *Never Let Me Go*, it is the development of a system of justice that fails to live up to the ideals of universal human and political rights that Habermas seeks to argue is possible. Both Shakespeare's Lavinia and Ishiguro's students are innocents in the ruined worlds that they respectively inhabit, and as such are all the more valuable as sacrifices for the purposes of others who

---

4   As translated in the New Revised Standard Version, my emphasis. The corporeal metaphor appears in the King James Bible as '… and the congregation was gathered together *as one man*, … unto the LORD in Mizpeh' (my emphasis).

stand to profit from their rape and deaths. Ishiguro's students and Shakespeare's Lavinia both make vain attempts to appeal to the humanity of those that oppress them, the failure of which serves to underline the vulnerability of the body and of justice in the face of political power. Before being dragged away to be raped and mutilated by Chiron and Demetrius, Lavinia turns to their mother (Tamora, the queen of the Goths) for help: 'O Tamora! Thou bar'st a woman's face' (II, iii, 136). Indeed, the figure of justice does bear a woman's face in the great majority of artistic and dramatic representations of her: as the blindfolded female figure of justice holding weighing scales that adorns the Royal Courts of Justice in London or in the form of Portia as equity in the court scene of *The Merchant of Venice*. But Tamora is determined to use Lavinia to have her revenge on her father Titus for earlier refusing to save her eldest son from sacrificial execution. Tamora's response to Lavinia's pathetic pleas seems to be as a perversion or perhaps an inversion of the 'woman's face' of justice that Lavinia tried to appeal to in solidarity:

> Remember, boys, I pour'd forth tears in vain
> To save your brother from the sacrifice;
> But fierce Andronicus would not relent:
> Therefore, away with her, and use her as you will,
> The worse to her, the better loved of me. (II, iii, 164–7)

In *Never Let Me Go*, the fates of Kathy and Tommy are as inevitably crushing as Lavinia's, not because of the demands of revenge, but by the realities of the society in which they live. If Tamora was a grotesque perversion of justice, then Miss Emily, the former head teacher to whom Kathy and Tommy appeal for a stay of execution, represents the absence of justice in a society driven by utilitarian need. Her explanation is full of resignation and the inevitability of injustice: 'You have to accept that sometimes that's how things happen in this world' (Ishiguro 2005, 243). In the only scene in the novel in which the consequentialist and principled ethical arguments concerning the creation and use of cloned humans as a source of organ donors are discussed (spanning just a few pages), Miss Emily explains that due to the impressive advancements in medical science, the students' moral status is irreversible: 'How can you ask a world that has come to regard cancer as curable, how can you ask such as world to put away that cure, to go back to the dark days? There was no going back' (Ishiguro 2005, 240). Miss Emily counsels Kathy and Tommy, who are mere clones after all, to feel grateful that their lives had been as good as they were, since most of their kind had not enjoyed such a happy childhood (Ishiguro 2005, 242–3). This scene of explanation and revelation (clumsily executed by Ishiguro it has to be said), is surely at the heart of Habermas's fear that the demonstrable advances in genetic science threatens to bring about radical changes in social attitudes. It is not a reasoned argument however – no empirical evidence for such a change has yet been convincingly adduced. Rather, it is an appeal to the imagination and to a physical, corporeal metaphor of justice and political society. On the journey back from their visit to

Miss Emily and Madame, Tommy asks Kathy to stop the car. He rushes out into the night and when Kathy tracks him down he is in the midst of a fit of rage. 'The moon wasn't quite full, but it was bright enough, and I could make out in the middle distance, near where the field began the fall away, Tommy's figure, raging, shouting, flinging his fists and kicking out' (Ishiguro 2005, 250). Tommy has no way to express his feelings coherently. Unlike Lavinia, his tongue has not actually been cut out, but nevertheless we may imagine that he feels that this is precisely what has happened to him in effect. His reaction to what he has discovered about his life and his role in society is inarticulate, expressible not as a reasoned argument but as a kicking and screaming. One might say that he is experiencing the dreaded, vertiginous realization that an essential part of his being has been determined and appropriated by someone else (that is, his identity, his organs and his lifespan). We are once again reminded of the reliance on bodily metaphors in mounting a critical argument of biotechnology.

Conclusion

To some, all theories of humanity as such – and especially notions of the essential nature of humanity – are romantic metaphysics formed in ignorance of the possibilities for change. But it is always necessary to reflect upon the bases of democratic society and ethical imperatives and the extent and nature of the challenge to these bases posed by technological developments that seem to promise/threaten fundamental changes to the way we live. I have suggested here that, although the material consequences for society and the quality of life of its members may be a matter for scientists, just how fundamental those changes are in a deeper sense is a question of imagination. What is at stake is the determination of the meaning of liberal principles of freedom and equality and the appropriate language for articulating these principles. The use of literature in this chapter has been directed towards addressing the problem of finding a language in which to speak about effects upon society and its bonds which have yet to come to pass, if they ever will. The conservative critique of biotechnology may have found itself struggling to show actual harm in a sense that Mill would recognize. Looking at this inability in the context of the literary texts, however, has enabled us to read the conservative critique in a more interesting way – invoking metaphorical allusions to the integrity and violation of the physical human body as a metaphor for the otherwise unnameable moral malaise. The next chapter develops this theme a little further, exploring the nostalgia of the conservative critique of biotechnology and the way in which this is reflected in science fiction literature.

Chapter 8
Science Fiction and the Sadness of Biotechnology: Deconstructing Conservative Nostalgia

It is not in doubt that, in the political sphere, moral squeamishness continues to frustrate consequentialists when it comes to debating biotechnologies such as embryo research, genetic enhancement, cloning and so on. When the Labour Government in the UK introduced its Bill for regulating the creation of human/animal embryos for stem cell research, it was expected to pass comfortably, given the Government's healthy majority in the House of Commons.[1] Nonetheless, members of the scientific community such as Sir Martin Evans, Professor of Mammalian Genetics, felt it necessary to publicly appeal for MPs to try to ignore the pro-life pressure groups and be guided instead by the scientific and medical benefits of stem cell research. It seems that conservative moral commentators on bioethics have succeeded in raising fears that the new Bill would allow 'immoral' scientific activity – the creation of Frankenstein monsters – even although the Bill contained explicit safeguards against research on any embryo beyond 14 days' development and could result in immensely beneficial possible consequences for the lives of living persons. As in other bioethics debates, the response from the scientific and liberal academic community to such arguments was to intensify its focus on attacking conservatives on consequentialist grounds, seeking to expose the flimsiness of conservative warnings of moral disaster by drawing attention to the liberal use of qualifiers such as 'may', 'might', 'could' and so on in conservative predictions for the future of humankind. While conservatives see biotechnologies as potentially undermining the conditions for a society committed to equal rights and participatory democracy, liberal consequentialists defend their development on grounds of the positive potential medical benefits of stem cell research, procreative liberty for parents and in some cases the purported duty on parents to use biotechnology to further the interests of their children, invoking Mill's principle that liberty must be protected against gloom-laden speculations about unknown futures and the fantasies of 'imaginative tyrants'. However, in concentrating on consequences, they have addressed only the weakest aspect of the conservative attack on biotechnology and largely ignored its more compelling aspect, at least in public political discourse. In this chapter I want to suggest a way

---

1   The Bill in question has now been passed as the Human Fertilization and Embryology Act 2008.

of challenging the conservative arguments at the level of their moral premises –
something that liberal consequentialists have so far felt to be unnecessary and
irrational. Conservatives have tended to premise their arguments on a broadly
conceived moral idea of what Leon Kass (1992, 99, 105) calls 'humanness'
and the 'human context' of our lives. Although such ideas are not vulnerable to
consequentialist critique, they can be deconstructed by engaging critically with the
ideals of the authentic human life relied upon. Part 1 of this final chapter rehearses
the existing liberal consequentialist critique of conservative positions as weak
speculation and incoherent scaremongering. Then through the literary science
fiction introduced in the previous chapter (namely Margaret Atwood's *Oryx and
Crake*, Kazuo Ishiguro's *Never Let Me Go* and Aldous Huxley's *Brave New World*),
part 2 deconstructs the moral distinction relied upon in conservative writings as
between what they regard as 'human' (ethical) and less than human (unethical)
forms of procreating, living and dying. In this part I argue that the conservative
prioritization of the distinctly 'human' conjures an ideal of authentic human life
which I liken to a myth because of the endless possibilities for rewriting and
recreating it. The mythic quality of this narrative of humanity lends it an enduring
strength in the face of consequentialist and other rational critique, but this does
not mean that it is beyond question or even defeat. As suggested in part 2 below,
it is through engaging in this process of imaginative mythmaking that an effective
challenge to conservative bioethics might be mounted.

1. Principles and Consequences: Interpreting Conservative Bioethics

As outlined above, this chapter considers the debate between conservative
and liberal commentators on the disputed ethical significance and/or danger of
biotechnology. A definition of what I mean by 'conservative' insofar as the moral
debate goes is given in Chapter 7.[2] That chapter examined the role of taboo and
metaphors of the physical human body in interpreting the conservative moral
position. This chapter now focuses more closely on the difficulties of mounting
a liberal response to the conservative position. The last chapter did not examine
in detail 'liberal' ethical positions. In contrast to the conservatives so defined in
terms of ethics, 'liberal' positions are understood here as those that defend the
development of biotechnologies on distinctly ethical grounds. The 'liberals'
presented in this chapter – represented by commentators such as John Harris – are

---

2   From Chapter 7: 'To be "conservative" for the purposes of this debate is interpreted
here as being opposed to the development of biotechnologies, in particular technologies
for the genetic enhancement of future persons, on *moral* grounds. This conservative moral
opposition to biotechnology is represented here chiefly by Jurgen Habermas, but also others
such as Leon Kass. Their objections to biotechnologies such as genetic enhancement,
cloning and PGD is definably "moral" since the arguments they advance relate to their
picture of the authentic human life.'

defined as such because their position is more or less permissive on ethical grounds: biotechnologies being regarded as good insofar as they seem to promote the interests of persons and do not cause demonstrable harm in Mill's sense. To be a liberal consequentialist on bioethics as defined here is to rest one's argument on demonstrable consequences of biotechnologies for individuals: if they in fact improve an individual person's life in some way without causing demonstrable harm, then they are to be encouraged and the harms to the principles that the conservatives identify, dismissed as phantom pains. Again, I acknowledge that the label of 'liberal' has implications far wider than this narrow sense of liberal consequentialist ethics, but as I stated above in relation to 'conservative ethics', those implications are not the subject of this chapter or indeed of this book. A starting point for our discussion is a scene from *Brave New World* in which the World Controller confronts John the Savage about his ideas on the possibility of freedom in a society dedicated to generalized satisfaction and comfort. John demands 'freedom', whatever the cost to comfort and physical and mental well-being. As he puts it: 'But I don't want comfort. I want God, I want poetry, I want real danger, I want freedom, I want goodness, I want sin' (Huxley 1974, 187). In response, the World Controller points out that to claim the right to freedom above material wellbeing means also claiming the right ...

> ... to grow old and ugly and impotent; the right to have syphilis and cancer; the right to have too little to eat; the right to be lousy; the right to live in constant apprehension of what may happen tomorrow; the right to catch typhoid; the right to be tortured by unspeakable pains of every kind. (Huxley 1974, 187)

John's reply is: 'I claim them all' (Huxley 1974, 187). That is to say, he claims the right to a future with the possibility of pain as well as pleasure, where he is free to make his own mistakes and moral choices. This exchange between John and the World Controller is of course very famous and is commonly cited as the kernel of Huxley's satire both of what he regarded as the bland comforts offered by American consumerism and restrictions on personal freedom for state purposes by Soviet socialism (West 1932, quoted in Watt 1975, 200).[3] But what relevance does the passage have for bioethics? The understanding of the relationship between 'real freedom' and 'unspeakable pains' that both characters seem to accept as an either/or choice can be read in (at least) two quite different ways. First, we might read the passage as making a weak and problematic consequentialist claim that *if* society manages to bring this list of pains under control – aging, impotence, syphilis, cancer, hunger, typhoid, pain in general – *then* we must also sacrifice those things we want to preserve – 'poetry, real danger, freedom, goodness, sin'. It is this interpretation that some conservative bioethicists have adopted – I will

---

3   Rebecca West in her 1932 review of *Brave New World* described the society that Huxley's World Controller represents as achieving Communism's desire to 'flatten out' emotional and intellectual life to achieve 'triumphant smoothness' (Watt 1975, 200).

argue, unwisely – as a template for an argument that opposes biotechnology on the basis of the possible consequent harm to those things we regard as valuable and important in human life. It is this interpretation and the liberal consequentialist critique of it that is considered immediately below. On the other hand, we might interpret the exchange as implying no particular empirical claim about the effects of biotechnology on the experience of individual freedom, but rather as a personal expression about what it means to live an authentic life, inviting critique not for its implied prediction for our own society but for its claim that a distinctly 'human' life can be coherently distinguished from and prioritized over an 'artificial' one. On this reading, there is no claim that the eradication of disease or the provision of comfort is in itself inimical to freedom, but rather that reflecting on the meaning of values that have in the past been identified as concerns for human identity and society (freedom, autonomy, belief, equality, democracy, and so on) involves prioritizing the recognisably 'human' over the artificial, unfamiliar or supposedly dehumanizing. Such an interpretation is a basis for an attempt to challenge conservative arguments on their own terms, engaging with the conservative appeal to a moral prioritization of the human(e) over the less than human(e), and we turn to that interpretation in Part 2 of this chapter.

a) The Biotechnology Debate on Consequentialist Terms: Liberty, Benefit and Harm

It is undeniable that the conservative commentators have indeed presented their own arguments as warnings about possible future harms resulting from biotechnology and in doing so have exposed themselves to withering criticism by liberal consequentialists. The argument from 'flourishing' or 'flowering' is one example a future-harm orientated conservative argument. Leon Kass's writings on the ethics of biotechnology come as close as anyone's to directly rehearsing the first interpretation I outlined of the exchange between John the Savage and the World Controller. Kass (2003, 16) makes an explicit link between vulnerability to disease and personal freedom and the link is forged by a claim that reducing vulnerability also reduces diversity and the different kinds of lives that can be lived. He argues:

> We are right to worry that the self-selected non-therapeutic uses of the new powers, especially where they become widespread, will be put in the service of the most common human desires, moving us toward still greater homogenization of human society – perhaps raising the floor but greatly lowering the ceiling of human possibility, and reducing the likelihood of genuine freedom, individuality, and greatness. (Kass 2003, 16)

Like John the Savage, Kass sees 'genuine' freedom in opposition to what he regards as the quick-fix happiness apparently offered by biotechnology and any future success in wielding biotechnology to deliver increased comfort as deleterious to freedom. It is well known that Huxley's own feelings on the matter were in part drawn from his reaction to visiting Los Angeles, which he called 'the City of Dreadful Joy'. Huxley regarded Los Angeles as offering standardized happiness (and therefore political and social stability) at the expense of intellectual and spiritual life (Firchow 1972, 125). Huxley (1927) wrote of the citizens of Los Angeles that many 'do not want to be cultured, are not interested in the higher life. For these people existence on the lower, animal level is perfectly satisfactory'. His critics have suggested that Huxley himself believed that a rationally ordered society and the life of passion and creativity were incompatible, that the death of high culture is a necessary condition for generalized order and happiness.[4] What seems to have appalled Huxley about Los Angeles was the ease with which its inhabitants seemed to be satisfied through 'low' physical and emotional pleasures (Firchow 1972, 128). Leon Kass makes it clear that the exacerbation of what he perceives as the superficial nature of modern consumer society would be a harm sufficient for ethical condemnation and perhaps also legal prohibition. However Kass, like Huxley, may simply be a bit snobbish. It may well be true that a man who is truly satisfied by the 'low' pleasures that Huxley and Kass find so depressing will probably not be moved to write the next *Anna Karenina*. But surely this has very little to do with freedom in the sense of liberty. A depressed person is likely to (and indeed is supposed to) experience life and make decisions differently if they begin using Prozac. The same might be said for, say, a man who takes Viagra to improve his sex life or someone else who becomes convinced that McDonald's is the right place for them to eat, since the sugar and salt content of the food gives them sufficient enjoyment. Would we say that such people's 'freedom' is thereby affected negatively? Huxley's Savage, who despised the use of soma for its capacity to prevent all kinds of unhappiness (and therefore minimize the risk of social unrest), may have done. However, even if we accept that commercialism brings about a degree of homogenization of taste and behaviour, this does not necessarily carry any negative implications for autonomy. In the case of interventions that affect those unable to consent, whether in the form of drugs for children or embryo selection or genetic enhancement, liberal consequentialists argue that this poses no special problem. Unless the intervention actually diminished one's intellectual or creative abilities it is unlikely that they would be a bar to freedom even if universally available, any more than, say universal availability of clean running water (Harris 2007, 128). Certainly an enhanced child has not had the opportunity to consent or object. But liberal consequentialists argue that such a child is not harmed by having such a decision made on their behalf if the intervention is broadly speaking beneficial to them. For Kass's argument against such interventions to succeed, we would need to accept a particular definition of freedom that demands not only the protection of the child's reasoning powers, but also a Romantic vision of freedom stemming from Rousseau's notion of the individual striving to free themselves

---

4   Thody, P. (1973), *Aldous Huxley: A Biographical Introduction* (London: Studio Vista), 49–50.

from the trappings of culture and society. Kass, who does seem to demand such a view of freedom, has generalized his own personal frustration at and disdain for certain kinds of lives and certain kinds of people, whose apparently unimaginative and conformist preferences tie them too closely with consumer society. It is very difficult to see how such disdain could inform a reliable view as to what should be permitted and what should not. Dena S. Davis' opposition to sex selection, similarly, is precariously balanced between concern for a child's right to an 'open future' and snooty disdain for certain kinds of people and the choices they make:

> I suspect that parents who choose the sex of their offspring are more likely to have gender-specific expectations for those children, expectations that subtly limit the child's own individual flowering. The more we are able to control our children's characteristics ... the more invested we will become in our hopes and dreams for them. (Davis 2006, 254–5)[5]

This may be true for many parents and thinking about this possibility may be a useful way for parents themselves to reflect upon their relationship with their children, but speculation about how parents may or may not feel or act towards their offspring does not sufficiently make out a case for invoking legal prohibition or identify *when* parental freedoms might give way to protection of children from harm. As various commentators have pointed out, such an argument does not give us sufficient reason to distinguish between acceptable and unacceptable pressures and expectations that parents bring to bear on their children (Savulescu 2006, 146). The potential for increased personal decision-making powers to impact negatively upon moral attitudes is an approach adopted by Margaret Somerville (2001, 298), who writes in a slightly different context, 'legalizing euthanasia would harm society and diminish the value of respect for human life. It would change the fundamental norm of society – that we must not kill one another – to one that we may do so in some circumstances, albeit for reasons of the utmost mercy and compassion.' This consequentialist argument about the implications for further slippage of social attitudes is discernable in various forms and across the range of the medical ethical battlefront. George W. Bush appealed to it when, surrounded by an audience of parents and children he announced his decision to veto a Senate Bill to provide US federal funding for stem cell research: 'These boys and girls are not spare parts' ('Bush Uses Veto on Stem Cell Bill' 2006). The then President, like Margaret Somerville, felt that legal prohibitions must be kept in place in order to guard against the danger of a deterioration of ethical views about human life. Habermas (2003, 71) likewise appeals to the same kind of argument when he warns: 'The desensitisation of the way we look at human nature, going hand in hand with the *normalization* of this practice, would clear the path for liberal eugenics.' As a warning about future possible harms, arguments of this kind stand in need of empirical verification. Later in this chapter we examine

---

5   See also Feinberg (1988, 124–53).

this argument through a society imagined in Kazuo Ishiguro's *Never Let Me Go* in which legal changes regarding cloning and organ donation have in fact brought about such a view of children.

As we have seen, Habermas's critique of biotechnology is a little more nuanced than Kass', since his objection to what he calls 'eugenic programming' seems to be torn between condemning it both as being wrong in principle and for possible harmful effects. However, insofar as he too predicts that biotechnology will have harmful effects, his forays into the subject have been met with a similar kind of criticism as Kass. The harms to individuals and society that Habermas identifies are the undermining of the conditions of equality and freedom necessary for open and universal communicative and discourse and hence liberal democracy itself. Habermas's painstakingly worked through notions of the conditions for universal communication within democratic society are a response to what he regards threats to the very idea of liberal democracy. He vociferously defends the distinction between serious, constructive speech capable of giving rise to universal moral and legal norms on the one hand and strategic deployments of rhetoric and coercion that serve only particular power bases on the other. The targets of his defensive attacks on behalf of liberal democracy over the past couple of decades have been postmodernism and poststructuralism (which prioritize playful rhetoric over serious speech) and also capitalist and commercial interests seeking to use financial influence in public discourse (Habermas 1997). Habermas's accusation against liberal consequentialists in favour of biotechnology is broadly in line with that which he levelled against postmodern writers: that the ideal of constructing the conditions for a truly universal liberal democracy are put in jeopardy by the problematizing of enlightenment notions of equality, participatory democracy, justice and freedom.

As discussed in the previous chapter, it is a moral problem for Habermas that eugenic programming allows essential aspects of a person's identity to be irreversibly determined in advance, ensuring radical inequality between the generations and closing off the possibility of the level communicative relationship necessary for liberal democracy. The individual is harmed by having such a decision made for them without their being able to communicate consent or refusal, even if the decision itself results in that child being born healthier, more intelligent and stronger than they would have otherwise been. In this sense it is not the effect but the fact of a decision having been made outside the realm of a communicative relationship that is unethical for Habermas. Would a child justifiably feel harmed by knowing that their parents used genetic enhancements to give their offspring, say, a stronger heart or a fine roman nose? Habermas seems to be arguing that such a child may, not on the basis of the physical effects, but on the principle of inequality underlying the decision. Habermas (2003, 68) states that his principled opposition to, say, PGD means that for him it is better to refrain altogether from determining which embryo is implanted than to select one either to avoid genetic disease or to provide some positive trait.[6] Understanding what Habermas is getting at requires one to accept that someone can be benefited and harmed at the same time and by the same act; the benefit is in the physical advantage conferred in advance and the harm is in the consequent alienation from democratic society.

The liberal consequentialist response to the above arguments has been to question the empirical justifiability of their predictions of harm. Recall the exchange between John the Savage and the World Controller in *Brave New World*, interpreted as warning that a society that embraces biotechnologies to eradicate disease and suffering and so on could not be inhabited by 'free' citizens. A reader in the early twenty-first century sympathetic to liberal consequentialism might reflect that it does seem possible to be 'free' in a moral sense of experiencing 'poetry, God, real danger, freedom, goodness, sin', and so on even though one's life may not seem to be at the mercy of 'unspeakable pains of every kind'. To such a reader, John's stoicism will seem misplaced, since the notion that the eradication of debilitating diseases and disabilities makes us unfree is simply not in evidence. In any case, Huxley's citizens' lack of freedom derives not from the fact of having been cloned nor from the comforts provided by medical and reproductive technology but from the state's success in chemically controlling intelligence, personality and systematically indoctrinating them to accept socially useful values. It is this state intervention in the tiniest details of both public and private life (for there is no discernable distinction) that ensures that Huxley's citizens feel satisfied with their pre-defined place in society to the extent that there is no social unrest or dramatic or unpredictable changes in consumer behaviour. Only the Savage can fully feel the full effects of the system on his freedom because he has not been subjected to the conditioning that would otherwise make him more pliant.

In response to conservatives, liberal consequentialists raise two related arguments; 1) Whatever is in a person's interest is a benefit not a harm; and 2) unless the conferring of a benefit will cause some empirically identifiable and sufficiently serious harmful effect, it cannot be wrong to provide it. On the contrary, for those with a parental or some other responsibility, it is a positive duty: '... we must not fail to make changes that could be made which will avoid harm to future people or which would benefit them in ways that cannot be achieved unless these enhancements are put in place' (Harris 2007, 80). Some liberal consequentialists have focused on the liberty of parents rather than that of children, since the restriction of biotechnologies that would otherwise help parents to have the children they want could be a violation of what Julian Savulescu calls 'procreative autonomy' – which must trump vague speculations as to harm, particularly 'social' harms. 'Parents know best their own circumstances, and ultimately it is parents

---

6   Habermas (2003, 68): 'Our unwillingness to legalize PGD is grounded in consideration of both the conditional creation of embryos and the nature of this condition itself. Bringing about a situation in which we might eventually reject an afflicted embryo is as dubious as selection according to criteria defined by one side only.'

who must live with and make sacrifices for their children. Procreative autonomy should not be sacrificed to correct social inequality' (Savulescu 2006, 148). For Harris, similarly, reproductive liberty is so important that prospective harm must be demonstrably present, serious and actual for legal prohibition is justified. As in previous publications, Harris's defence of biotechnology in general and genetic enhancement in particular is based on Mill's idea that liberty must prevail unless exercising it causes definable harm. '[U]nless I can show that what you propose to do, or are doing, is harmful to others or society, then a commitment to liberal democratic values means that I must leave you room to differ from me' (Harris 2007, 73). In fact, Mill probably understood the concept of 'harm' even more narrowly than does Harris, since while Harris includes 'society' as a possible victim of harm, Mill denied that there existed 'social rights' attaching to society as a whole. On the subject of whether individual liberty could be justifiably curtailed to protect society in general from violations of equality and security, Mill's response is fiercely negative: 'So monstrous a principle is far more dangerous than any single interference with liberty; there is no violation of liberty which it would not justify' (Mill 1863, 173). On this view, anyone who opposes a certain practice, belief, words and so on bears the burden of showing 'real and present' harm. If the rights and freedoms in liberal democratic society are to have any practical meaning, liberty must not be allowed to be held hostage to 'imaginative tyrants' (Harris 2007, 74). Therefore, provided that parents' decisions are not 'grossly against their interests or manifestly dangerous', Habermas's worries about a possible violation of communicative encounter is predictably insufficient for legal prohibition since on such grounds, most parenting decisions for very young children would be ruled out. Savulescu (2006, 147) denies that there is a duty to consider possible psychological harms resulting from technologies whose purpose is to create life because without the pre-natal decisions that led to the uniting of the particular gametes that created the person, that person would not exist: 'Even if the child is disadvantaged psychologically, this is only wrong from the child's perspective if its life is so bad that it is not worth living.' Presumably this would justify interventions such as sex selection and cloning that directly lead to the creation of a person, but not necessarily those that simply alter its characteristics, such as PGD and genetic enhancement. This view that harm caused by the act of procreation itself is only morally relevant if it makes the created person's life so bad as to be not worth living is one that is not universally accepted however. Seana Valentine Shiffrin (1999) argues that since procreation is not an activity made necessary to avert greater harm (like a rescue), then those involved owe a duty not to thereby inflict harm to future children:

> Causing another to exist may well be all-things-considered justified, but the conditions in which it may be justified seem different from those in which

inflicting harm to prevent harm is justified. Specifically, this justification would yield a permission only if the bestower is accountable for harm that results. (Shiffrin 1999, 134)

... [T]he procreative acts will set in motion a series of events that will impose a set of significant, burdensome conditions on the person; being subject to these unchosen harms, assuming they persist so long, will violate the person's consent rights at whatever point these rights vest. (Shiffrin 1999, 137–8)

Whether or not we would hold progenitors of a cloned child liable for resulting 'harms', the difference between liberal and conservative consequentialists lies firstly in what we recognize as harm at all, and secondly in what suffices as evidence that such a harm will result. Drawn into an empirical discussion of how a future individual might actually experience a supposed violation of identity as an autonomous person on an equal footing with the previous generation, Kass and Habermas and other conservatives inevitably struggle to demonstrate harm as Mill would recognize it as the threshold necessary to justify curtailing the liberty of parents to make genetic interventions for their children. To the contention that eugenic programming is an 'instrumental determinism' by one generation of the next, Harris (2007, 139) replies that although Habermas is indeed correct that the latter is permanently affected by the former, this is equally true of any other kind of child-rearing. This being so, it makes no sense to speak of the future generations as harmed by genetic intervention. Ordinarily, the two parents' genetics determine the outcome of their child's genome and they make various decisions for the child that the latter cannot later alter, such as vaccination, language, nursery education, and so on. Harris (2007, 142) identifies Habermas as falling short of Mill's test precisely because, his contentions that biotechnology represents an especially troubling order of control and influence are merely gloom-laden speculations, which could as well turn out to be false as true. Habermas's warnings that a genetically determined person would or might find it difficult to participate fully in democratic society on account of a feeling of degraded equality and/or autonomy, Harris (2007, 141) dismisses as mere 'scaremongering'. He goes on: 'If [the eugenic control that Habermas objects to] is inimical to equality or autonomy, then neither equality not autonomy exist nor have they ever existed' (Harris 2007, 140). Harris (2007, 81) dismisses Habermas's argument that pre-natal decisions are unethical because they are not made against a background of a communicative relationship as 'simply absurd'. We readily accept the necessity of making decisions for those incompetent to decide for themselves in the interests of preserving 'family life' and 'parental discretion' without any perceived negative implications for the autonomy of children as they develop (Harris 2007, 83, 124–5). Interpreted as a debate on whether the consequences of biotechnology are commensurable with liberal democracy's commitments to equality, diversity and autonomy, the liberals have sought to undercut the conservative assertions of possible future harm. This liberal attack on conservative consequentialist arguments has been applied also to cloning. A clone or a person genetically enhanced or in some other way manipulated before birth might believe that their choices have been determined by their parents' genetic decisions, but as Michael Tooley (2006, 168–70) argues, they would be wrong to believe such as thing, since this belief would be founded on a prior belief in genetic determinism, itself lacking credibility. For many conservatives, the mere possibility that a cloned child will feel somehow disadvantaged by his difference from peers born through 'normal' means is reason enough to ground an ethical objection. For liberals, such possibility is to be dismissed as irrelevant and prejudiced as an objection to a mixed race or homosexual couple desiring to have children to protect the children's feelings. 'Natural' people might regard human clones with disdain but, again, their disdain might be dismissed as mere prejudice. The risk of harm is too remote and too abstract to justify imposing restrictions on the exercise of free choice which is designed to confer a benefit on the future person in any case.

2. Bioethics without Consequentialism: Deconstructing Conservative Mythology of 'Humanness'

It is not conservatives' consequentialist claims that have had the most impact in political discourse, but rather their moral claims about promoting a certain ideal of human life. As a matter of policy the biotechnologies we have discussed may be, and in many cases are, rejected in political debate irrespective of the possible benefits. The more compelling interpretation of Huxley's interrogation scene and of conservative bioethics itself is as a view on the recognizably authentic 'human' life rather than an empirical claim that artificially enhanced comfort is inimical to freedom, because liberal consequentialism has no response to this. Liberal consequentialists may have stripped away conservatives' dire warnings, but have left untouched a set of ideas about human nature and its relationship to the material world and consumer society that is itself vulnerable to a different sort of critique, which I lay out below.

a) Bioethics as Presence: Prioritizing 'Human Context'

It is no coincidence that conservative denunciations of various forms of biotechnology are accompanied by approval for 'natural' life. We have seen above that Kass (2003, 16) favours natural physical attributes, talents and mental states over enhancements irrespective of consequences and that Habermas considers that to refrain to interfere with embryonic life altogether is better than acting to enhance it. But to interpret these conservative positions being premised on naturalness alone would be to ignore signs of awareness of the shortcomings of such appeals in conservative writings on bioethics, in particular that naturalness is a 'moral conclusion, not evidence that can be offered in a moral argument' (Gorvitz 1992, 121). Even most conservatives would now concede that since there is no appreciable moral problem with interventions such as painkillers, vaccinations, organ transplants and so on, then there cannot be any necessary moral relevance to artificiality in itself. This being so, there must be something else that grounds the conservative argument once we have left arguments as to whether the consequences of artificial interventions are harmful or beneficial to one side. The 'something else' needed to provide the foundation is a moral prioritization of the recognizably 'human' over that which displaces 'human context'. The moral focus of the conservative writings is to try to sustain a narrative that effectively invokes an idea or ideal of humanity – what I call a mythologizing of humanity – in order to foster a feeling that certain things are wrong simply because they stand in opposition to the ideal. This narrative is underpinned in the conservative bioethical writings by a set of binary distinctions that will be familiar to readers of Jacques Derrida: life/death, vivaciousness/sterility, joy/reason, spontaneity/calculation, love/indifference and speech/writing. In each case, the first part of the binary opposition represents an aspect of authentic and hence definitively *human* experience, and hence that which is morally prioritized over the second part. And this moral order pertains irrespective of empirically discernable consequences.

Consider once more Huxley's *Brave New World*, and particularly two scenes depicting death and birth respectively, in which Huxley seems to contrast an authentic, human perspective against cold utilitarianism. First, there is a moving scene in which John's mother Linda, who spends her final days drugged on soma and watching electronic tennis, finally gains enough consciousness to recognize her son and understand that she really is dying (Huxley 1974, 183). As later recounted by his widow, Aldous Huxley had strong beliefs about the significance of death, believing that the dying process itself must not be shrunk from, feared or avoided through heavy sedation, but rather approached positively, with 'joy, peace, love' (May 1972, 114; Woodcock 1972, 40–1). Second, there is the novel's opening scene, depicting the London Hatchery in which babies are 'decanted' by scientists according to a Platonist idea of the correctly balanced society;

> [A] harsh thin light glared through the windows, hungrily seeking some draped lay figure, some pallid shape of academic goose-flesh, but finding only the glass and nickel and bleakly shining porcelain of a laboratory. Wintriness responded to wintriness. The overalls of the workers were white, their hands gloved with a pale corpse-coloured rubber. The light was frozen, dead, a ghost. (Huxley 1974, 15)

Huxley's description evokes not the mixture of optimism and uncertainty associated with birth but the dull depressing inevitability of a factory line or even a mortuary. The 'corpse-coloured workers' are responsible for bringing into being lives that will be every bit as 'spiritually dead' as themselves (May 1972, 105). Although no argument has yet been advanced as to why such a society is to be rejected, readers are in doubt that all is not well. Even if the consequences of such a system are universally good and beneficial, readers of Huxley's novel will typically recoil at his futuristic society. Consequences are hardly the point: where there ought to be life, spontaneity and joy, there is instead stillness, rationality, sterility, indifference. Through a set of binary oppositions between life and death, a particular narrative about the nature of authentic human life and also what is inimical to such a life is created. Thus human life itself reveals itself as a myth, that is, a story that, lacking an official version, may be endlessly recreated and rewritten. And it is the very re-writability of this story that is the key to challenging the conservative critique of biotechnology in terms of moral rhetoric. Leon Kass has said that the perversion of the natural process of childbirth depicted in *Brave New World* is in itself sufficiently horrible for criticism in its own right, and from a consequentialist viewpoint this is the thinnest of all possible arguments. If consequences were the key to resolving the debate, Kass and other conservatives would be of no relevance whatsoever to contemporary bioethics. The lingering impact of such arguments may relate to what Derrida describes as a general tendency for texts in the Western tradition to prioritize 'speech' over 'writing'. Concepts associated with speech imply *presence*, in particular the presence of a living, speaking person and hence a source of authentication and verification. Conversely, concepts associated with writing imply *absence*, or in other words being cut off from a living source of authentication (Derrida 2002). To associate a practice or concept with writing is to denigrate it as secondary, supplementary, inauthentic and unreliable. The metaphor of a piece of writing as a form of expression implies a formal and physical disconnection from its original source in living thought and hence the risk of it being misread and misused (Wolfreys 1998, 68).[7] Derrida's own early writings trawl the history of Western philosophy to reveal how writing has been disparaged as a 'dangerous supplement' to living speech (Rousseau 1986), and a 'usurper of natural memory' (Plato 1990, 157; Derrida 2002, 353).[8] Derrida reads the traditional commitment within Western philosophy to distinguishing the true from the false as a repeated invocation of the presence/absence opposition, and in particular the concern that writing should not be allowed to endanger the primacy of people's natural faculties.

Writings in conservative bioethics provide ample examples of this hierarchy between speech (presence) and writing (absence). We will again draw from Kass and Habermas. In order to support his argument, Kass (1992, 104–5) evokes the 'dehumanising' environment of Huxley's London Hatchery to argue that to permit human babies to be born through ectogenesis would disrespect human life by denying the foetus the 'human context' it deserves. A rhetoric of 'humanness' or 'humanity' is one that is familiar to Huxley's readers. For instance, Huxley's

---

7   The special status of authenticity accorded to speech is arguably identifiable in the legal process. For instance, a trial witness's testimony is regarded as more likely to be authentic if it is spoken in court, following a spoken oath. If the witness him or herself is not able to testify personally then it is generally excluded as mere hearsay.

8   Plato warns that writing 'will implant forgetfulness in their souls ... calling things to remembrance no longer from within themselves but by means of external marks ... it is no true wisdom but only its semblance ...'

rejection of American consumerism as a model for future society was based on his own preference for the internal and personal aspects of life over the external (that is, happiness through acquisition), a hierarchy that is itself based on what Firchow (1972, 121–2) calls a concern for a 'genuinely human society'. The human context that Kass refers to in relation to reproduction and gestation is the physical bodily presence of a mother to the foetus growing inside the womb, which for Kass guarantees the authenticity of natural birth. The absence of a human mother in the case of ectogenesis is what guides Kass to the view that it is unethical. Scientists and their machinery are unwelcome third parties that replace vivaciousness with sterility, love with exactitude and speech with writing.

Second, consider Habermas. Defending his assertions that pre-natal genetic decisions are unethical even if the health of the resulting child is thereby enhanced, Habermas argues that legal prohibitions are necessary in order to protect the moral image of man as a *subject* within a society committed to universally free and equal deliberative discourse. For Habermas, it is important continually to reinforce the distinction between subjects ('the grown') and objects ('the made') in public democratic discourse because they ensure that the liberal conception of the person of rights and dignity who cannot be treated like an object in the realm of consumer goods is maintained. Preserving this distinction involves Habermas himself using language strategically in order to mark the distinction as he sees it between the authentic life as 'subject' and the inauthentic life as 'object', in at least two ways in particular. For instance, he argues that birth is symbolic of a person's uniqueness; as an opportunity for a fresh start, birth 'goes back beyond the lines of tradition and the contexts of interaction [constituting] a life history' (Habermas 2003, 59). To deny someone the opportunity for a clean break by predetermining their identity through 'eugenic programming' is therefore to blur the distinction between subject and object. Furthermore, his use of the expression 'eugenic programming' – a consciously pejorative expression – to describe a range of technologies and techniques involved in fertility treatment indicates the distinction. Some of these technologies, such as genetic enhancement and sex selection for family balancing can perhaps be justifiably be regarded as forms of positive eugenics. To describe them all as eugenic programming has particularly nasty historical associations in Germany, and particular the strategic and partial attitudes fostered by the Third Reich towards human life (which of course in the case of many people deemed draining on society meant death, whether literally in the case of the eugenics programmes for the disabled or the death camps for others, or symbolically in the form of the death of civil and political rights). Using the word 'programming' implies not only the practice of selecting genes to avoid certain genetic diseases or even for selecting in particular physical characteristics, but that the resulting persons will themselves be 'programmed' in the sense of lacking autonomy – even if those 'programmed' in fact do not feel any loss of autonomy at all. Whereas Habermas associates 'natural' reproduction with an ideal of human life, universality, freedom and being treated with respect, he associates 'eugenic programming' with their opposites: with arbitrary death, partiality of favour, slavery, being treated like an object. For both Habermas and Kass then, biotechnologies such as artificial reproductive technologies are to be viewed as a 'dangerous supplement' to natural life, which must be kept from usurping that which it is supposed only to serve by continually reinforcing the primacy of the recognizably and authentically 'human'.

b) The Failure of Presence: Conservative Bioethics as Nostalgia for the 'Authentic'

To deconstruct a text is to demonstrate how the metaphysical premises on which an argument is based – namely the underlying moral distinction between what is favoured and what is disfavoured – unravel. Derrida devoted much of his own career to showing how the prioritization of speech over writing – which he regarded as the basis for all further philosophy in the Western tradition – was itself flawed. He argued that Western philosophers, once having asserted the primacy of spontaneous and trustworthy 'speech' over dead and unreliable 'writing' (and thus the stability of moral judgments as such), have then tended to admit anxieties about the possibility of sustaining the priority of speech. Both Rousseau and Plato, for instance, worry that the necessity for writing to supplement the natural and inevitable limitations of living speech (for example, the death or physical absence of the original speaker) may lead to writing – the symbol of absence and thus inauthenticity – eventually replacing speech as the primary communicative form. It is this anxiety that points to the failure of the hierarchy itself as a basis for coherently prioritizing one concept over another, since if speech – apparently symbolic of authenticity and truth – stands in need of supplementation by the supposedly secondary 'writing', then it surely must fail to do the work needed – that is, to guarantee *presence*. The insidious characteristics of 'writing' (a mere supplement to original expression in the absence of its source) come to characterize the prioritized concept as well (Derrida 1993, 102–3). Deconstructing conservative bioethics in this way means considering the success or otherwise with which conservatives mobilize the binary associations of life/death, vivaciousness/ sterility, joy/reason, spontaneity/calculation, love/indifference in the cause of establishing that only the practices they believe are ethical (natural reproduction, non-interference with embryonic life, and so on) and not supposedly unethical ones are authenticated by the presence of 'human context'. Take, for example, Kass' argument about the moral superiority of natural reproduction over artificially assisted method. Kass himself shows a certain anxiety about whether his own prioritization of 'human' over 'artificial' reproduction is stable. Reading Kass, it quickly becomes clear that a principled distinction between the different types of reproduction is undermined since the presence or absence of 'human context' seems to depend on wholly arbitrary factors not related to the physical presence of, say, a mother's womb or a loving couple, or even on a reliance more abstract signs of human physicality. Take, for example, his admission that IVF technology does not raise the same magnitude of ethical difficulty as ectogenesis. Kass (1992, 106) bemoans the lack of sexual intimacy involved in IVF technology, a technology not quite as awful as others, but to be treated with suspicion since it lacks a 'fusion of souls' and involves the unwelcome intrusion into a couple's private life in the form of a clinician. 'Even in the best of cases', he writes, 'do we not pay in coin of our humanity for electing to generate sexlessly?' His preference for reproduction based on sexual intercourse is consistent with his generally conservative bioethics, as this demonstrates the conservative association of the natural, vivacious means of procreation with the ethical (presence of human context), and the clinical, scientifically controlled, measured, professional environment of the IVF clinic shares with the unethical (absence of human context). However, despite his view that humanity is diminished by 'electing to generate sexlessly', he nevertheless accepts that IVF in fact poses no ethical problems and that it is ectogenesis rather than IVF that 'dehumanizes' gestation and birth. So not all technology dehumanizes, but what is the principled distinction between IVF and ectogenesis? Kass (1992, 104) gives no argument beyond asserting that ectogenesis is a 'repugnant Huxleyan prospect'. Both IVF and ectogenesis involve replacing the natural accident and uncertainty of the reproductive functions of the unaided human body with those of the processes of reproductive technology which ought to mark both processes with the characteristics of absence. Since Kass himself gives no coherent reason to think otherwise we are left to suppose that the difference is merely one of arbitrary feeling, based on the familiarity of IVF and unfamiliarity (and currently beyond the capabilities of technology) of ectogenesis. The hierarchy itself therefore loses its coherence and Kass's championing of natural reproduction on the grounds that it supports the 'humanness of our human life and the meaning of or embodiment' (Kass 1992, 99) is in fact a nostalgic longing for an original purity of human life that he imagines must have existed before humans invented the means to supplement natural infertility and thereby endanger the definably human character of formally vital human processes (Derrida 1993, 102–3).

Reading the arguments in this way, the mythology – or re-writiability – of the idea of 'humanness' becomes apparent inasmuch as it becomes clear that it does not belong to the conservatives alone. It cannot be fixed except by associations that are themselves arbitrary and fluid. Secondly, consider Habermas's invocation of the birth event. If Habermas were really confident that the birth event carried the symbolic significance that he accords to it, then surely the fact that the gametes were provided by two people rather than one, or that a particular embryo was chosen for implantation on grounds of having the combination of genes that its progenitors desired, would not affect the status of birth itself as representing a baby's individuality. If the significance of this momentous event is so easily undermined, the very idea of maintaining a distinction between natural and unnatural is itself open to doubt. The fear of the dangerous effects of supposedly secondary, supplementary technological interventions on the primacy or uniqueness of birth as authentic marks it with the signs of absence that Habermas wants to confine to the former and calls the primacy of the latter into question. Why limit the failure of the significance of birth to instances in which the progenitors have chosen their offspring's genetic characteristics using PGD and other technologies? The decision to limit it is thus surely an arbitrary one which merely reflects Habermas's own ideas about the significance of genetic accident and mystery and his nostalgia for a simpler life. All of these factors contribute to Habermas' understanding of the myth of the authentic life.

The nostalgic yearning for the definitively 'human' life is inexhaustible due to the infinite malleability of the concept in question. No one particular version of it is wholly true or wholly authentic and thus the 'speech' metaphors invoked to defend it – life, vivacity, spontaneity, chance, and so on – can do no more than supplement repeated failure to guarantee the prioritization of what conservatives regard as the authentic life over the artificial one. Derrida coined the expression 'différance' to describe what he regarded as the logical conclusion of the structuralist notion of meaning as difference: that if a signifier (such as a word) comes to have meaning not through any natural signification but rather through its difference from other signifiers (hence making up a system of differences we recognize as a language), then meaning itself must be an *infinite* chain of significations. To speak of difference, therefore, is to speak of the endless *deferral* of meaning and hence of the endlessly slippery nature of truth (or 'truth') itself, including moral truth, and the nostalgia of the search for it. In Caryl Churchill's play *A Number* a man in his early 60s, Salter, who abandoned his son at the age of four meets Michael, 35, one of 'a number' of men whom he discovers had been cloned from his abandoned child. Hitherto a stranger to him, Salter wants some reassurance that Michael really is unique in some way; that Michael is authentically human like himself. He interrogates him at length about what it is about this young man that is unique and specific *to him*. Of course, there is no answer that can satisfy the father, since everything the young man says relates not to himself alone, but to his relationships with and differences from other people. The exchange, quoted below from Caryl Churchill's script (Churchill 2002), can be read as demonstrating the infinite difference and deferral that takes place in trying meaningfully to separate authentic from inauthentic human life (the moral basis of conservative critiques), a difficulty that calls into question the binary opposition itself:

SALTER: I was hoping I don't know something more personal something from deep inside your life. If that's not intrusive.

MICHAEL: Maybe what maybe my wife's ears?

SALTER: Yes?

MICHAEL: Because last night we were watching the news and I thought what beautiful and slightly odd ears she's got, they're small but with big lobes, big relative to the small ear, and they're slightly pointy on top, like a Disney elf or little animal ears and they're always there but you know how you suddenly notice and noticing that, I mean the way I love her, felt very felt what you said something deep inside. Or the children obviously, I could talk about, is this the sort of thing?

SALTER: It's not quite

MICHAEL: No

SALTER: Because you're just describing other people or

MICHAEL: Yes

SALTER: Not yourself

MICHAEL: But it's people I love so

SALTER: It's not what I'm looking for. Because anyone could feel

MICHAEL: Oh of course I'm not claiming

SALTER: I was somehow hoping

MICHAEL: Yes

SALTER: Further in

MICHAEL: Yes

SALTER: Just about yourself

MICHAEL: Myself

SALTER: Yes

MICHAEL: Like maybe I'm lying in bed and it's comfortable and then it gets slightly not so comfortable and I move my legs or even turn over then it's

SALTER: No

MICHAEL: No

SALTER: No that's

MICHAEL: Yes that's something everyone

SALTER: Yes

MICHAEL: Well I don't know. I like blue socks. Banana ice-cream. Does that help you?

The conversation goes some way to demonstrating what Derrida might mean by 'différance' and how it might apply to conservative arguments on biotechnology. Salter's repeated demand to learn something uniquely significant that does not refers to others asks more than it is possible to achieve in language, since linguistic meaning works by a network of signification, the meaning of a particular word being determined by its difference from other words.[9] The meaning that Salter wants to find is endlessly deferred and different from what can be expressed since like other words, the meaning of 'me' in Michael's case is only expressible by locating it in the wider network of signification in which x might be married to y, whereas z is unmarried, and so on. The exchange leads us back to the two possible interpretations of conservative unease about biotechnology. One possible 'lesson' of the scene and the play as a whole is that although a person might be cloned from a previous person, this does not mean that their character and identity are thereby determined. This is the familiar liberal consequentialist riposte to the unconvincing warnings by some conservatives that technologies such as cloning will be deleterious to a unique human identity and an 'open future'. More than this though, Salter's persistence in seeking a defining feature of Michael's uniqueness in the face of the obvious impossibility of the task as he understands it represents the impossible desire that motivates conservative bioethics – to somehow uncover the elusive, true and authentic defining feature of a person's unique life – and thus to distinguish it from the less than human kinds of life offered by biotechnology.

In the discussion above I have tried to sketch the outline for reading science fiction as doing more for contemporary debates on biotechnology than simply offering warnings for future society. Science fiction novels are often overtly nostalgic and nostalgia is deployed as a narrative device for reflecting on and satirizing contemporary society. Huxley himself seems to have regarded his early childhood as an idyllic haven, and remembered as all the brighter and more joyful because of a series of tragic events – his mother's death when he was fourteen and then his brother's suicide when he was twenty – which he felt had cut him off from his early happiness. As Woodcock (1972, 29) writes: '[Huxley] looked back with nostalgia to childhood in the twilight of Victorian England. He remembered it, seen from the brutal chaos of the 1940s as the end of one of history's Golden Ages.' This may have contributed to Huxley's own feelings of suspicion towards 'progress' as a removal from human essence which comes through in his science fiction (Calder 1976, 13), but science fiction novels can also be read as deconstructing

---

9   Following Saussure's synchronic' theory of language, we know what is signified by, for instance, d-o-g because we differentiate it (and thus attach a different significance) from, say, c-a-t.

this sort of nostalgia for apparently 'lost humanity'. Recall that *Never Let Me Go* is a novel in which children are cloned to be sources of organs for other people and are brought up to accept this fate without challenging it, including the central characters Kathy and Tommy. There is much material in the novel to serve the conservative association of a brutally utilitarian pursuit of health with absence or loss of humanity. As students, the donors have no families and are brought up within a boarding school called Hailsham somewhere in the English countryside, disconnected from the rest of the world. If their disconnection itself symbolizes an absence of human context, their situation after graduation becomes a whole lot worse, and they come to regard themselves as having been very lucky to have the privileges that Hailsham afforded them. Towards the end of the novel and with the time for Tommy and Kathy to 'donate' drawing near we find them becoming obsessed with clinging to memories of their happier, more secure past in order to cope with the terror of their impending deaths.[10] They take comfort by recalling their upbringing at their old fashioned English boarding school, from which in later life they find themselves cut off. The symbolic importance of Hailsham's role in the collective memory of its young graduates is underlined at several points in the novel. They are pathologically attached to their old boarding school. Recalling a donor close to death, Kathy as narrator writes:

> He could hardly breathe, but he looked towards me and said: "Hailsham. I bet that was a beautiful place" … What he wanted was not just to hear about Hailsham, but to *remember* Hailsham, just like it had been his own childhood. … That was when I first understood, really understood, just how lucky we'd been – Tommy, Ruth, me, all the rest of us. (Ishiguro 2005, 5)

It is certainly odd to try to remember something of which one has had no experience. His behaviour can only really make any sense if we understand it as representing a more general comment about a society that has already lost its connection with its humane aspect. From a conservative perspective the death of the boy in the scene as Kathy narrates it is the death of human society as such, and a society that wants to remember what it was like to have had a humane past. For both conservative bioethicists and the characters of Ishiguro's novel, a symbol of the authentic and comforting is conjured and mourned in order to demonstrate what has been lost on the road to utilitarian gain. When Kathy, now in her early thirties and working as a carer for clones who have reached the socially crucial end of their lives, hears a rumour that Hailsham is to close down, she imagines herself and her fellow graduates as helium balloons cut free from their source. Of course, there is no joy in being 'free' from Hailsham. Her remark is full of the sadness of being fully disconnected from the one thing that provided

---

10   As Ishiguro explained in an interview, 'I wanted to show the human life concertinaed into thirty years; by the end of the novel, they are like old people'. See K. Ishiguro (2004), 'Faber and Faber' official interview.

her life with meaning. Neither does freedom bring any joy for Habermas or Kass. In the face of the freedom that genetic enhancement and other forms of 'eugenic programming' promise, they too mourn what they believe is consequently lost. To Habermas and Kass, the road to accepting genetic enhancement is one that vanishes behind us – cutting future generations off from the possibility of a society that is recognizably human. This idea that there is a necessary connection between a 'human' society and a good society is certainly important for conservative bioethicists. Like the use of the word 'humane' as a synonym for kind or civilized, it draws a connection between the physical changes that biotechnologies make possible for future people and a moral change (usually regarded as a degradation) as well. The concern to preserve a society populated by humans and not something that due to genetic control might be something else, represents the conceit that a person's capacity for feelings, identities and associations that we recognize in ourselves and in each other come from our being the species that we are. If this is so, then it is not difficult at all to appreciate why conservative bioethicists would regard a departure from the *human* to represent also a departure from the *humane*. The response from liberal consequentialists is, predictably, consistent with their response to other conservative worries about the moral health and status of future beings. Gregory Stock (2002) argues that, given current advances in reproductive and genetic technologies, a future in which humans themselves enhance their own evolution is inevitable, and to resist it would be to try to 'hold ourselves apart from the biological heritage that has shaped us' (Stock 2002, 7). Rather than being unethical in itself, such an age of self-design presents challenges which must be faced rather than resisted (Stock 2002, 17). John Harris (2007, 16) accuses conservative moralists of intellectualizing a parochial view of the human genome in its present form:

> If our ape ancestor had thought about it, she might have taken the view adopted by so many of our contemporary gurus, Leon Kass [etc]. ... I personally am pleased that our ape ancestor lacked either the power of the imagination, or indeed avoided the errors of logic and/or morality, which might have led her to preserve herself at our expense.

However, *Never Let Me Go* does not simply affirm the conservative view of society tragically losing touch with its humanity. The novel also deconstructs it by undermining the reassurance that the memory of this old boarding school provides for its graduates. While they are pupils there, Hailsham is shrouded in a Sleeping Beauty-esque mystery. Sleeping Beauty, it may be recalled, slept for a hundred years in a castle surrounded by a forest so thick and deadly with thorns that it would kill any man who attempted to pass through it before the hundred years had passed. The pupils of Hailsham are kept from being tempted to leave its grounds by terrible stories of violent fates befalling children who long ago strayed into the woods that now surround them. The taboo against leaving the confines of Hailsham effectively ensures its physical separation from the rest of the world (Ishiguro 2005, 45–7) and it means that once they graduate, they are effectively lost in a cruel world that will take away their organs before they grow old. As in Ishiguro's other novels, memory is unreliable and takes on a mythical, almost ghostly characteristic. In later life, Kathy herself experiences the memory of Hailsham as something like a dream, and her thoughts about it take on an unearthly quality:

> Driving around the country now, I still see things that will remind me of Hailsham. I might pass the corner of a misty field, or see part of a large house in the distance as I come down the side of a valley, even a particular arrangement of poplar trees up on a hillside, and I'll think: "Maybe that's it! I've found it! This actually *is* Hailsham!" Then I see it's impossible and I go on driving, my thoughts drifting on elsewhere. (Ishiguro 2005, 5–6)

The very existence of the school becomes doubtful and obscure for the ex-students, whose collective obsession with it is both sad and disturbing. As the adult Kathy reflects: 'You still hear stories about some ex-Hailsham student trying to find it, or rather the place where it used to be. And an odd rumour will go round sometimes about what Hailsham's become these days – a hotel, a school, a ruin' (Ishiguro 2005, 262). How can it be that Kathy and the other characters have no idea where their old school is or whether it still operates as such? My view is that Hailsham and its mysteriousness in *Never Let Me Go* is readable as deconstructing the conservative invocation of the presence of human context and its loss through resorting to biotechnology because it raises the possibility that the school (and by analogy the presence of an authentic human context) never existed outside its collective imagination.

Of course, a conservative interpretation of the novel would point out that the inadequacy of the memory of Hailsham to make up for the characters' less than fully human lives does not deconstruct but instead actually supports the conservative warnings that a society that uses biotechnology to adapt human life for utilitarian purposes is one that ceases to care for individual human lives. Furthermore, if the existence of the school was always in doubt, this only demonstrates that the society in which the donors live is truly one in which the human context of reproduction and medical technology has been lost. On this reading, the overriding theme of the novel is the absence of human context that marks the characters' attempts to come to terms with their place in the world. As products of a dehumanized and dehumanizing society, their lives are something less than fully human. However, I would say that this interpretation of *Never Let Me Go* is vulnerable to two criticisms. First, it falls into the same trap as we discussed in part one of this chapter; that is, it attempts to take an account of a specific set of social circumstances that *in fact* dehumanizes a given set of characters through treating them in a way that ought to be regarded as a violation of human rights, and turn that account into an ethical argument about the dire effects of biotechnology itself. Like conservative interpretations of *Brave New World*, this reading tries to turn the fictionalization of a society that permits human rights abuses for the greater good into a general warning about what will happen if we use biotechnology for utilitarian ends. What I argued in part one of this chapter applies here: such warnings of possible harms cannot amount to a persuasive argument about biotechnology as such since in order for society to permit such rights violations there needs to be much more than simply the development of the technological means of, say, cloning humans. Reading *Never Let Me Go* as deconstructing the conservative position means reading the unreliability of the students' memories of Hailsham as denoting, not that in such a society there is nothing human to cling to, but that the simplistic binary opposition between human and less than human ways of doing things is not reliable. In the same way, apparent markers of what Kass calls the 'humanness of our human life' are in themselves not enough to make the kinds of ethical distinctions that the conservative bioethicists rely on.

In Margaret Atwood's *Oryx and Crake,* the theme of loss and mourning are at least equally as strong as in *Never Let Me Go.* Like Ishiguro's, the action of Atwood's novel is split temporally into two parts. First, there is American society not very far into the future with political, social and economic structures that are geared towards serving the financial interests of huge biotech companies. Secondly, there is a post-apocalyptic one where all human beings except protagonist Jimmy have been wiped out by a rogue happiness/sexual virility drug. The potential for reading it as a very simplistic cautionary tale is obvious, and indeed reviews at the time of publication suggest that Atwood's novel has been typically read as a straightforward warning of the dangers of biotechnology for human life and the environment. However, it can also be read as a deconstruction of the conservative critique of genetic enhancement. Both parts of Atwood's novel depict Jimmy as trying and failing to find meaningful connections with other people. In Atwood's imagined *pre*-apocalyptic America, the breakdown of social solidarity and interaction has brought about a far-reaching atomization and alienation. The prioritization of scientific progress is underlined not only by the reorganization of political society to suit the research and marketing needs of the biotech companies but also the virtual annihilation of live theatre for public health and security reasons. Mirroring Huxley's imagined future in which all high art has been made redundant by the living conditions of the people, the only forms of entertainment left to the citizens of Atwood's pre-apocalyptic America are cable and electronic, broadcasting a constant supply of hardcore porn and violence, desensitizing and disconnecting people. Like Huxley's noble savage, Jimmy finds the discovery of Shakespeare a welcome respite (Atwood 2004, 97). Jimmy spends his youth as a perpetual underachiever – drifting between unsatisfying sexual relationships and meaningless ad-writing jobs. However, there is a scene that jars against this alienating background. While the teenage Jimmy and his friend Crake are watching a particularly ugly scene involving a group of girl-children pleasuring a man, one of the girls – who years later turns out to be the girl Oryx who in adult life becomes Jimmy's lover – turns around to look at the camera. Jimmy is transfixed and terrified by this moment, because he feels that she is looking at him specifically, and further, that she is looking right into his soul (Atwood 2004, 104). Like Hailsham for Ishiguro's Kathy and Tommy, the face of the child Oryx becomes a source of obsession for Jimmy. He downloads the image and keeps a printout of it into adulthood. The feeling of proximity that Jimmy experiences contrasts starkly against his more general feeling of remoteness and alienation and portrays in dramatic form the nostalgia for the loss of the vital, authentic physical connection between human beings that is at the heart of conservative bioethics.

In the second part of the story, Jimmy finds himself in a post-apocalyptic America. The rest of the human race having been eliminated by biotechnology gone wrong, Jimmy is entirely alone in the world save for herds of highly aggressive and super-intelligent GM pigs (that had originally been created to provide organs) and a small race of peaceful humanoid creatures who were created to survive human extinction, with which Jimmy has nothing in common. At this stage of the novel, Jimmy spends his days sitting in a tree sheltering under an old bed-sheet from the blistering sun, talking to himself. Atwood (2004, 11) tells us that he 'feels the need to hear ... a fully human voice, like his own' and indeed he consoles himself by imagining that he is being watched over and listened to by someone, possibly Oryx, whom he finally met and fell in love with shortly before she along with the rest of humankind died, or his mother who vanished from his life while he was still a young boy. Like Hailsham for Ishiguro's clones, Jimmy's memories of Oryx and his mother are marked by both acute longing and anxious uncertainty simultaneously. It is never entirely clear that Oryx returns Jimmy's love, and the mother of his imagination is always one in the margins of his memory – not quite present and not quite absent. In Atwood's novel there is no doubt at least that the subject of the protagonist's memory (and the object of his desire) did actually exist, but in terms of a present human context, is equally ambiguous. Note the dramatic contradictions at the beginning and end of the following passage:

> In the small hot room he dreams; again, it's his mother. No, he never dreams about his mother, only about her absence. He's in the kitchen. Whuff, goes the wind in his ear, a door closing. On a hook her dressing gown is hanging, magenta, empty, frightening.

> He wakes with his heart pounding. He remembers now that after she'd left he'd put it on, that dressing gown. It still smelled of her, of that jasmine-based perfume she used to wear. He'd looked at himself in the mirror, his boy's head with its cool practiced fish-eye stare topping a neck that led down into that swaddling of female-coloured fabric. How much he'd hated her at that moment. He could hardly breathe, he'd been suffocating with hatred, tears of hatred had been rolling down his cheeks. But he'd hugged his arms around himself all the same.

> Her arms. (Atwood 2004, 325)

The kitchen door closing, an empty dressing gown, the smell of jasmine, the arms that hug around him: Jimmy's recollections of his mother contain all the necessary details except mother herself. Instead of her he remembers only his reflection and his own arms, and his grief arises from his belief that he lacks the thing he needs to achieve the *re*-humanization he craves. Reading the scene as we have read *Never Let Me Go*, we can say that Margaret Atwood's narration of Jimmy's memories deconstructs the yearning for human context in the conservative bioethics of Habermas and Kass. The passage above can be read as a series of supplementations in Jimmy's mental reconstruction of 'real' life before the biotechnological apocalypse: each remembered detail about his mother representing a vain attempt on Jimmy's part to compensate for a felt lack of human presence. He recalls putting on his mother's dressing gown as if this will resurrect her, but since he is forced by her absence from the memory to substitute her body for his own, he intensifies the illusion by representing to himself that his own arms – clad as they are in her dressing gown – are in fact 'her arms' as they wrap around his body. The closeness that Jimmy momentarily finds – the presence, or human context that he wills into existence – is of course only imagined. In rethinking or rewriting the past, Jimmy has created a myth for himself about how life ought to be and this is what makes this passage and Atwood's novel as a whole relevant for a critical perspective on the 'meaning' that Kass, Habermas and arguably Huxley read into what they regard as ethical forms of managing human reproduction, living and dying, and find lacking in those they find unacceptable. The effectiveness of Habermas' bioethics or the science fiction discussed here in affecting the way ethical questions about biotechnology are publicly understood, lies not with any claim to know or predict its possible benefits or harms, but with presenting a particular narrative about what is necessary for the possibility of an authentic human life.

Conclusion

The conservative bioethicists share a nostalgic view of aspects of human life because the conservative perspectives are oriented backwards towards a mythic past, imagining and recreating an ideal past that is not tainted by artificiality that renders life less recognizably human. Like any kind of myth, the myth of the 'authentic' human life is a narrative with no official version and is infinitely flexible and endlessly rewritable. It is used by Habermas and Kass and others to lend substance to conservative claims, but at the same time it can be enlisted to contradict conservative denunciations of artificial technologies. Just as the characters in the science fiction novels discussed here resort to a conjured or imagined past to distinguish themselves from the ruined worlds they later inhabit, so the conservatives' distinction between original or authentic human processes and the apparently dehumanizing artificial methods depends upon invoking a particular version of the 'humanity' myth. In this chapter I have tried to show that the moral hierarchy constructed by the conservative bioethicists is demonstrably unstable due to the impossibility of pinning down (or summoning to presence) such a slippery idea, but its flexibility is also the source of its enduring potency. Despite showing real and compelling reasons why the conservative warnings of harm are weak, liberal consequentialists have yet to address this much more heavily entrenched retrospective aspect of Kass' and Habermas' arguments. For anyone who really wants to bring about a paradigm shift in attitudes towards, say, genetic enhancement, cloning, sex selection and other technologies, it may be necessary to leave the comfort zone of consequences in terms of harms and benefits, and to engage instead with imaginative mythmaking and thereby challenge the conservatives on their own ground.

List of References

Adler, A. (2001a), 'The Perverse Law of Child Pornography', *Columbia Law Review* 101, 209–273.

Adler, A. (2001b), 'Inverting the First Amendment', *University of Pennsylvania Law Review* 149, 921–1002.

Aeschylus (1977), *The Oresteia: Agamemnon; The Libation Bearers; The Eumenides*. Trans. R. Fagles, Introduction and notes by R. Fagles and W.B. Stanford (London: Penguin Classics).

Aiken, W. and LaFollette, H. (eds) (1988), *Whose Child? Children's Rights, Parental Authority, and State Power* (Totowa, NJ: Litlefiled, Adams and Co.).

Allen, D.S. (1999), 'Democratic Dis-ease: Of Anger and the Troubling Nature of Punishment' in Bandes (ed.).

Allen, D.S. (2001), 'Sounding Silence', *Modernism/Modernity* 8:2, 325–34.

Alpern, K.D. (ed.) (1992), *The Ethics of Reproductive Technology* (Oxford: Oxford University Press).

Aristodemou, M. (1999), 'Fantasies of Women as Lawmakers: Empowerment or Entrapment in Angela Carter's *Bloody Chambers*' in Freeman and Lewis (eds).

Aristodemou, M. (2000), *Law and Literature: Journeys from Her to Eternity* (Oxford: Oxford University Press).

Armitstead (2006), *A Complete Collection of State Trials for High Treason and Other Misdemeanours, London. 1776: XIX. The Trials of Robert Winter, Thomas Winter, Guy Fawkes, John Grant, Ambrose Rookwood, Robert Keyes, Thomas Bates and Sir Everard Digby, at Westminster for High-Treason, being Conspirators in the Gunpowder Plot. 27 Jan. 1605. 3 Jac. l.* [Online]. Available at <http://www.armitstead.com/gunpowder/verdicts.html> [accessed 7 December 2008].

'Arrest After "Sarah's Law" Call' (2008), *BBC News* [Online: 19 September]. Available at <http://news.bbc.co.uk/1/hi/england/7625877.stm> [accessed 3 December 2008].

Ashliman, D.L. (2008), 'Incest in Indo-European Folktales', *Folklore and Mythology Electronic Texts* [Online: edited by D.L. Ashliman, University of Pittsburgh]. Available at <http://www.pitt.edu/~dash/incest.html#> [accessed 8 December 2008].

Ashworth, A. (1976), 'The Doctrine of Provocation', *Cam LJ* 35, 292.

Atwood, M. (2004), *Oryx and Crake* (London: Virago).

AVERT: AVERTing HIV and AIDS [Online]. Available at <http://www.avert.org/aofconsent.htm 2008> [accessed 3 December 2008].

'Baby P Petition Reaches 850,000' (2008), *The Sun*, 24 November.

Bacchilega, C. (1997), *Postmodern Fairytales: Gender and Narrative Strategies* (Philadelphia: University of Philadelphia Press).

Bandes, S.A. (ed.) (1999), *The Passions of Law* (New York and London: New York University Press).

Barnett, H. (1998), *Introduction to Feminist Jurisprudence* (London and Sydney: Cavendish Publishing).

Barthes, R. (1977), *Image, Music, Text* (London: Fontana).

Basile, G. (2005), 'Sun, Moon and Talia', *Folklore and Mythology Electronic Texts* [Online: edited by D.L. Ashliman, University of Pittsburgh]. Available at <http://www.pitt.edu/~dash/type0410.html#basile> [accessed 8 December 2008].

Bataille, G. (1962), *Eroticism*. Trans. M. Dalwood (London: Penguin).

Bataille, G. (1982), *Story of the Eye* (London: Penguin Books).

Bataille, G. (1989), *The Tears of Eros*. Trans. P. Connor (San Francisco: City Lights).

Baudrillard, J. (1988), *Selected Writings*. Trans. M. Thomas (Stanford: Stanford University Press).

Belsey, C. (1999), *Shakespeare and the Loss of Eden: The Construction of Family Values in Early Modern Culture* (Basinstoke: Macmillan).

Bettelheim, B. (1976), *The Uses of Enchantment: The Meaning and Importance of Fairytales* (London: Thames and Hudson).

Bradley, A.C. (1952), *Shakespearean Tragedy* (London: Macmillan).

Brindle, D. (2008), 'Baby P Case Raises Questions Over Child Protection Practice', *The Guardian*, 11 November.

Brothers Grimm, The (2004), *Selected Tales*. Trans. D. Luke (London: Penguin).

Brothers Grimm, The (2005), 'Cat's Skin', *Grimm's Fairy Tales* [Online: 1812 edition]. Available at 'The Literature Page' <http://www.literaturepage.com/read/grimms-fairy-tales-258.html> [accessed 8 December 2008].

'Bush Uses Veto on Stem Cell Bill' (2006), *BBC News*, [Online: 19 July]. Available at <http://news.bbc.co.uk/1/hi/world/americas/5193998.stm> [accessed 10 December 2008].

Calder, J. (1976), *Huxley and Orwell: Brave New World and Nineteen Eighty-Four* (London: Edward Arnold).

'Calvin Klein's Dirty Obsession' (1995), *NY Daily Mail*, 29 August.

Camus, A. (2000), *The Outsider* (London: Penguin Classics).

Carter, A. (1996), *Burning Your Boats: Collected Short Stories* (London: Vintage).

'Child Maltreatment: Current Series' (2008), *The Lancet* [Online: 2 December]. Available at <http://www.thelancet.com/series/child-maltreatment> [accessed 4 December 2008].

'Child Porn They Call Art' (2001), *News of the World*, 11 March.

Childnet International (2002), *Home Affairs Select Committee – Sexual Offences Bill: The Need for the New Clause 17 Grooming Offence* [Online]. Available at <http://www.childnet-int.org/downloads/SOBclause17.pdf> [accessed 8 December 2008].

Churchill, C. (2002), *A Number* (London: Nick Hern).

Clymer, L. (1999), 'Cromwell's Head and Milton's Hair: Corpse Theory in Spectacular Bodies of the Interregnum', *Eighteenth Century: Theory and Interpretation* 40:2, 91–114.

Corngold, S. (2001), 'Allotria and Excreta in "In the Penal Colony"', *Modernism/Modernity* 8:2, 281–293.

Dalrymple, T. (2002), 'It is Irrelevant Whether Hindley Felt Remorse', *The Telegraph*, 17 November.

Dante (2003), *The Divine Comedy Volume I: The Inferno*. Trans. M. Musa, with Introduction, notes and commentary by M. Musa (London and New York: Penguin Classics).

Davis, D.S. (2006), 'Genetic Dilemmas and the Child's Right to an Open Future' in Kuhse and Singer (eds).

Derrida, J. (1993), *Dissemination* (London: Athlone).

Derrida, J. (2002), *Writing and Difference*. Trans. A. Bass (London: Routledge).

Diamond, C. (1995), *The Realist Spirit: Wittgenstein, Philosophy and the Mind* (Cambridge, MA: MIT Press).

Dolphin, L. (2004), *Belshazzar's Banquet and Daniel in the Lion's Den (Daniel 5, 6)* [Online]. Available at <http://ldolphin.org/daniel/daniel03.html> [accessed 5 December 2008].

Dostoyevsky, F. (1998), *Crime and Punishment*. Trans. J. Coulson (Oxford: Oxford University Press).

Douzinas, C. and Nead, L. (eds) (1999), *Law and the Image: The Authority of Art and the Aesthetics of Law* (London and Chicago: University of Chicago Press).

Duff, R.A. (1996), 'Penal Communications: Recent Work in the Philosophy of Punishment', *Crime & Justice* 20, 1–97.

Duff, R.A. (1999), 'Punishment, Communication and Community' in Matravers (ed.).

Duff, R.A. (2001), *Punishment, Communication and Community* (Oxford: Oxford University Press).

Duff, A. and Hirsch, A. von (1997), 'Responsibility, Retribution and the "Voluntary": A Response to Williams', *Cam LJ* 56:1, 103–113.

Dullmen, R. (1990), *Theatre of Horror: Crime and Punishment in Early Modern Germany*. Trans. E. Neu (Cambridge, MA: Polity Press).

Dunker, P. (1984), 'Re-Imagining the Fairytale', *Literature and History* 10:1, 3–12.

Dworkin, R. (1977), *Taking Rights Seriously* (London: Duckworth).

Economist (2008), 'Most Foul', 15 November, 40.

Edge, S. and Baylis, G. (2004), 'Photographing Children: The Works of Tierney Gearon and Sally Mann', *Visual Culture in Britain* 5:1, 75–89.

Edger, E. (1986), 'Still Hamlet: An Historical and Comparative Study' in Price.

Euripides (1994), *Electra*. Trans. J. Lembke and K.J. Reckford (New York and Oxford: Oxford University Press).

Feinberg, J. (1988), 'The Child's Right to an Open Future' in Aiken and LaFollette.

Fenner, A. and Standora, L. (1999), 'Designer Klein has Nixed Ads with Kids', *NY Daily News*, 18 February.

Firchow, P. (1972), *Aldous Huxley: Satirist and Novelist* (Minneapolis: University of Minnesota Press).

Fitzpatrick, P. (1992), *The Mythology of Modern Law* (London and New York: Routledge).

Foakes, R.A. (2003), *Shakespeare and Violence* (Cambridge, MA: Cambridge University Press).

Forell, C.A. (2006), 'Gender Equality, Social Values and Provocation Law in the United States, Canada and Australia', *Journal of Gender, Social Policy, and the Law* 14:1, 27–69.

Foucault, M. (1991), *Discipline and Punish: The Birth of the Prison*. Trans. A. Sheridan (London: Penguin Books).

Fowler, R. (1995), 'Julia Somerville Defends "Innocent Family Photos"', *The Independent*, 5 November.

Freeman, M. and Lewis, A. (1999), *Law and Literature* (Oxford: Oxford University Press).

Freud, S. (1950), *Totem and Taboo*. Trans. J. Strachey (London: Routledge & Kegan Paul).

Freud, S. (1991), *On Sexuality: Three Essays on the Theory of Sexuality and Other Works*. Trans. J. Strachey, edited by A. Richards (London: Penguin Books).

Gailus, A. (2001), 'Lessons of the Cryptograph: Revelation and the Mechanical in Kafka's "In the Penal Colony"', *Modernism/Modernity* 8:2, 295–302.

Gavin, M. (2007), 'Tierney Gearon: Daddy Where Are You?', *Hotshoe International: Fresh Perspectives on Contemporary Photography* [Online: October 2007]. Available at <http://www.hotshoeinternational.com/book_details.do?b=49> [accessed 10 December 2008].

Gearon, T. (2001), 'Where is the Sex?', *The Guardian*, 13 March.

Gorvitz, S. (1992), 'Progeny, Progress and Primrose Paths' in Alpern (ed.)

Green, T.A. (1972), 'Societal Concepts of Criminal Liability for Homicide in Mediaeval England', *Speculum* 47:4, 669–694.

Green, T.A. (1976), 'The Jury and the English Law of Homicide, 1200–1600', *Michigan Law Review* 74, 413–499.

Grimm, J.L.C. and W.C. (1993), *Grimm's Fairytales* (Ware: Wordsworth's Classics).

Grimm, J.L.C. and W.C. (2002), 'Little Red Cap' (1857 edition), *Folklore and Mythology Electronic Texts* [Online: edited by D.L. Ashliman, University of Pittsburgh]. Available at <http://www.pitt.edu/~dash/grimm026.htm> [accessed 8 December 2008].

Grimm, J.L.C. and W.C. (2005), 'Little Briar Rose', *Folklore and Mythology Electronic Texts* [Online: edited by D.L. Ashliman, University of Pittsburgh].

Available at <http://www.pitt.edu/~dash/type0410.html#grimm> [accessed 8 December 2008].

Grimm, J.L.C. and W.C. (2007), 'Little Red Cap' (1812 edition), *Folklore and Mythology Electronic Texts* [Online: edited by D.L. Ashliman, University of Pittsburgh]. Available at <http://www.pitt.edu/~dash/type0333.html#grimm> [accessed 8 December 2008].

Guilfoyle, C. (1990), *Shakespeare's Play within Play: Medieval Imagery and Scenic Form in Hamlet, Othello and King Lear* (Michigan: Western Michigan University Press).

Gurnham, D. (2003), 'The Moral Narrative of Criminal Responsibility and the Principled Justification of Tariffs for Murder: Myra Hindley and Thompson and Venables', *Legal Studies* 23:4, 605–622.

Gurnham, D. (2004), 'The Otherness of the Dead: The Fates of Antigone, Narcissus, and the Sly Fox, and the Search for Justice', *Law and Literature* 16:3, 327–351.

Habermas, J. (1997), *Between Facts and Norms: Contributions to a Discourse Theory of Law and Politics* (Cambridge, MA: Polity Press).

Habermas, J. (2003), *The Future of Human* Nature (Cambridge, MA: Polity Press).

Hanawalt, B.A. (1976), 'Violent Death in Fourteenth- and Early Fifteenth Century England', *Comparative Studies in Society and History* 18:3, 297–320.

Hanson, M. (2008), 'Teachers Who Have Affairs with Pupils Over 16 are Behaving Appallingly. But They're Not Sex Offenders', *The Guardian G2*, 7 October.

Harris, J. (1998), *Clones, Genes and Immortality: Ethics and Genetics* (Oxford: Oxford University Press).

Harris, J. (2007), *Enhancing Evolution: The Ethical Case for Making Better People* (Princeton and Oxford: Princeton University Press).

Haydn, H. (1950), *The Counter-Renaissance* (New York: Harcourt, Brace & World).

Hoff, L.K. (1990), *Hamlet's Choice* (Lewiston: The Edwin Mellen Press).

Horder, J. (1992), *Provocation and Responsibility* (Oxford: Clarendon Press).

House of Lords Journal (1660), *Journal of the House of Lords: Volume 11: 1660–1666*, 204–205 [Online: 10 December]. Available at <http://www.british-history.ac.uk/report.aspx?compid=14082> [accessed 10 December 2008].

Huxley, A. (1927), 'The Outlook for the American Culture: Some Reflections on the Machine Age', *Harper's Magazine* 155 (August) 265–70 [Online]. Available at <http://www.harpers.org/archive/1927/08/0013415> [accessed 12 December 2008].

Huxley, A. (1974), *Brave New World* (London: Penguin Books).

Ishiguro, K. (2004), *Faber and Faber Interview* [Online: Kazuo Ishiguro discusses *Never Let Me Go*]. Available at <http://uk.youtube.com/watch?v=-SmuYqKeTTs> [accessed 12 December 2008].

Ishiguro, K. (2005), *Never Let Me Go* (London: Faber and Faber).

Jenkins, H. (1982), *Hamlet: The Arden Shakespeare* (London: Methuen).

Jenkins, S. (2008), 'Officialdom Cannot Hammer Straight the Crooked Timber of Mankind', *The Guardian*, 14 November.

Johnson, J. (1967), 'The Concept of the "King's Two Bodies" in Hamlet', *Shakespeare Quarterly* 18:4, 430–434.

Kafka, F. (1961), 'In the Penal Settlement' in Kafka, F. *Metamorphosis and Other Stories*. Trans. W. and E. Muir. (London: Penguin Books).

Kant, I. (1998), *The Metaphysics of Morals* (Cambridge: Cambridge University Press).

Kass, L. (1992), 'The Meaning of Life – in the Laboratory' in Alpern (ed.).

Kass, L. (2003), 'Ageless Bodies, Happy Souls: Biotechnology and the Pursuit of Perfection', *The New Atlantis* 1, 9–28.

Kaye, J. (1967), 'The Early History of Murder and Manslaughter', *LQR* 365, 569–601.

Keenan, C. and Maitland, L. (1999), '"There Ought to be a Law Against it" – Police Evaluation of the Efficacy of Prosecution in a Case of Child Abuse', *Child and Family Law Quarterly* [Online: 11(4) 397]. Available at <http://www.lexisnexis.com/uk/legal/delivery/DnldWorking.do?fromCart=false&disb=0_T5277668383&hideSource=false&estPage=19&delFmt=QDS_EF_WORD60TYPE&docRange=Current+Document+(1)&dnldFileName=Research_%27There_Ought_To_Be_A_Law_Against_i&jobHandle=1822%3A128264280> [accessed 2 December 2008].

Kemp, L. (2008), *BBC Prom 41: Programme Notes*, 16 August.

Kincaid, J.R. (1992), *Child-Loving: The Erotic Child and Victorian Culture* (New York and London: Routledge).

Kincaid, J.R. (2000), *Erotic Innocence: The Culture of Child Molesting* (Durham and London: Duke University Press).

Kitzinger, J. (1988), 'Defending Innocence: Ideologies of Childhood', *Feminist Review* 28, 77–87.

Knight, G.W. (1989), *The Wheel of Fire: Interpretations of Shakespearean Tragedy with the Three New Essays* (London and New York: Routledge).

Kuhse, H. and Singer, P. (2006), *Bioethics: An Anthology* (Oxford: Blackwell Publishing).

Lack, J. (2008), 'Censoring Provocative Art is the Worst Advert for 2012', *The Guardian*, 26 August.

Laming, Lord (2003), *The Victoria Climbié Inquiry: Report of an inquiry by Lord Laming*, CM 5730 [Online]. Available at <http://www.victoria-climbie-inquiry.org.uk/finreport/report.pdf> [accessed 10 December 2008].

Landau, A. (2001), 'Let Me Not Burst in Ignorance: Scepticism and Anxiety in Hamlet', *English Studies* 82:3, 218–30.

Law Commission (2004), *Law Com 290: Partial Defences to Murder* (London: TSO).

Law Commission (2006), *Law Com 304: Murder, Manslaughter and Infanticide*, HC 30 (London: TSO).

Lembke, J. and Reckford, K.J. (1994), 'Introduction' in *Euripides' Electra* (New York and Oxford: Oxford University Press).

Lesnik-Oberstein, K. (ed.) (1998) *Children in Culture: Approaches to Childhood* (Basingstoke: Macmillan), 178–203.

Levin, Y. (2003), 'The Paradox of Conservative Bioethics', *The New Atlantis* 53–65.

Linklater, M. (2007), 'This Misguided, Old Testament Approach to Paedophiles', *The Times*, 20 June.

Lords Hansard (2007) [March 1, Online]. Available at <http://www.publications. parliament.uk/pa/ld200607/ldhansrd/text/70301-0012.htm#07030154000317> [accessed 5 May 2009].

Marks, A. (1980), *Tyburn Tree: Its History and Annals* (London: Brown and Langham) [Online]. Available at <http://www.archive.org/stream/ tyburntreeitshis00markuoft/tyburntreeitshis00markuoft_djvu.txt> [accessed 7 December 2008].

Matravers, M. (ed.) (1999), *Punishment and Political Theory* (Oxford and Portland, Oregon: Hart Publishing).

May, K.M. (1972), *Aldous Huxley* (London: Elek).

McGlathery, J.M. (1991), *Fairytale Romance: The Grimms, Basile and Perrault* (Urbana and Chicago: University of Illinois Press).

Mill, J.S. (1863), *On Liberty*, 2nd edition (Boston: Ticknor and Fields).

Miller, I. (2006), *Eye for an Eye* (Cambridge: Cambridge University Press).

Millien, A. (2007), 'The Grandmother', *Folklore and Mythology Electronic Texts* [Online: edited by D.L. Ashliman, University of Pittsburgh]. Available at <http://www.pitt.edu/~dash/type0333.html#millien> [accessed 8 December 2008].

Ministry of Justice (2008), *Murder, Manslaughter and Infanticide: Proposals for Reform of the Law*, Consultation Paper CP 19/08.

Ministry of Justice (2009), *Murder, Manslaughter and Infanticide: Proposals for Reform of the Law: Summary of Responses and Government Position*, Response to Consultation CP(R) 19/08.

Mitchell, B. and Cunningham, S. (2006), 'Defences to Murder in the Law Commission', *Law Comm 304: Murder, Manslaughter and Infanticide* 184–191.

'MPs Fail to Impose Smacking Ban' (2008), *Epolitix* [Online: 9 October]. Available at <http://www.epolitix.com/latestnews/article-detail/newsarticle/mps-fail-to-impose-smacking-ban/> [accessed 2 December 2008].

'Murder Law Proposals Criticised' (2008), *BBC News* [Online: 7 November]. Available at <http://news.bbc.co.uk/1/low/uk/7715230.stm> [accessed 10 December 2008].

Nead, L. (1999), 'Bodies of Judgment: Art, Obscenity, and the Connoisseur' in Douzinas and Nead (eds).

New Revised Standard Version Bible: Anglicized Edition with Apocrypha (1995) (Oxford: Oxford University Press).

Norris, C. (1990), *What's Wrong With Postmodernism: Critical Theory and the Ends of Philosophy* (Baltimore: Johns Hopkins University Press).

Nussbaum, M.C. (1999), '"Secret Sewers of Vice": Disgust, Bodies and the Law' in Bandes (ed.).

Ost, S. (2002), 'Children at Risk: Legal and Societal Perceptions of the Potential Threat that the Possession of Child Pornography Poses to Society', *Journal of Law and Society* 29:3, 436–60.

'Panorama: Myra Hindley Debate' (1997), *BBC TX* [Online: 24 November]. Available at <http://news.bbc.co.uk/hi/english/static/audio_video/programmes/panorama/transcripts/transcript_24_11_97.txt> [accessed 12 December 2008].

Perrault, C. (1988), *Tales from Perrault* (Oxford: Oxford University Press).

Perrault, C. (2005), 'The Sleeping Beauty, in the Wood', *Folklore and Mythology Electronic Texts* [Online: edited by D.L. Ashliman, University of Pittsburgh]. Available at <http://www.pitt.edu/~dash/type0410.html#perrault> [accessed 8 December 2008].

Perrault, C. (2008a), 'Little Red Riding Hood', *Folklore and Mythology Electronic Texts* [Online: edited by Ashliman, D.L., University of Pittsburgh]. Available at <http://www.pitt.edu/~dash/type0333.html#perrault> [accessed 8 December 2008].

Perrault, C. (2008b), 'The Donkey's Skin', *SurLaLune Fairytales* [Online: edited by H.A. Heiner]. Available at <http://www.surlalunefairytales.com/donkeyskin/index.html> [accessed 9 December 2008].

Plato (1990), *Phaedrus*. Trans. R. Hackworth (Cambridge: Cambridge University Press).

Pope, S. (2008), 'Locked Up for Smacking My Son ... How a Slap Brought Police and Social Services in to Tear a Family Apart', *Daily Mail*, 7 April.

Price, J.G. (1986), *Hamlet: Critical Essays* (London: Garland).

Prosser, E. (1971), *Hamlet and Revenge* (Stanford: Stanford University Press).

'Provocation – Homicide Act 1957, s.3 – Defence of Provocation' (1995), *Crim LR* 739–740.

Rackley, E. (2006), 'Narrative in Judging: When Hercules Met the Happy Prince: Re-imagining the Judge', *Texas Wesleyan Law Review* 12, 213–232.

Raffield, P. (2008), '"Terras Astraea Reliqui": Titus Andronicus and the Loss of Justice' in Raffield and Watt (eds).

Raffield, P. and Watt, G. (eds) (2008), *Shakespeare and the Law* (Oxford: Hart Publishing).

Ratcliffe, S. (1998), 'What Doesn't Happen in *Hamlet*: The Ghost's Speech', *Modern Language Studies* 28:3/4, 125–150.

Rawls, J. (1993), *Political Liberalism* (New York: Colombia University Press).

Rawls, J. (1999), *A Theory of Justice* (Oxford: Oxford University Press).

Rice, A. [writing as A. Roquelaure] (1999), *The Claiming of Sleeping Beauty* (London: Penguin Books (Plume)).

Robertson, D. (2008), 'Why a Smacking Ban Must be Slapped Down', *Western Mail*, 29 July.

Rosenberg, J. (2008), 'Homicide Reforms Would be "Nightmare" for Juries, Says Top Law Lord', *The Daily Telegraph*, 1 November.

Rousseau, J.J. (1986), *Essay on the Origin of Languages*. Trans. J.H. Moran and A. Gode (London and Chicago: University of Chicago Press).

Rutherford, D. (2001), 'The Foreignness of Power: Alterity and Subversion in Kafka's "In the Penal Colony" and Beyond', *Modernism/Modernity* 303–313.

Sade, Marquis de (1999), *The Misfortunes of Virtue and Other Early Tales*. Trans. D. Coward (Oxford: Oxford University Press).

Sarat, A. (1999), 'Remorse, Responsibility and Criminal Punishment: An Analysis of Popular Culture' in Bandes (ed.).

Savulescu, J. (2006), 'Sex Selection: The Case For' in Kuhse and Singer (eds).

Sayer, F.B. (1932), 'Mens Rea' *Harvard Law Review* 45, 974–1026.

Schneller, C. (2007), 'Little Red Hat', *Folklore and Mythology Electronic Texts* [Online: edited by D.L. Ashliman, University of Pittsburgh]. Available at <http://www.pitt.edu/~dash/type0333.html#italy> [accessed 8 December 2008].

Sellers, S. (2001), *Myth and Fairytale in Contemporary Women's Fiction* (New York: Palgrave).

Sentencing Advisory Panel (2005), *Murder by Provocation: Advice to the Sentencing Guidelines Council* [Online]. Available at <http://www.sentencing-guidelines.gov.uk/docs/advice_manslaughter.pdf> [accessed 5 December 2008].

Sentencing Guideline Council (2005), *Manslaughter by Reason of Provocation: Final Guideline* [Online]. Available at <http://www.sentencing-guidelines.gov.uk/docs/Manslaughterbyreasonofprovocation-final.pdf> [accessed 5 December 2008].

Shakespeare, W. (1998), *The Complete Works of Shakespeare*, edited by S.W. Wells and G. Taylor (Oxford: Oxford University Press).

Sharpe, J. (2005), *Remember, Remember the Fifth of November: Guy Fawkes and the Gunpowder Plot* (London: Profile).

Shiffrin, S.V. (1999), 'Wrongful Life, Procreative Responsibility, and the Significance of Harm', *Legal Theory* 5, 117–148.

Smith, R.K.M. (2004), '"Hands-Off Parenting?" – Towards a Reform of the Defence of Reasonable Chastisement in the UK', *Child and Family Law Quarterly* 16:3, 261.

Somerville, M. (2001), *Death Talk: The Case Against Euthanasia and Physician-Assisted Suicide* (Montreal: McGill-Queen's University Press).

Sontag, S. (1982), 'The Pornographic Imagination' in Bataille.

Sophocles (2001), *The Complete Plays*. Trans. P. Roche (London: Penguin Books [Signet Classics]).

Spencer, J.R. (2004), 'The Sexual Offences Act 2003: (2) Child and Family Offences', *Crim LR* 347–360.

Stainton Rogers, R. and W. (1998), 'Word Children' in Lesnik-Oberstein, K. (ed.).

Stock, G. (2002), *Redesigning Humans: Our Inevitable Genetic Future* (Boston and New York: Houghton Mifflin Co.).

Swann Jones, S. (1995), *The Fairytale: The Magic Mirror of the Imagination* (New York: Twayne Publishers).

Tatar, M. (1987), *The Hard Facts of the Grimm's Fairy Tales* (Princeton: Princeton University Press).

The Bible: Authorized King James Version (2008), R. Carroll and S. Prickett (eds). (Oxford: Oxford World's Classics).

Thody, P. (1973), *Aldous Huxley: A Biographical Introduction* (London: Studio Vista).

Tooley, M. (2006), 'The Moral Status of the Cloning of Humans' in Kuhse and Singer (eds).

Toynbee, P. (2001), 'The Voyeurs Have Won', *The Guardian*, 13 March.

Tulloch, J. (2006), 'The Privatising of Pain', *Journalism Studies* 7:3, 437–451.

Ward, I. (2007), 'Terrorists and Equivocators', *Law and Humanities* 1:1, 111–131.

Warner, M. (1994), *From the Beast to the Blonde: On Fairytales and their Tellers* (London: Chatto and Windus).

Watt, D. (1975), *Aldous Huxley: The Critical Heritage* (London and Boston: Routledge & Kegan Paul).

Wegert, K. (2003), 'The Social Context of State Terror in Early Modern Germany', *Canadian Journal of History* 23:1, 21–4.

White, J.B. (1985), *Hercules' Bow* (Wisconsin: University of Wisconsin).

Williams, M. (2002), *Empty Justice: One Hundred Years of Law, Literature and Philosophy* (London: Cavendish Publishing).

Wolfreys, J. (1998), *Deconstruction: Derrida* (Basingstoke: Macmillan).

Wolfson, A. (2003), 'Why Conservatives Care About Biotechnology', *The New Atlantis* 55–64.

Womack, S. (2006), 'Punishing Children by Smacking Wins Widespread Adult Approval', *Daily Telegraph*, 21 September.

Woodcock, G. (1972), *Dawn and the Darkest Hour: A Study of Aldous Huxley* (London: Faber and Faber).

Young, A. (2005), *Judging the Image: Art, Value, Law* (New York and Oxford: Routledge).

Zipes, J. (1988), *The Brothers Grimm: From Enchanted Forests to the Modern World* (London: Routledge).

Zipes, J. (1991), *Fairytales and the Art of Subversion: The Classical Genre for Children and the Process of Civilization* (New York: Routledge).

Index